Mr. McNamara's vivid description of fighting the throes
of addiction as a Christian in today's society gives a compelling and moving experience to the reader. He offers
an authentic account of the horrific obstacles of the past
that one must conquer in order to surrender and allow
God to transform us so that we might turn from our sin
and accept His grace. Mr. McNamara's personal account
of strength and perseverance offers a fresh and optimis-
tic hope for those of us who strive to lead a healthy and
Christ-centered life.

—Debbie Leoni, MA, LPC, NBCC

NO MORE
HIDING
NO MORE
SHAME

NO MORE HIDING NO MORE SHAME

Freedom

from

Pornography

Addiction

BRENT EDWARD MCNAMARA

TATE PUBLISHING & Enterprises

The opinions expressed by the author are not necessarily those of Tate Publishing, LLC.

Published by Tate Publishing & Enterprises, LLC
127 E. Trade Center Terrace | Mustang, Oklahoma 73064 USA
1.888.361.9473 | www.tatepublishing.com

Tate Publishing is committed to excellence in the publishing industry. The company reflects the philosophy established by the founders, based on Psalm 68:11,
"The Lord gave the word and great was the company of those who published it."

Book design copyright © 2010 by Tate Publishing, LLC. All rights reserved.
Cover design by Kristen Verser
Interior design by Nathan Harmony

Published in the United States of America

ISBN: 978-1-61739-268-9
1. Religion: Christian Life: Social Issues
2. Religion: Christian Life: Personal Growth
10.10.14

Dedication

To my loving wife, Tricia. God used you to set me free at last.

Special thanks to my mother, Elaine Boisvert. Mom, this book would not have been possible without your love and encouragement. Thank you for taking me to church so that I could hear and accept the gospel of Jesus Christ.

In loving memory of my brother, Kevin Boisvert. I miss you, little brother.

I would also like to thank Dr. Gary Steven Shogren, Joe Frey, Jim Smith, Mark Barnish, Noel and Chetna Macwan, Dan Gavin, Steve Keith, Glenn Rambo, Debbie Leoni, Dr. Bruce Betner, my wonderful nephew Colin McNamara, and many others who read my manuscript and offered many excellent suggestions to make this the best book possible. I am indebted to you and your constructive criticism.

If you hold to my teaching, you are really my disciples. Then you will know the truth, and the truth will set you free.

John 8:31b, 32 (NIV)

Table of Contents

Foreword

At the time of Jesus's ministry, Tiberius was the emperor of Rome. He had a dark reputation; among his issues, he was a famous porn addict. The emperor created a pleasure palace for himself, which was stocked full of pornography and sex manuals. Each page was hand copied and each picture hand drawn. A single book was incredibly expensive and would take weeks to produce. Meanwhile, the average peasant had no chance of seeing pornography or, apart from marriage, even of catching a glimpse of a nude person. The poor had all they could do to buy food and had no riches to waste on pornographic pictures or books. The highest technology available for them was to drill a peephole through a wall.

Fast-forward two thousand years. All of the information technology that we use every day is used for pornography.

In the seventies, I remember someone preaching that one day soon they would begin to transmit X-rated movies on television. The audience gasped at such an idea, and many of us thought he must be mistaken. As it turns out, he was off only by only a few years, and he could not have begun to imagine how digital technology would one day be at the service of the porn industry.

Over the last half-century, there has been an exponential growth in the instant transmission of more pornography to a greater number of people at less cost and with tighter secrecy.

Anyone with a computer may now access free pornography. And it will not end there: if there is two-dimensional material today, it will be three-dimensional tomorrow. If the appeal is to the eyes today, it will be linked to all five senses tomorrow. If a person has to go to a computer screen to view it today, it will be available at all times through portable technology tomorrow. We must prepare for a world where people will be secretly watching pornography while they are sitting in the pew and listening to this week's sermon.

The war against pornography—like the war against drugs—must be fought on two fronts. One strategy is to block the transmission of pornography. Brent's book concentrates on the second, more personal, front: persuading people not to use pornography, even when it is available.

No More Hiding, No More Shame reveals how pornography addiction, like any addiction, is enslavement to a behavior that runs contrary to God's desires for us. An addiction begins with a person making a conscious choice

(I will do this unusual thing, that is, go to a pornographic Web site). Next, that person has less choice in the matter (opening this Web site now seems like normal behavior). Finally, that same person has no choice (I cannot choose *not* to open this Web site!). He or she has become enslaved to a new master, a master who comes to steal and batter and give nothing in return.

Jesus told us that God has no interest in sharing us with another lord: "No one can serve two masters" (Matthew 6:24). Slaves to sin, says Jesus, are not on the road to salvation; they will not be shooed into the kingdom by an indulgent Father. Rather, sin addicts must act on the assumption that they are not followers of Jesus and are far from heaven.

Brent writes about the choices that people need to make if they are to follow Christ. These are hard choices. Yet the old saying is true that what we do now will echo for eternity. The decision for or against pornography is one that will have unending consequences because it is the choice between God and a god. I urge you to follow the true and living God.

—Gary Steven Shogren, PhD
Author, *Running in Circles:
How to Find Freedom from Addictive Behavior*
Coauthor, *Addictive Behavior*

Introduction

I had a difficult time in deciding whether or not to write this book. I've actually been advised by some well-meaning individuals not to be so transparent, open, and honest about my past addiction to pornography. After much prayer and consternation, I believe that the Lord wants me to tell my story. If it were up to me, I would have just as soon kept this a secret. However, God has been so gracious to me in helping me recover from the addiction that was my master for so many years that I feel compelled to help others who may be suffering from this addiction as well. Rather than play it safe I've decided to be as direct and forthcoming about my addiction as is possible while maintaining a manner of discretion with this not-so-savory subject matter. As I am an assistant pastor who has his heart set on serving God and others, this may look to some like suicide at first glance. On the other hand, I had no ministry whatsoever for all of the years that pornography controlled me.

God is the "great reclaimer." He specializes in taking sinful, broken, ordinary people and turning their lives around and using even the horrible experiences that he never intended for them in a way that brings Him honor and glory. If I am to be used by God in any way, shape, or form, perhaps this is the manner in which He has chosen to "reclaim" me. If I'm not transparent about my sin, I believe I have no chance to be used by God at all.

If our churches would let transparency and public confession become the rule rather than the exception, I believe we could see a spiritual revival in this country in our lifetime. Rather than covering up and hiding the sin we all know exists in our churches, the willingness to be open and honest about our sin could become a powerful tool in the hand of God and could bring about real change in the lives of Christians. Unfortunately, I don't see it ever happening in our perfect little churches.

There are some in the church that actually discourage transparency. What a shame. James, the brother of Jesus, knew about the power of public confession and transparency when he wrote, "Therefore confess your sins to each other and pray for each other so that you may be healed. The prayer of a righteous man is powerful and effective" (James 5:16, NIV). It is my prayer that Christians will begin humbling themselves before one another and that real life change will sweep through our churches. We need revival today more than ever.

Why this book? Why do I feel I need to be so transparent? Well, many years ago, as a student at Philadelphia College of Bible (now Philadelphia Biblical University) I envisioned myself the pastor of a large, suburban church with a thriving ministry and congregation. That vision never materialized due to the rampant sin in my life. As God has brought me back into a right relationship with himself in recent years, my longing to be used by him has returned. It is my prayer God will use this book to bring honor and glory to himself through what he has done in my life. Secondly, if you suffer from addiction, I pray he will use this book to help you to overcome this horrible sin and to get clean.

The statistics are startling. Fifty percent of Christian men and 20 percent of Christian women admit they are addicted to pornography (Christiannet.com June 07). Fifty-one percent of pastors say cyber porn is a possible temptation; 37 percent say it is a current struggle (*Christianity Today* Leadership Survey, December 2001). Of Promise Keepers attendees—one of the largest Christian men's conferences in the U.S.—53 percent admitted to viewing pornography regularly (*Internet Filter Review*, 2006). Forty million adults in the U.S. regularly visit porn sites on the Internet (*Internet Filter Review*). Forty-seven percent of families say pornography is a problem in their home (Focus on the Family poll, October 2003).

As is clearly seen from the statistics, pornography is a monstrous problem in our day. And, make no mistake about it, pornography addiction is sin. As a matter of fact, it is several sins: idolatry, adultery, and fornication all rolled into one. I'm not trying to sugarcoat the situation by calling this sin an addiction. By referring to this sin as pornography addiction I am simply trying to isolate the specific type of sin that enslaved me for so long. Without going into graphic details, it is my wish to attempt to share as much as possible about my addiction to pornography, as well as the devastating effect it had on my spiritual life, marriage, ministry, and family. I praise God that for the first time in my life, I am living porn-free. It's been "all God and no me" in overcoming this addiction.

As any addict knows, I'll never be fully cured from this addiction. In fact, while I was taking a break from writing this introduction, I discovered a CD in my collection that had pornography on it. I was searching for a Windows 2000 CD for a laptop I was repairing. I thought I had destroyed any and all of the remnants of my huge porn collection. However, from time to time I'll find porn hidden on what appears to be an innocent CD. The temptation to look at the images was so great that I had to pray to the Lord for the strength to cut the CD in two and render it powerless. Thank God I was able to resist the temptation through his strength. Porn addiction, like all addiction, is a second-by-second, minute-by-minute, hour-by-hour, day-by-day battle that will be fought in the battleground of my heart and mind for the rest of my life. But it is a battle that can be won.

You, too, can be free from porn addiction, or any addiction for that matter. Please allow me to qualify this statement. If you rely on your own strength to overcome this sin, you will fail every time. It is only when you rely completely on God's grace and the power of the Holy Spirit that you can experience victory over pornography or sex addiction.

What do you want most in your life? If you want to continue to wallow in the filth of pornography, you will do just that. If you want to continue hiding, living a double life, lying to your loved ones, and feeling terrible about yourself, you'll keep your sin a secret. However, if you truly want to be holy—if you want to be free from sin— you can choose to cry out to God to save you from this sin and confess what you've been doing to those around you. God knows your heart. If you truly want to be holy more than you want your addiction, he will free you from your chains. I'm free at last. He can free you too.

Warning: Some content may be of an objection-able nature due to the subject matter. In attempting to be transparent about the problems that males encoun-ter, it was necessary to describe some situations and use terminology that may be offensive. Please use discretion in allowing minors to read this material. I apologize in advance to anyone who is offended by the accounts and descriptions used herein. It is not my intention to offend. It is my hope that by getting this out in the open that real healing can take place.

How It Started

> Therefore confess your sins to each other and pray for each other so that you may be healed.
>
> James 5:16a (NIV)

Early Childhood

My father and mother divorced when I was six years old. I was devastated by this awful turn of events. Dad was at work. Mom left my sister, my brother, and me alone in our second-story apartment. I can still see her walking up the hill that led away from our house while my sister and I banged on the window and cried for her to please come back. Even though I have forgiven my mother many, many years ago, that memory haunts me to this very day. Mom had suffered a nervous breakdown. We didn't know what that meant, but one thing for sure was that our lives would never be the same. My sister, my brother, and I lived with our father and only saw our mother on the weekends. We moved from rental apartment to rental apartment every year or so but stayed within the same city.

When I was in the first or second grade, I recall my father inviting a young man named Cliff to stay with us for a short while. He seemed to be a drifter. Maybe he just needed some temporary shelter, so my father took him in for a few weeks. This all seemed harmless enough, but the lasting effect that his visit would have on me is all too clear to me even to this day.

Cliff was a hippie. He had long hair, a beard, a guitar, and something I'd never seen before: pornography. I caught him looking at it while he thought we were all asleep. I watched where he hid them and whenever I could, I'd sneak them out and have a look. I was just a boy, but I was already experiencing lust. I don't really understand it, but looking at pictures of naked women became an obsession to me that lasts to this day. As a boy, I desired to know more about such things, and over the years I secretly went about gratifying those desires.

It's important to note here that my father had no idea I had been exposed to porn by Cliff. In fact, I only learned recently that one day my father came home to find Cliff shaking me and yelling at me about something. Evidently, he had caught me looking at his magazines. My father grabbed him by the neck and lifted him as high as he could. He told him that if he ever caught him laying a hand on his son again, he would kill him, and he threw him out of the house. I must have blocked out this memory over the years because I honestly have no recollection of it at all. If I had remembered this episode of my father's love and protection for me, my life would probably have gone in a much different direction. Since my father never really showed his feelings, I grew up not really knowing if my father loved me or approved of me.

It was at this very tender time in my life that my father met Barbara. Barbara was to become my stepmother in the next several months. She was an attractive woman. If I had to venture a guess, I'd say she must have only been twenty-one or twenty-two at that time. Barbara had never been married, and here she was about to marry a man who was raising three kids by himself. The next few years would prove to be some of the worst years of my life as I endured the wrath of Barbara.

Barbara never knew it, but my brother and I had drilled a hole in the bathroom door so that we could watch her bathe and towel off. I suppose she knew what we were doing. I mean, how could she miss the hole in the bathroom door? My brother and I would take turns standing on a chair outside the door as often as Barbara was in that bathroom. We were nearly caught one day when Barbara unexpectedly hurried out of the bath as if she was suspicious and trying to catch us at our nasty game.

In later years, my friends and I satisfied our appetite for pornography and sex by stealing our father's *Playboy* magazines. We would hide them in our tree forts and look at them whenever we could. It all seemed harmless enough—just a bunch of curious little boys—but my curiosity didn't stop there. Unknown to my friends, I was stealing magazines from the grocery stores where they still, at that time, displayed *Playboy*, *Penthouse*, and other men's magazines right alongside the *Good Housekeeping* and *Glamour* magazines. I took them home and hid them in my bedroom where I looked at them every chance I got.

Over the next several years, Barbara inflicted more physical, mental, emotional, and sexual abuse on three innocent children than can be imagined. She was a vicious tyrant who seemed to delight in torturing the three of us. Actually, Barbara delighted much more in torturing my brother and me. She pretty much left our sister alone—at least physically and sexually. For my brother and me, it was sheer agony.

Barbara would hold our hands over the open flame of the gas stove if we ate some of her ice cream. She would whip us with a metal coat hanger if we were too loud. She even shot my brother with a pellet gun because of something he had done. When I was a teenager, Barbara ripped handfuls of hair from my head when I refused to get a haircut. This was just after she made me eat an entire bar of Irish Spring soap. The physical abuse was bad enough, but somehow I think the mental abuse— the constant fear—was even worse. We lived on pins and needles, never knowing what horrible abuse Barbara was going to subject us to next.

In an ironic twist, Barbara seemingly took delight in exposing herself to my brother and me. She would lie on the bed in full view of the living room sofa and expose herself to us as we watched Saturday morning cartoons.

Adolescence

This abuse continued into my teenage years. I reached puberty, and I noticed a sudden change in my body. I became quite adept at pleasuring myself while looking at pornographic images. It made looking at pornographic images even more exciting to me. If I didn't have the images to look at, the pleasure wasn't nearly as gratifying. My escape from reality had begun. When things were bad—and they were always bad—I simply retreated into my fantasy world. All I needed was my paper ladies to get that feeling again. The girls on the pages never hurt me. They never disappointed me. They never broke my heart. They never left me. I felt safe with them. They made me forget, for the moment, my mom and dad had just divorced. They made me forget I had a stepmother who abused me. They made me forget I felt alone and scared in this cold and meaningless world.

This pattern of behavior continued unabated into my high school years. I had some girlfriends, but I never even dreamed of daring to put my hands on them or having sex with them. I was too afraid of being rejected. I preferred the safety of my paper ladies to the real thing. Sure, we would kiss and hold hands but that was the extent of it. The only sexual release that I had was when I was all alone with my fantasies.

One of the bright spots in my otherwise dismal life was the time I spent with my dad and our horses. We didn't have much money, but somehow my dad managed to own a few horses, which he boarded at a friend's farm. We would go there and ride, clean stalls, feed, and water the horses on a regular basis. I became a very good rider and enjoyed the time with my dad.

His friend was an older, retired man who lived in a log cabin out in the middle of the country. He had a wooden leg from some previous accident or injury. I never knew the story behind it. He also had a funny way of talking. Perhaps it was his false teeth that made him talk in a sort of halting, *clickety-clackety* manner. Anyway, I always found him an odd fellow. I liked visiting his farm because there were always ice-cold glass bottles of Pepsi-Cola on-hand as well as peanut butter and saltine crackers for a snack. Oh, and I nearly forgot to mention that he always had *Playboy* magazines on his bookshelf.

One weekend, my father arranged for me to stay overnight at the farm. This seemed like a good idea at the time, but it turned out to be one of the worst nights of my life. In the middle of the night, I was awakened from a sound sleep only to see my dad's friend standing over me. He said he wanted to have sex with me. When I refused, he became insistent that it would be okay, that no one would ever know. I continued my refusal and tried to go back to sleep. I was terrified and lay there awake until morning. I spent the next day there with him, but I don't think I said a word to him that entire day. I never returned to the farm, and I didn't say a word about what had happened to anyone until many years later. As a boy, I didn't understand why my father allowed this to occur.

I suppose that this ugly encounter may have contributed to my general awkwardness and discomfort around adult men. I played football and basketball. I was captain of both the football and basketball teams. I had good, strong male coaches. I had strong male pastoral leadership as a teen. I'm not sure why but to this day it seems that, for some reason, I don't have many close male friends.

Because of my father's failure to protect me from the aforementioned sexual predator, and from Barbara, I have lived most of my life with the impression that my father let me and my siblings down. I have only learned recently that many of the assumptions I made about my father—his perceived lack of love for my mother and for his children—could not have been farther from the truth. But, when you're a little boy, perception is reality and can leave deep and lasting scars. Because my father was not one to show his feelings, I assumed he just didn't love me—that he just didn't care. I have said many times that he did the best that he could under the circumstances.

I carried a wound for most of my life that was based on a wrong impression of my father's love. This wound may have been even deeper than the wound my mother inflicted by leaving. I have forgiven my mother for her wound years and years ago. Many years later, as a man, I would need to forgive my father for his wound before I could experience true freedom from my addiction.

I misunderstood much about my father and the things he did after my mother left us. Quite unintentionally, I was exposed to some of his illicit sexual behavior while a very young and hurting little boy. I remember my father being with many different women in our apartment. He used no discretion when he was having sex with them in the very next bedroom to mine. This was all passed off as normal behavior. Again, it has only become clear to me very recently why my father behaved in this manner. Because he loved my mother unconditionally, forgave her completely, and wanted her back, he had a deep, bleeding wound in his heart. Just like me, my father used sex to dull the pain, thus beginning a vicious cycle that would enslave father and son for many, many years to come.

As a teenager I had girlfriends, but those relationships never became sexual in any way. I never even thought of having sex with a real girl. I was terrified of just asking a real girl out on a date. I honestly don't know how I ever got up the nerve to ask a girl out. My father had no knowledge of this terror. I preferred my safe paper women. I hid my sin and my stash of porn because I was ashamed. How could my father possibly understand? How could anyone understand when I didn't even understand it myself?

Broken Relationships

If we say that we have no sin, we deceive ourselves, and the truth is not in us. If we confess our sins, he is faithful and just to forgive us our sins, and to cleanse us from all unrighteousness.

1 John 1:8, 9 (KJV)

In May of 1973, the most important event of my life took place: I accepted Jesus Christ as my Lord and Savior after the evening service at Perth Bible Church in Amsterdam, New York. I was fifteen years old and in the tenth grade at Amsterdam High School. I was truly lost and confused. I had no meaning or purpose in my life. I existed, but that was about the extent of my life.

Even at this young age, I had already contemplated suicide. I tried drugs, drinking, and cigarettes, but these brought me very little pleasure. I was very good at football and basketball. I played both sports as often as possible.

Sports were about the only place that I found any meaning or enjoyment.

I believed in God, but I hadn't really attended church much. We were a Roman Catholic family, but we almost never attended church. God was not a part of my life—but that changed one evening in May of 1973. My brother and sister also accepted Christ that same evening. We were all led to the Lord by the late Frieda Frazier, a dear woman of God and longstanding member of the church.

We had been visiting our mother on weekends for years. Now, we began attending church with her and our youngest brother, Kevin. Kevin was the first to go to Perth Bible Church for Sunday school. The church had a bus ministry. The buses would go out into the neighboring cities and towns and bring children to Sunday school. This is how our family was introduced to Perth Bible Church.

Kevin took the bus and invited Mom to church. Mom accepted Christ and invited my siblings and me. We accepted Christ, and our lives were changed forever—all this because someone cared enough to bring children to church on old, refurbished school buses.

We all became very active in the youth group, bus ministry, Bible studies, youth sports, music ministry, and any other activities offered. We were all baptized soon after our conversions. I grew in the Lord quickly and became one of the leaders of the youth group.

I led other teens to Christ, including the future wife of one of my best friends. The two of them have since spent many years in a full-time Christian ministry. It felt great to be used by God to lead another soul to Christ.

I spent two summers working at Word of Life Ranger Camp (WOL) in Schroon Lake, New York. These were tremendous summers. I never felt such happiness and peace in my entire life.

From the time I accepted Christ through my summers at WOL, I had great victory over sexual sin in my life. While at WOL, I met a girl. We fell in love and dated for two years. Her father was a pastor in Hicksville, New York, and I visited her at her home a few times. She also came to visit me at my home in Amsterdam, New York. Even while away from the glaring eyes of parents and WOL staff, we had conducted ourselves according to Christian dating principles. We hadn't given in to temptation at all during our two years together. On the contrary, we had shown complete respect for one another's body during our time together. However, the last time we were together, we gave in to temptation and went a bit too far. She broke off our relationship after that time, but never gave a reason for the break-up.

Finally, my senior year of high school arrived. I was only seventeen but ready to go off to college in the fall. I never thought it would come. I was living with my mother at this time. She had been diagnosed with phlebitis and was having a difficult time. So, I decided to go live with her and care for her before I left home for college. This meant that I would have to change schools, as my mother lived in Perth, which was just outside of the Amsterdam school district.

Changing schools made my senior year extremely difficult. I didn't know anyone at Perth Central School. The school and everyone in it were highly antagonistic toward anyone who attended Perth Bible Church (PBC.) You see, the church had more buses than the school, and the church was right across the street from the high school. In this mostly Roman Catholic area, the people surrounding the church did not understand the ministry of PBC, nor did they care to learn about it. I think they saw us as a strange cult or something. This is understandable. I had never seen a church with buses before either.

At this time, my relationship to God was the most important thing in my life. I carried my Bible to class with me every day. At school, I was an outcast. There was some taunting and needling but mostly just the silent treatment for my entire senior year. Very few students were willing to risk befriending me for fear of being ostracized from their various cliques. This was quite a change for me. Back at Amsterdam High, I had been well liked. I had many friends. Even though my life changed dramatically after I accepted Christ, my classmates still seemed to like me. It was after I accepted Christ that I was elected captain of the football team. I didn't play football my senior year at Perth. Instead, I concentrated on my grades so that I could get into college. It was a very difficult senior year, but God was faithful to me and blessed me with three scholarships upon graduation.

Feeling led by God, I decided to follow in the footsteps of my pastor and youth pastor and attend Philadelphia College of Bible (PCB) to pursue a full-time pastoral ministry. I started at PCB in the summer of 1976.

The college's strict code of conduct forbade such items as dancing, drugs, drinking, card playing, and movies. Of course, illicit sexual activity of any kind was also strictly forbidden. Upon agreement, my very first day at PCB, I met the woman who was to later become my wife. She was a beautiful, young woman who also had sexual issues in her past. Only months before coming to PCB, she had given up a baby for adoption. She had run away from home out of shame.

While away, she had rededicated her life to Christ and longed to serve him in a music ministry. She was an excellent pianist and enrolled in PCB's music program. I was drawn to her. Upon hearing her story, I wanted to rescue her. I wanted to be her knight in shining armor.

Within a few weeks, we were going steady. Before long we were pushing the limits of sexual exploration and breaking the college's code of conduct. This presented the real risk of being discovered and kicked out of school. So we were careful to hide our problem from everyone. Even when confronted by the dean of students and asked if we needed help in this area, we denied any wrongdoing and continued to cover our sin. Many times, we felt extremely guilty and prayed for forgiveness together. Still, we were incapable of controlling our sexual desires.

At that time, the campus of PCB was in Center City, Philadelphia. This presented many temptations that I really didn't have to face in small-town Amsterdam. With millions of people who didn't know me, I found the risk in smuggling some pornography into my dorm room seemed rather small. Surely no one would suspect that I had a magazine in my briefcase—besides, I had a private room.

The temptation was too hard to resist, and I smuggled a magazine up to my room.

This was the first of many times that I would fall prey to this temptation. Later, my appetite for sex would take me to live sex shows, strip bars, and even prostitutes—all conveniently located only two blocks from my college dorm room. All this, mind you, while I was studying to be a pastor at PCB. There was no reconciling my behavior with my desire to serve the Lord in a pastoral position. I struggled with temptation and thought about quitting the Pastoral Studies program every day that I lived in Center City, Philadelphia. Even my part-time job at a Philadelphia law firm became a source of temptation.

I was employed as a messenger for most of the time that I attended PCB. This meant that I was constantly out in the city to deliver papers to other law firms or filing papers in the court systems. If a delivery of more than six blocks had to be made, the law firm gave me bus or subway fare. Rather than ride the bus or subway, I pocketed the money, walked the city, and used it at porn shops. For a few quarters, I could watch a live sex show or an X-rated movie.

There were brothels not-so-cleverly disguised as modeling studios all over Philadelphia at that time. Some of them were within a few blocks of the law firm. The police must have just closed their eyes to them or taken money to let them stay open. Sometimes, at lunch, if I had enough money, I'd go to the brothel and get whatever sex I could for the amount of money I had. This went on day after day for years. Not surprisingly, overcome with guilt, in about my junior year, I decided against the ministry. I could not reconcile my sinful behavior with my desire to serve the Lord in a full-time ministry. I finished my studies and graduated from PCB, but I had no intention of ever going into the ministry.

Between my sophomore and junior year, I went ahead and married my college sweetheart. We found an apartment in Center City, Philadelphia. I continued in school while my new bride found employment in the city. Within weeks of our marriage, she discovered a *Playboy* magazine in my briefcase. She was greatly disturbed by this and didn't understand why I would need pornography when I could have her anytime. Truthfully, I didn't really understand why I still needed pornography either. Wasn't this urge for elicit sexual pleasure supposed to go away when you got married? Now I could have sex anytime I wanted it. Why did I still feel it necessary to satisfy myself with pornography? This was the first of many incidences that would occur over the next twenty-three years. Unfortunately, neither of us sought help or counsel at this or any other time for this problem.

My new wife became pregnant during my senior year and the first of our three daughters was born in February 1980. After graduation, we moved to Amsterdam, New York, where I began looking for work. We attended Perth Bible Church where I had accepted Christ just a few years before. I was out of work during most of the nine months we lived there. Unknown to my wife, family, and church, I also struggled with temptation and sex addiction for the entire time we were there.

Surprisingly, I received a call from Southwood Baptist Church in Woodbury, New Jersey, about an interim youth pastor position. I say surprisingly because I wasn't actively seeking a position in the ministry. One of my college professors was the youth pastor at Southwood. He was leaving for the mission field and recommended me as his replacement. I interviewed and received an offer. I accepted the position, and we moved back to the Philadelphia area. I wasn't sure that I wanted to be in the ministry, but it was a job, so I gladly accepted the position. Inside, I hoped that the Lord had led me there and had affirmed my earlier calling. Maybe I would finally be able to overcome this sin now that I was officially in the ministry, as if the title of youth pastor would magically remove temptation and my inability to cope with it.

Among the youth was a pretty, young girl with blonde hair and blue eyes. She looked more like an eighteen-year-old than her actual age. She was actually only sixteen years old. I was twenty-three and married. The two of us formed a bond that began when we participated in a two-week wilderness trip with the other youth. The trip consisted of hiking, canoeing, mountain climbing, etc. She played the guitar. She taught me to play, and we sang songs together. She lived only a few houses from the church and stopped in to see me every day that summer. We would play ping-pong, play the guitar, and sing songs. Sometimes we would just sit and talk. It wasn't long before I began to have obsessive feelings for her.

My wife was pregnant at this time with our second daughter. I was already feeling overwhelmed with marriage, fatherhood, and my inability to resist the temptations in my life. Here was a young, vibrant, attractive girl who thought I walked on water. I began to fantasize about her. We never touched. Not even once. But I confessed my infatuation with her to my wife. She was very confused and hurt once more by my need to have something or someone in addition to her. I immediately resigned from my position as youth pastor, and I looked for work in a secular field.

I was ashamed of what had happened while I was on staff at Southwood. This made it very difficult for me to continue to attend church there. I didn't know who knew about what had happened, and I became very self-conscious about the entire sorry situation. Church attendance became sporadic at best over the next several years.

My wife and I struggled financially as I looked for a way to make a living. I finally found work in commission-based recruiting, or headhunting. I liked recruiting, and before long I was earning more money than I ever thought possible. Within a few years, we purchased our dream home in Mullica Hill, New Jersey. The house had belonged to my boss at the recruiting firm. My wife and I really loved the house. So, when my boss decided to sell, she gave us the first opportunity to buy it.

My boss was an attractive, professional woman, and we enjoyed working together very much. I learned everything I know about recruiting from her. Our friendship extended beyond the office. My wife and I began spending more and more time with her and her husband. We went golfing and took weekend antiquing excursions to

Saratoga and other places. This was all very nice, but it wasn't long before I developed a strong infatuation for my boss just as I had for previous women. When it became obvious we could never have a relationship, I fell into a deep depression. In 1987, I was diagnosed with manic depression and began treatment that included hospitalization, lithium, and regular counseling. I missed several months of work while I recovered. I never returned to my previous level of success.

Over the years that I was a recruiter, there were many other emotional affairs—infatuations, if you will—with many women. Most of these situations were confessed to my wife, which only added to her considerable pain and confusion about me and my supposed commitment to our marriage. None of these relationships ever turned into sexual relationships, but the fact that I was emotionally involved with other women hurt my wife all the same.

In 1990, my wife confessed to me that she had been having a year-long affair with the husband of one of her friends. This revelation landed me in the hospital again—this time for a two-week stay, another long recovery, and the inability to work. My wife had been working as a nurse's aid while studying for her RN license at a local community college. She met him while visiting her friend at their home. He made advances toward her and she accepted them. Their sexual affair had gone on undetected and included dinners, hotels, and talk of a future together.

I believed my wife felt genuinely bad about what she had done when she asked for my forgiveness. She ended the affair, and I forgave her completely—at least I thought that I had at that time. The hurt was severe, and I had lost my trust for her. We participated in one or two counseling sessions and went about trying to put our marriage back together. Things were rough at first, and I'm not sure we ever totally rebuilt the trust that we had lost. Things were never quite the same from that point on, and we drifted apart on an emotional level.

With the advent of the personal computer and the Internet, I was working from home those days. This was the perfect way for me to make a living yet hide away from those who knew about my depression. A nice basement office was built, enthusiasm was high, and the money started rolling in. We became interested in horses during these years and purchased several for our daughters and ourselves. Showing and competing with our horses became our passion. We spent every penny we had on horses, trucks, trailers, clothing, and accessories, not to mention show fees, hotels, and meals. We became highly successful in the horse show circuits all over New Jersey, Pennsylvania, Delaware, Maryland, Virginia, New York, and as far away as Kentucky.

Since most horse shows were on Sundays, church attendance became impossible. Pretty soon—even though the show season only ran from April to October—we stopped going to church altogether. We had never been much for daily Bible reading or prayer anyway since we had been married, so the little bit of spiritual influence we had pretty much ended.

Our daughters grew and lost their interest in horses, preferring boys and cars. As our interest in horses waned, we spent less and less time together as a family. I found myself spending more and more time at my computer. Soon, I discovered that the pornographic material I had been paying for could be had for free right there on my PC. This discovery changed my life. I couldn't get enough porn. I downloaded it and downloaded it. When I had more than my hard drive could handle, I burned it on a CD. I built a phenomenal system specifically designed to download as much porn as possible. Not only did I partake of the available porn, but I soon became a well-known contributor in Internet porn circles.

It was also during this time I developed an infatuation for country-pop music star Shania Twain. This, of course, was just another form of idolatry. I was worshipping the creation rather than the creator. I was so crazy over her that I collected everything that I could possibly get my hands on if it had anything to do with Shania Twain. I spared no expense. Many times I spent money that we needed to pay bills so I could collect more and more of her merchandise. This led to my having to file Chapter 11 bankruptcy.

I started a Web site that was all about Shania. It quickly became one of the best-known Shania sites on the Internet. I started a Shania Twain fan club that to this day is still the biggest and best known of the online Shania Twain fan clubs on the Internet. I stood in line for four hours to meet and have my picture taken with Shania at a local K-Mart. I went to see her in concert three times in the space of a year. The last time I saw Shania, I stood in line for twelve hours to be first in the ticket line. I scanned and posted the best pictures of Shania Twain anywhere on the Internet.

Of course, much of the time that I spent pursuing my obsession, I was supposed to be working. I was being paid quite well by my employer and was doing precious little work. I also spent most of my free time in the pursuit of anything related to Shania. As you might expect, my wife was extremely distressed over my behavior and we were at odds much of the time. After years of being ignored, she turned to the man she had an affair with all those years ago. Evidently, they had stayed in touch over the years, and he was aware of her unhappiness. When he propositioned her about spending some time together, she couldn't resist.

She had been telling me for more than a year she was going to leave me. I didn't listen. To tell you the truth, I didn't even care. I was so wrapped up in my Shania Twain and pornography addiction that it didn't matter to me if she stayed or left. After all, her leaving would give me all the more time and freedom to satisfy my lust.

In July 2000, my wife and I sat down to talk and she told me she was involved with her illicit lover again. She also told me that she was leaving me within a few weeks, just as soon as she could find an apartment. I listened in disbelief but did very little to stop her. Just as she had said, within a few weeks she packed up her things and moved out. It hit me hard. I never thought that this could actually happen to us. I never thought that our marriage would end. I was wrong. The end was here, and there was nothing I could do to change it.

I fell on my knees and begged God to forgive me and to rescue me from the sin that had so completely enslaved me. I confessed what I had been doing to my wife, all of my children, all of my family, and all of my wife's family. I begged for their forgiveness. I turned back to God and sought help from the church, which was quite ironic since I had turned my back on the church many years ago. I began attending SLAA meetings (Sex and Love Addicts Anonymous), and Harvest USA, which is a Christian addiction recovery ministry.

With the help of my children and a friend who also is an addict, I got rid of all of the porn in my home and in my computer. Upon hearing my confession and apology, my children were very gracious and forgiving. They even helped me password-protect my computers so that I couldn't access adult content. They password-protected the cable television so that I couldn't access adult movies. We carried out boxes and boxes full of magazines and CDs and threw them in a dumpster. I sold all of the Shania Twain collectibles I had accumulated and used the money to pay off my bankruptcy.

I began to go to church again at Southwood. I also began to go to Pastor Joel MacDonald for counseling. Pastor MacDonald was very helpful and gracious to me in the way he handled my confession. Rather than make me feel isolated and dirty, and without naming names, he told me about others he had counseled for the same addiction. He even told me about a pastor at his old church who fell into this same sin. Knowing I wasn't alone was somehow reassuring.

At this time I began to seek restitution with my wife. She had moved into my daughter's apartment while waiting for her own apartment to be ready. For weeks,

I wrote to her every day about what had gone wrong in our marriage, especially in forgetting about God and his rightful place in our life. Unfortunately, she was no longer able to trust me, and she couldn't see herself ever giving me another chance to hurt her. I couldn't blame her for not trusting me again. I had repeatedly hurt her for twenty-two years. Why in the world would she want to go through that anymore?

We're friends today. We care about our children and want to raise them the best we can, albeit separately. We care about each other, but we don't talk all that often. When we do, the conversation inevitably turns to the mistakes we made and how much we regret the past. We made every mistake that you can make in a Christian marriage. It's a shame. Isaiah 48:18 says, "If only you had paid attention to my commands, your peace would have been like a river, your righteousness like the waves of the sea." But we didn't pay attention to his commands. Instead of peace and righteousness, we have a broken marriage and a broken family.

Getting Clean

For from the heart come evil thoughts, murder, adultery, all other sexual immorality, theft, lying, and slander. These are what defile you. Eating with unwashed hands could never defile you and make you unacceptable to God!

Matthew 15:19, 20 (NLT)

It was at this time that God sent the woman who would become my second wife. She has become one of the greatest blessings that God has ever bestowed on me. I had known her for quite some time from the Shania Twain fan club I had established. She was a big fan and one of the regular contributors to the message board and our weekly online chat room.

I had always enjoyed her contributions to the online chats, especially her wit and sense of humor. Even though I had never met her or spoken with her, I felt some sort of a connection with her. We certainly had at least one thing in common in Shania Twain. I was soon to find out there was much more there.

Taking a chance, I confided in her about my wife leaving me. I was honest with her about the reasons why. I told her about my obsession with pornography, Shania Twain, and all the sordid details. I needed someone to talk to. I really wanted to work things out with my wife and asked her to pray for me. I asked her to pray God would bring my wife back to me.

Months went by. It became more and more obvious my first wife wasn't coming back. Within weeks, she and her new man had moved into an apartment together. Less than a year later, they bought a house together and reside there to this day. I had to face the fact that my marriage was over. Two years later, the divorce made it legal and final.

Over the next few years, I continued to struggle with sexual addiction. I knew that God designed sex to be a good thing—a beautiful thing between a husband and wife. Yet for most of my life, I think I completely misunderstood this truth or I was incapable of comprehending it. I certainly wasn't capable of applying this truth to my own life.

It is man who has perverted God's original plan for sexuality. Beginning with the fall of man in the garden of Eden, man has chosen to worship the created rather than the Creator. Man has also chosen to satisfy his own selfish sexual needs over those of his faithful wife. Unfortunately, it seems this is the norm these days rather than the exception. We need to get back to a biblically based understanding of sex.

We need to take sex back from the Hugh Hefners and Bob Gucciones of the world. There is nothing more beautiful than the act of love between a husband and wife. Unlike the world's selfish, sexual love, godly love enables one partner to put the needs of the other ahead of his or her own. This is true, unselfish, unconditional love. It's a beautiful picture of what God did for us in sending his own Son to die for us. He put our need ahead of his own need.

In February of 2002, my second wife and I were married. We had a small, private ceremony attended by just my children, my granddaughter, a few friends, and the pastor of the church we had been attending. A justice of the peace performed the wedding ceremony. Pastor attended the ceremony but wouldn't marry us because I was divorced. I understood his stance on this issue but his decision hurt nonetheless. We lived in the home I had shared with my first wife for all of those years. I know this was an especially difficult time for my new wife. Here she was, far from her family, living in a home that would never be hers with her husband and his fully grown daughters. There were some tense and troubled times.

It wasn't long before my new bride caught me with pornography on the computer. She was hurt. She was furious. She knew quite a bit more about computers than my first wife ever knew, so it wasn't going to be easy for me to hide what I was doing. Even though I had confessed my sin to everyone and gotten rid of all the pornography I had collected, my habit remained.

I continued to collect new pornography on the computer. Sometimes I would just look at pornography on the computer but not save the image or images to the hard drive. I hadn't yet fully dealt with ridding my life of this awful habit. This would come about in the next several months but not without some painful experiences.

In December of 2002, I was diagnosed with stage three, level IV melanoma. The cancer had penetrated all of the layers of the derma and had reached my lymph nodes. My situation was quite grave. The doctors estimated that I had five years to live. After telling my daughters and the rest of my loved ones the bad news, I had two surgeries—one to remove the tumor and a second surgery to remove the infected lymph node. Four months of chemotherapy awaited me at the Hospital of the University of Pennsylvania.

During that time, I did a lot of reflecting on my life. I began writing my memoirs. I went back to the very beginning of my life and wrote down the events as I remembered them. This was a very powerful exercise for me. I was able to identify where my problem with sexual addiction started. I was able to pinpoint events and individuals that contributed to the problem. Once identified, I began to think and pray about these things. It was suddenly very clear to me how and why I became addicted to love, sex, and pornography.

I attempted to complete our family genealogy. I'm the fourth generation of McNamaras to be born in America. Unfortunately, I still haven't been able to complete the genealogy back to our Irish ancestors.

I wanted to visit Ireland before I died. In 2003, my sister gave us a trip to the Emerald Isle. We spent eight glorious days traveling from town to town all over County

Clare and many other counties in the west of Ireland. We also made a quick two-day trip up to Dublin.

Visiting Ireland and experiencing firsthand the history of my family roots was a spiritual experience for me. When I sat on the throne in the grand hall of Bunratty Castle, which was one of eighty-plus castles built by the McNamaras, I felt an eerie chill come over me. Climbing up the stairs in the castle turrets, I also experienced this same chilling feeling. It was as if the ghosts of my ancestors were glad to see me and happy that I'd finally made the trip to Ireland. For all I knew, thanks to my cancer, I would be joining them soon in that great beyond.

In learning that I was descended from royalty I began seeing myself in a different light. I didn't have much to be proud of for most of my formative years. We were a broken family. We were dysfunctional in every sense of the word. I can't say that I ever felt particularly proud of my heritage. Heck, I didn't even *know* my family heritage.

Why didn't the knowledge that I was a child of the King of kings change my self-image and self-perception? It's one thing to be descended from some ancient Irish kingdom no one has ever heard of. It's quite another to know you are a child of the King of the universe. This knowledge should have changed me. It should change you. The Bible tells us that we have been adopted into God's family and given all of the same rights and privileges as his own son. We are sons of the King. In his letter to the Ephesians, the Apostle Paul tells us just some of the benefits of our adoption as sons:

Praise be to the God and Father of our Lord Jesus Christ, who has blessed us in the heavenly realms with every spiritual blessing in Christ. For he chose us in him before the creation of the world to be holy and blameless in his sight. In love he predestined us to be adopted as his sons through Jesus Christ, in accordance with his pleasure and will—to the praise of his glorious grace, which he has freely given us in the One he loves. In him we have redemption through his blood, the for-giveness of sins, in accordance with the riches of God's grace that he lavished on us with all wisdom and understanding. And he made known to us the mystery of his will according to his good pleasure, which he purposed in Christ, to be put into ef-fect when the times will have reached their fulfill-ment—to bring all things in heaven and on earth together under one head, even Christ.

Ephesians 1:3–10 (NIV)

This knowledge should change us. It should make us want to live differently. It should make us want to bring honor and glory to the family name. If finding out that I was descended from human royalty had an impact on my mind-set, how much more should the knowledge that I have been adopted as God's son?

I'm not sure why my family history and genealogy became so important to me at this time. I worked and worked to try to find the missing information and to com-plete the puzzle. I suppose I looked at this as part of my legacy. If I was going to die, I wanted to leave something behind for my children and my grandchildren. I wanted them to know their heritage and to be proud of who they were. Lord knows I wasn't proud of what I had done up to that point. For me, this was another step in getting clean.

The biggest change in me was a spiritual change. I had claimed to be a Christian for many years. I came to know the Lord at the age of fifteen. Yet it's still quite difficult for me to understand how I could have been a genuine believer and still fallen so deeply into sin. I have considered that maybe I wasn't actually saved back in 1973. Perhaps I made only an emotional decision or an intellectual decision for Christ. Was Jesus truly my Lord and Savior for all of those years? Did I turn my back on my sin and submit myself to his lordship for all of those years? No. Rather, I wanted my sin more than I wanted to be holy.

There were many times I wrestled with guilt and shame because of what I was doing. For many years, after I would either buy or steal a porn magazine, I would burn it or throw it away immediately after using it. This pattern repeated itself over and over for many, many years. I would fall. I would get up and pray for forgiveness. I would fall again. I would get up and pray for forgiveness.

What am I to conclude from this? Was I a Christian all these years? Or did my salvation occur at this later time when I had finally been broken by the awesome love and discipline of the Father? I may never know the answer in this lifetime, but I know this: until I surrendered my life completely to Jesus Christ and his lordship, I had no victory over this or any other sin in my Christian life. Since the day I surrendered to him, he has given me great victory over this sin. Nothing I had ever done could free me from these chains. It wasn't until I surrendered completely that God gave me power over sin through the Holy Spirit.

Now, I don't want to get into a detailed theological debate about lordship salvation. Space does not permit, and it is not the purpose of this book. I would recommend, however, that you read *The Gospel According to Jesus* by John MacArthur for the clearest explanation of what it truly means to be a born-again believer. If you're not sure that you have actually experienced the new birth, if you have any question whatsoever about your eternal salvation, by all means, purchase this book and read it.

Jesus's message of salvation is very clearly outlined and discussed in this book. MacArthur goes into great detail to make Christ's terms of salvation crystal clear to the reader. Buy it. Read it. Study it. Don't make the mistake of assuming you are on the narrow road that leads to heaven, when you may, in fact, have been deceived and are actually on the wide road that leads to eternal damnation. Jesus said: "Enter through the narrow gate. For wide is the gate and broad is the road that leads to destruction, and many enter through it. But small is the gate and narrow the road that leads to life, and only a few find it" (Matthew 7:13, NIV).

If you're willfully committing sin and hiding it from all those around you, you need to take a close look at your salvation. Those who have truly repented of their sin and put their faith and trust in our Lord Jesus Christ cannot continue to commit willful sin. "No man can serve two masters. Either he will hate the one and love the other" (Matthew 6:24, NIV). Don't be deceived. If you are a true child of God, he will chasten and discipline you because he loves you. Sometimes, as in my case, this chastening can be severe.

Get right with God. Repent and turn away from your sin. Fall down before him and acknowledge him and who he is: Lord and Master. Submit yourself to his authority from that day forward. After all, he *owns* you. He bought you with a price—his own shed blood on the cross. He paid the penalty that each and every one of us could never have paid for ourselves. Being a slave to Jesus Christ will finally free you from your bondage to sin. You will never be free from sin any other way. Only complete and utter submission to Christ will set you free. How ironic that to be truly free we must become a slave. John 8:36 says, "So if the Son sets you free, you will be free indeed." And let me tell you something, it feels so good to be free at last.

There is a difference between *willful sin* and *slavery to sin*. The addict knows this all too well. Whereas we began our addiction *willfully*, it wasn't very long before we had no choice in the matter. We became enslaved to the addiction. This is a true master-slave relationship. Our master controlled us and we were powerless to do anything to stop the addictive behavior. We had to obey our master because this was no longer willful sin. We had become completely and utterly enslaved to the sin in every sense of the word. The only way to break the master-slave relationship is for the slave to be set free. In Jesus Christ, we have already been set free. He paid the price to redeem us from the slave block. We were in chains. We were being treated harshly by our slave master. We had no choice. We had to willingly suffer and obey—that's what slaves do.

But Jesus bought us with his own blood and set us free. We no longer have to live in bondage.

So, if we have been set free, why do we still live in bondage? It's very simple. Like some freed slaves in ancient times, we have chosen to remain with our master. Now, if the master had been kind to us, I can see why we might decide to remain enslaved to him. But our addiction to pornography and other sins has been anything but kind to us. It has destroyed our lives. It has destroyed our families. It has cost us our ministries. Why in the world would we willingly stay with this wicked taskmaster? We will explore this in the following chapter and lay out the steps that are necessary to finally break free from slavery and experience true freedom.

Getting to the Root of the Problem

Then Jesus turned to the Jews who had claimed to believe in him. "If you stick with this, living out what I tell you, you are my disciples for sure. Then you will experience for yourselves the truth, and the truth will free you."

John 8:31, 32 (MSG)

Webster defines addiction:

1: the quality or state of being addicted <addiction to reading>

2: compulsive need for and use of a habit-forming substance (as heroin, nicotine, or alcohol) characterized by tolerance and by well-defined physiological symptoms upon withdrawal ; broadly : persistent compulsive use of a substance known by the user to be harmful.

In his book *Running in Circles: How to Find Freedom from Addictive Behavior*, Dr. Gary Steven Shogren defined addiction like this: "Addiction is bondage to the rule of a substance, activity, or state of mind, which then becomes the center of life, defending itself from the truth, and leading to estrangement from God's kingdom."[1]

Addiction manifests itself in many different forms, which differ from addict to addict. There are many types of addictions. Even aversions and phobias are forms of addictive behavior.[2] Some common addictions include heroin, nicotine, and alcohol but there are many, many more. In fact, you can become addicted to just about anything. I recently heard about a man who became addicted to Ping-Pong.

This book is written with the sex, love, and/or pornography addict in mind. However, the principles discussed within this book are equally applicable in defeating any addiction.

Vincent J. Felitti, M.D., in his white paper entitled "The Origins of Addiction: Evidence from the Adverse Childhood Experience Study" asserts that a large percentage of addictive behavior stems from painful childhood experiences, much of it sexual, physical, or emotional in nature.[3]

A 2004 study by Peter Stock of The Canadian Institute for Education on Family entitled "The Harmful Effects on Children of Exposure to Pornography" stated that:

> Numerous scientific studies have demonstrated a strong correlation between exposure to pornography and subsequent deviant sexual behavior by children. The explosive growth of the Internet

over the last decade and the freely available pornography to be found on this new medium pose an additional significant public health and safety threat to children.

Both of the previous factors entered into my addiction to pornography. Everyone is different. Every addiction has come about in its own unique set of circumstances. In order to understand and stop the addiction, you must go back to the root cause of the addiction. Where did it start? Why did it start? How did it start? What was the resulting behavior? When you understand the root cause, you are on the way to finally experiencing freedom from addiction.

Understanding the root cause of your addiction may be the single most important exercise you will ever undertake in your search for freedom. As I mentioned back in the introduction to this book, I did not believe that it was possible for an addict—especially me—to ever be free from the power of addiction. I was wrong. I have since learned firsthand that you *can* be freed from the power of addiction. I cannot take any credit for this discovery. It was something God had to bring to my attention through a number of very difficult situations in my marriage and family life.

I will go into full detail in the following paragraphs, but let me summarize here: The heart is the key. As human beings, our hearts typically desire the wrong things—the things that God has warned us are harmful to us. Unfortunately, we don't listen to him. We covet our neighbor's wife. We commit adultery. We commit fornication. We worship false gods. God never intended this for us, and he tried to protect us from the resulting pain, heartache, and addiction.

The heart is the key in another respect as well. If your heart is not right—f you are carrying open wounds that have never truly healed—then you will continue to struggle with addiction. Why? Because the reason you started the addictive behavior in the first place was to dull the pain from these open, bleeding wounds. You may not have realized it at the time. You may not even realize it now, but if you search your heart, you will come to know that this is the truth.

A key passage in regard to our heart problem is Hebrews 3:7–15 (NIV):

> So, as the Holy Spirit says: "Today, if you hear his voice, do not harden your hearts as you did in the rebellion, during the time of testing in the desert, where your fathers tested and tried me and for forty years saw what I did. That is why I was angry with that generation, and I said, 'Their hearts are always going astray, and they have not known my ways.' So I declared on oath in my anger,
> 'They shall never enter my rest.' See to it, brothers, that none of you has a sinful, unbelieving heart that turns away from the living God. But encourage one another daily, as long as it is called Today, so that none of you may be hardened by sin's deceitfulness. We have come to share in Christ if we hold firmly till the end the confidence we had at first. As has just been said: Today, if you hear his voice, do not harden your hearts as you did in the rebellion."

This passage is referring to Israel's deliverance from 400 years of slavery to the Egyptians. The Lord did miracle after miracle right in front of their faces as he singlehandedly defeated Pharaoh's armies and guided them toward the promised land. It's so hard to understand how the Israelites could have rebelled against the Lord, especially since he was actually present with them for much of their journey. Because of their rebellion, Israel wandered in the desert for forty years.

Like Israel, when we repeatedly sin against the Lord our heart will become rock hard. We must protect our heart against the deceitfulness of sin. I never thought my heart could become hardened against the Lord. I was wrong. After willfully sinning against the Lord for years, I found that my heart had become as hard as rock. I stopped feeling guilt or shame about my sin. Of course, this made it possible to sin all the more. I didn't want to hear anything about God, Christ, or the Christian life. It took radical action by God to break through the hardness of my heart.

With my heart hardened against God, I discovered that it was only a matter of time before my willful sin became an addiction. Addiction is pure cause and effect. No one becomes an addict in a vacuum. The object of our addiction fulfills a very real need in our lives. We might not ever realize it, but when we use, we are attempting to cover up something that hurts.

The alcoholic drinks himself into a drunken stupor because a drunk feels no pain. The heroin addict shoots up because, when he's high, the hurt is temporarily gone. The sex addict uses sex in the very same way. It's a different high, but it's a high nonetheless. And, just like any addiction, due to tolerance, it will take more and more to produce the desired effect. This is why addiction is so dangerous. You need more and more to get the feeling you're looking for. The more you need, the more you use. The more you use, the more enslaved you become until you finally die or until you are set free.

Getting to the root of the problem is essential in overcoming your addiction. Once you realize when and why you started using, you can finally heal the open wounds and overcome the addiction. It sounds simple, but this process can take years. Depending on the wound, or wounds, you may need to speak with your parents, your brother, sister, or friends, maybe a priest—whoever it was who hurt you.

Once you have identified the root cause and you know whom you need to speak with about the wound, you must decide to forgive this individual or individuals *regardless of whether they deserve to be forgiven or not.* This is key. You must forgive this person whether you get an apology or not. You have to tell him or her how he or she hurt you because he or she may not even realize it. Honestly, when I had this conversation with my father, he did not even know he had hurt me or that I had been carrying the hurt with me for forty-four years.

If the person who hurt you is your mother, father, or a family member, please understand this: you must let him or her know that you love him or her *unconditionally* and that you forgive him or her completely. Why? Unconditional love by its very essence can never die. Since it's unconditional, there are no strings attached. It is pure love—the kind that comes from God.

Why do you have to forgive them whether they deserve forgiveness or not? Well, theologically speaking, that's how God loves us as well. Not only does he love us unconditionally, but he forgave us when we certainly did not deserve forgiveness at all. On the contrary, we deserved eternal punishment and damnation. In other words, God has been *gracious* to us. The very essence of grace is God giving us that which we don't deserve and withholding from us that which we deserve. As a believer, if you can wrap your arms around this concept, you will enjoy years of close fellowship with God and man.

There is also a very practical reason for forgiveness. Forgiveness is a choice. You have the power to forgive someone who has wronged you. When you choose to forgive this person, you are freeing yourself from the chains of bitterness, resentment, and even hatred that have imprisoned you all these years.

So many people refuse to forgive. They would rather hold on to the bitterness. In so doing, they sentence themselves to a life of misery and bondage. These people leave a trail of broken relationships wherever they go. The really sad part is that many behave in this way because they have never forgiven themselves for something they have done.

This is a vicious cycle. Follow me here. Somewhere along the line, usually at a very tender age, someone has hurt you. Because you refused to forgive him or her, you carried the bitterness and resentment with you. The pain only increased over the years. To cover the pain, you started using something—you may not have even realized it at the time or even now—porn, drugs, alcohol, food, whatever. The more you used, the more you hated yourself. The more you hated yourself, the more you used. You can't forgive yourself for your weakness and how you are hurting those who love you, so you can't forgive anyone else either. Do you see what has happened here? And this goes on and on and on, replicated in the lives of those we hurt and who have hurt us. How do we stop the cycle? We stop it by loving unconditionally and choosing to forgive those who hurt us even when they don't deserve to be forgiven. Take away the hurt and the magic potion we used to cover it up no longer has any power. The pain is gone—no need for a pain reliever.

This process took years for me. I had some wounds I didn't even realize were still open. One of the wounds had to do with my father and me. When my mother left when I was six, I was left with a gaping wound. A longing to be loved had been created. I know this to be true and have forgiven my mother many, many years ago.

However, I don't think I realized how badly my father had hurt me. He certainly didn't realize it at the time. In fact, he only learned of it when I confronted him about it recently. I'm fifty years old now as I sit here at my PC. I carried a hurt for most of my life that was based upon a misconception, a misunderstanding, and a false interpretation. Believing this lie made me doubt my father's love for me all of these years. I didn't even realize how much it hurt until the pain was brought to the surface as I read a book called *Wild at Heart* by John Eldredge.

Wild at Heart talks about the importance of the father-son relationship. Besides knowing his father loves him, a boy also needs to be initiated into manhood by his father. This is a rite of passage that has been passed down from generation to generation from father to son. The author cited many examples from his own childhood and his relationship with his children. He also cited examples from other cultures. For instance, Eldredge tells us the Mesai warriors of Africa have a custom that a boy is not considered a man until he has killed a lion. He is only allowed to marry once he has accomplished this feat. There are many other initiation rites and traditions in every culture around the globe.

When I confronted my father, I made him aware that I didn't know if he loved me. He told me some stories from my childhood that made it crystal clear that he loved me more than I could have ever dreamed of. I asked him when he thought I became a man. He didn't hesitate for a second in telling me that I became a man when my first daughter was born. The only problem was that he never told *me* at that time, so I never really knew it.

My father explained his deep love for me, his unconditional love for my mom, and how he tried to get her to come back. He explained how he had risked his life for me and my mother on more than one occasion, how he knew that I was a man when my daughter was born. I was finally free. I no longer had or have a desire to commit sexual sin. As an added bonus, I also no longer had a desire to overeat. Unknowingly, I had replaced porn addiction with food addiction for the last several years as I was getting clean. After hearing these things from my father, I dropped twenty-six pounds in three weeks without even trying. I never wanted to lose weight before because I believed I wasn't worth it. Nobody loved me. Nobody cared. I didn't love myself, so why should I take care of myself? I had tried to commit suicide twice back in the late eighties and early nineties. I've come to see that obesity and overeating are simply prolonged suicide. I was killing myself with food and I did nothing to stop it.

My second wife and I were struggling in our marriage. The problems were getting so big that I wondered if we would end up divorced. However, the revelation my father really did love me and considered me a man brought about a dramatic change in me. I no longer blamed my wife for everything that was wrong with my life. I stopped blaming my mother and father for everything that was wrong in my life. The picture became crystal clear. *I* was the problem. *My* heart needed fixing.

I had believed a lie for my entire life. As a young boy, I didn't understand my father wasn't a very expressive person. I interpreted his aloofness as a sign that he didn't really love me. I didn't know my father had actually risked his life to get my mother back. I didn't know my father nearly killed the man who inadvertently introduced me to pornography. My mind interpreted all of these occurrences incorrectly. I lived forty-four years of my life not knowing if my father loved me or my mother. I lived forty-four years of my life not knowing if my father considered me a man. I believed a lie.

Believing this lie had a devastating effect on my life. Combined with the wound from my mother leaving, an abusive stepmother, and the resultant painkiller of pornography, these other wounds produced a low self-image, shame, insecurity, self-doubt, fearfulness, meekness, and many other negative traits.

Just like my overeating issues, I've recently realized anything can become an addiction—even Ping-Pong. Take anger for example. I have recently suffered from some anger issues. It would be easy for me to blame my anger on genetic disposition. But that would be absolutely, one hundred percent like justifying fornication due to genetic disposition; lying or stealing due to genetic disposition. Jesus said that:

> You have heard that it was said to the people long ago, "Do not murder, and anyone who murders will be subject to judgment." But I tell you that anyone who is angry with his brother will be subject to judgment. Again, anyone who says to his brother "Raca," is answerable to the Sanhedrin. But anyone who says, "You fool" will be in danger of the fire of hell.
>
> Matthew 5:21–22 (NIV)

Raca is a quasi-swear word in Aramaic. It means "empty-headed" or "good for nothing." Jesus wouldn't have listed anger here if it wasn't a sin. So, as adultery is to lust, murder is to anger. This is very clear from Jesus's teaching here.

If you are a Christian and you suffer with anger issues, get your anger under the control of the Holy Spirit. Your anger issues are hurting people and destroying relationships. Confess these anger issues for what they are: sin.

Seek to find out where the anger stems from and you will be in a position to be freed from it. Maybe you failed miserably at something as a child and it has produced fear of failure in you. Genetics didn't produce your anger. Only a wound can produce anger.

Anger is often the result of fear. Fear can manifest itself in many ways, some of which include control and trust issues. You're probably a very good Christian in every other area of your life. You just need God's help in controlling your anger. Surrender it to him and just see what he does. He'll give you the victory over this sin just like any other sin.

You may need to take a hard look at your past to find out where the anger began. You may have to work through some unresolved issues surrounding its origin. You may have to ask forgiveness from some people you have hurt by your anger. Once you do this, you are on your way to freedom from this sin.

Dr. David Burns of the University of Pennsylvania Hospital has written a book entitled *Feeling Good: The New Mood Therapy*.[4] In it he describes the "thought-feeling-behavior" triangle or, as he calls it, the Guilt Cycle (see Figure 2). Though I read the book many years ago while I was a patient of Dr. Burns, I have only now fully grasped the magnitude and application of this paradigm.

The mind reacts to a stimulus, action or word from another individual. The mind processes the stimuli, actions, or words, and a feeling is instantly created according to that interpretation. This is where the wound comes into play. Whether the interpretation is correct, based on a lie, misconception, or misunderstanding or not, the hurt is still very real.

When wounded, the mind cannot immediately distinguish whether the thought was based on a true or a false interpretation. All it knows is that it has been hurt. The hurt produces a behavior or reaction. This behavior can be as gentle as shedding a tear or as dangerous as murder. All of this depends on the individual; the severity of the wound, and the length of time the individual has been carrying the wound.

THE GUILT CYCLE

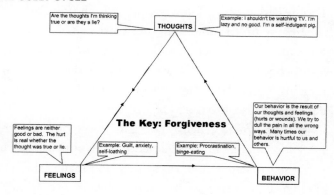

I have added "The Key to Freedom: Forgiveness" to Dr. Burns's original "Guilt Cycle." To the best of my recollection, this was not a part of his original paradigm. I have added it here because without forgiveness, the cycle will continue unabated. You see, just knowing you have believed a lie that produced a wound that resulted in addiction is not enough. Dr. Burns's cognitive therapy can only take you so far. You can "talk back" to your mind all day long in response to false thinking, but if you don't forgive those who injured you, the pain and addiction will persist.

Forgiveness is making a big comeback these days in the worlds of professional psychiatry and psychology. Once criticized as "too religious" or "not researchable," forgiveness is now being taught at some of our major universities as part of their psychiatric and psychology curriculum. Fredric Lushkin of Stanford University offers a course entitled "The Steps to Forgiveness." A charity group in London, England, has a program that seeks to look for alternatives to revenge. The program is called "The Forgiveness Project." Slowly but surely the secular world is catching on to something that Christians have known for centuries. Forgiveness is the secret to happiness.

In choosing not to forgive when wounded, the wound remains open. Non-forgiveness causes the relationship between the two parties to be damaged or destroyed. The longer the wound remains open, the more bitter, resentful, and even hateful the injured party will become. This can result in depression, aggression, and many other psychological problems. Many people never recover from the wound and eventually take their own lives—all because they could not forgive. And the really sad thing is that they may not have even known the truth. Like me, they may have believed a lie for their entire lives.

Loving communication is so important between husbands and wives, parents and children, siblings, and even friends. When someone is hurt, rather than hide the pain, it is vital that the injured party makes the other aware of the hurt. This individual may not even be aware that he has caused pain. By being made aware of the pain he has caused, there is now an opportunity for restitution, forgiveness, and healing. Instead of bitterness, suffering, and depression, a relationship can be fully restored and trust rebuilt. It sounds so simple. So why is it so difficult for us to do?

As human beings, we find it difficult to love unconditionally and to truly forgive. This is because we can't fully understand the kind of love and forgiveness that God has demonstrated to us. This is also why we have more difficulty forgiving *ourselves* than even others who have hurt us. Until we fully understand God's love and forgiveness toward us, we will never be able to forgive ourselves and to truly forgive others.

Making Changes

> Repent, then, and turn to God, so that your sins
> may be wiped out, that times of refreshing may
> come from the Lord.
>
> Acts 3:19 (NIV)

Getting clean and staying clean are two entirely different things. Temptation is everywhere for anyone who calls himself a Christian. Even if you haven't filled your eyes and mind full of pornographic garbage like I did, you will still face the struggle of fighting temptation. For someone like me, it is a minute-by-minute, hour-by-hour, day-by-day battle. But it's a battle I can win now that I am not relying on my own strength. I have surrendered my life to God and am counting on his strength and his grace.

Let's stop here to define some terms. For instance, what exactly is pornography anyway? How much of a stickler do we have to be when categorizing pornographic material? Is so-called "soft porn" considered pornography and why? What about the *Sports Illustrated* swimsuit issue? What about the *Victoria's Secret* catalog that comes in the mail? Is it okay to look at these things?

The word *pornography* comes from two Greek words: *pornea* and *graphe*. We get our English word *fornication* from *pornea*. *Graphe* means "to write." So a literal definition of *pornography* would be any graphical representation that causes us to commit fornication. A fornicator, according to scripture, is "the person who commits immorality sins against his own body" (1 Corinthians 6.18).[5] Compare this to 1 Thessalonians 4:3, which says. "This is God's will: to be consecrated to him and to abstain from sexual immorality."[6]

Pornography and fornication are very closely related. We could say that anything that we use to commit sexual immorality could be considered pornography. That means that there is no such thing as "soft porn." Pornography is pornography. As a matter of fact, the object of lust could be a fully clothed image of Shania Twain or that *Victoria's Secret* catalog. Pornography doesn't have to be hardcore images or movies. George Costanza used a *Glamour* magazine in an episode of *Seinfeld*. Pornography is anything that we use to commit sexual immorality—period.

For the Christian to seek to categorize magazines or images as "soft" or "hardcore" pornography is simply a way to try to rationalize and justify our sin. There is no justifying lust or fornication. Remember, Jesus said to look at a woman with lust is the same as committing adultery with her (see Matthew 5:27, 28). The same principle applies to fornication.

We need to surrender our eyes and the other parts of our body to God in order to break free from sexual sin. The problem is we can "un-surrender" to God in any given moment. Referring to Romans 12:1–2, Chuck Swindoll once said, "The trouble with a living sacrifice is that it can crawl off of the altar." We are human. We will never be 100% percent totally free from temptation or sin while we are living on this earth. Our only hope is to throw ourselves on the grace and mercy of God. Left to our own devices, we do not have the power to overcome sin or addiction. As long as I am walking in the spirit and am surrendered to God, I don't have the desire to look at pornographic images or at a woman with lust. Why? What is the connection here? What in the world does *surrender* have to do with addiction? We will answer that question in detail in later chapters.

To become free from addiction, I began by not letting sin "*reign* in my mortal body" (Romans 6:12, NIV, emphasis added.) Rather, when I sinned, I confessed and got right with God (see 1 John 1:9). The sin became less and less frequent. Eventually, the sin no longer controlled me and dominated my every waking moment as it had previously done. Now, much more than not, God gave me the strength to resist and flee from temptation. You don't get clean by accident. You have to work at it. You have to make some changes.

This doesn't mean that I will never commit the sin of fornication again. It would be unrealistic to anticipate I will live the rest of my life and never, ever look at a woman with lust. The difference is I don't *want* to commit fornication any longer and—finally—I don't have to, thanks to the awesome power of the Holy Spirit. In the past, I *lived* to commit fornication and to satisfy my own lust. Now, the chains of addiction have been broken, yes, but I will definitely be tempted again. As surrendered as I am to God in my heart right now, I can easily "un-surrender" in a moment of weakness. I will still have to guard my eyes and my heart to sexual imagery. I can never let my guard down and think that I'm above it. Never. In order to remain free, I will have to work at it.

Spiritual Changes

Important changes must be made in order to overcome addiction. These changes need to occur in every area of our lives beginning with our spiritual lives. Without God's help we will fail miserably.

Church

Find yourself a good, Bible-believing church and go to it every Sunday. What is a Bible-believing church, you ask? A Bible-believing church believes the Bible is the inspired word of God—infallible in its original autographs. There is no wavering on this point. Not all churches believe this about the Bible. Some churches and denominations want to pick and choose which part of the Bible they accept and which part they deny. The problem is who decides this? How do we know if they decided correctly? No, my friend. Don't mess around with this. The Bible is the holy word of God. We either accept all of it or none of it.

Not only should you find and attend this Bible-believing church, you also get involved in the church's programs and ministries. Why? Because spiritual growth does not occur in a vacuum—you need to be with other Christians. One of Satan's favorite strategies is the divide-and-conquer ploy. He convinces Christians they are the only ones who are struggling with sin. One of the greatest tools he uses to do this is other Christians. When we are not transparent with one another about the sin in our life, we can actually discourage other believers by making them believe they are alone in their sinfulness. This produces needless discouragement and can cause a believer to quit the church and the Christian life altogether.

You need to have accountability. At the appropriate time and in the appropriate setting, you need to be transparent regarding your spiritual condition. You need to use great discretion in this. As a male, I have not been comfortable telling women in my church that I am a former pornography addict. I'm not sure that too many women could handle hearing that sort of thing at church, especially from the assistant pastor. Rather, if you are a male with this problem, be transparent with other trustworthy men who may have a similar struggle in their own lives. Transparency is the key. If we hide our sin, we can hold onto it. You must confess your sin in order to ever be truly free from it: "Therefore confess your sins to each other and pray for each other so that you may be healed" (James 5:16, NIV). "So humble yourselves under the mighty power of God, and in his good time he will honor you" (1 Peter 5:6, NLT).

If you've ever read Psalm 51, you know David was transparent about his sin. David committed adultery with Bathsheba and then had her husband murdered. How do we know David was transparent? Well, he had the record of his sin and his repentance published. The Lord made sure his sin and repentance were made public and part of the Holy Scriptures. God did this because transparency is a good and godly activity. Transparency and confession are good for the soul. David committed these gross sins against God and others, yet the Lord called him "a man after God's own heart."

Reading the Bible

The Bible is our roadmap, our manual on how to do life. For the new or struggling Christian, not reading the Bible is akin to a baby not drinking milk. Without nourishment we cannot grow. As a matter of fact, if a baby doesn't have nourishment, it will have a hard time surviving at all. A good mother makes sure her baby has plenty of nourishing milk so that her baby will grow and be in good health. The same is true with the Christian life. If we neglect to read and study the Scriptures, we cannot grow. Just like the undernourished baby, survival, to say nothing of growth, will be almost impossible.

If you are a new Christian, you might want to start out by reading a paraphrased version of the Bible, like *The Living Bible* or an enhanced translation like *The Message*. These versions of the Bible use modern English and fill in the gaps left by the Greek-to-English translation to make it easier to read and understand.

Prayer

No one should spend more time in prayer than the recovering addict. It doesn't matter what the addiction—without God's help, we cannot take even one step toward freedom. My good friend Rick Sawyer wrote a song entitled "Strongholds." Here's a snippet from the song: "When in my heart I forsake them; on my knees I will break them."[7] We need to be in constant prayer to break down the strongholds in our life.

If not for God's grace and mercy, we stand no chance against our enemies. And our enemies are numerous: the world, the devil, and our own heart and mind. "The heart is deceitfully wicked above all things" (Jeremiah 17:9, NIV). Spend as much time in prayer as you possibly can. The Apostle Paul told us to "pray without ceasing" (1 Thessalonians 5:17, NIV).

Service

Service is just another word for *worship*. Biblical worship is offering to serve God. On many occasions Israel offered herself to serve other gods rather than the God of Israel. This is idolatry. Whatever we offer ourselves in servitude to—that is our god. It could be God. It could be sex, money, alcohol. It could be drugs—whatever. So, now that you are on the road to true freedom, offer yourself in service to God. It doesn't matter what it is that you do for him. It could be anything. There are usually many opportunities for ministry available at most local churches. Start small. Maybe there is some painting that needs to be done at the church. Maybe you could volunteer as an usher. Start serving others and, in so doing, you are serving God. He will accept your service of worship as long as it comes from your heart.

Relational Changes

If you haven't done so already, seek out those who you have hurt by your addiction. If it's an estranged spouse, confess your sin and ask for forgiveness. Confess your sin to your mother, your father, your children—anyone who you have hurt through the lies, deceitfulness, and pain that comes with addiction. This is a huge step in breaking free from addiction, and it is not one that you can just skip over. Again, this comes back to transparency. By confessing your sin, you can no longer hide it and hold onto it.

Accountability

Accountability is going to be very important in your recovery. If you are married, you will be accountable to your spouse and to everyone you have hurt. I strongly recommend you seek out an accountability partner or even a few people with whom you can be honest about your past problems with addiction. When there is no accountability, it is very easy to slip back into our old ways and to cover up our sin again.

Becoming part of an accountability group is not as daunting a task as it might sound. Once you get involved with a good, Bible-believing church, you may want to speak with the pastor about your addiction issues. He may be able to point you to someone in the church who shares the same problem. I realize that this can be uncomfortable at first, but once you have established a relationship with this individual, you have the beginning of an accountability group. There may even be an accountability group already in existence at the church. All you have to do is ask someone, and he or she'll be glad to help you.

You should also take advantage of the many Christian recovery groups that are out there. Some recovery groups in my area are Harvest USA, Celebrate Recovery, and Addictions Victorious. These groups are confidential, free of charge, and facilitated by men and women who, before surrendering to Christ, have struggled with addiction themselves.

Like Alcoholics Anonymous, many of these programs utilize a Twelve-Step process. The difference is that instead of praying to a higher power, Christian addiction recovery names and prays to the God of Abraham, Isaac, and Jacob through his Son, our Lord Jesus Christ. AA's Twelve Steps have been modified for Christian addiction recovery. There are a few different versions. Here's the one from Rapha Christian Ministries. Rapha is a Christian counseling organization based in Florida.

Rapha's Twelve Steps

1. We admit that by ourselves we are powerless over chemical substances or other addictions—that our lives had become unmanageable. See Romans 7:18.

2. We came to believe that God, through Jesus Christ, can restore us to sanity. See 2 Corinthians 12:9.

3. We make a decision to turn our lives over to God, through Jesus Christ. See Luke 9:23.

4. We make a searching and fearless moral inventory of ourselves. See Lamentations 3:40.

5. We admitted to God, to ourselves, and to another human being the exact nature of our wrongs. See James 5:16.

6. We commit ourselves to obedience to God, desiring that He remove patterns of sin from our lives. See Isaiah 1:19.

7. We humbly asked God to renew our minds so that our sinful patterns can be transformed into patterns of righteousness. See James 4:10.

8. We make a list of all persons we have harmed and become willing to make amends to them all. See Matthew 5:23, 24.

9. We make direct amends to such people where possible, except when to do so would injure them or others. See Luke 6:38.

10. We continue to take personal inventory, and when we were wrong, promptly admitted it. See Romans 12:3.

11. We seek to grow in our relationship with Jesus Christ through prayer, study of His Word, medita-

tion and obedience, praying for wisdom to carry out His will. See Romans 12:3.

12. Having had a spiritual awakening; we try to carry the message of Christ's grace and restoration power to others who struggle with addictions and to practice these principles in all of our affairs. See Romans 12:3.[8]

It's not a magic formula or anything, but Rapha's Twelve Steps point the addict in the right direction.

Professional Changes

In order to break free from addiction, you may need to make some changes in your job, the people you associate with and even what you do for a living. This is going to be different for every person. I had to leave my home office and go to work for a company where I had to work in a cubicle. It was too easy for me to conceal my addiction at home, too easy to lie to my wife and to the rest of my family about what I was doing. Going out into the workplace made it risky to download and view porn while sitting in an office cubicle. For me, those years were extremely important in helping me to break free from the habit I had become so accustomed to.

The Internet

For the sex, pornography, or Internet addict, the Internet is truly a garden of good and evil. There is so much good that can be done via the Internet, but it certainly seems like it's being used for much, much more evil than good. If you make your living using a computer, you have to make your computer safe.

I asked my wife to install a software program on all of the computers in our home that prohibits adult sites, porn sites, image searches, etc. There are many different software packages out there that can be downloaded for free. I recommend K-9 Web Protection by Blue Coat. This software is free, easily installed and configured, and very effective in keeping an addict from getting his fix.

Implementing Internet filtering is very important because it takes a long time to get hooked on porn. It has now become a habit. Your mind and your body have developed a dependency on this sinful activity. In order to begin recovery, you must break this dependency. Sometimes we are too weak to do it ourselves. That's where a spouse or trusted friend can come to your rescue. By safeguarding your computer, you will be forced to stop looking at the images that have polluted your mind for so long. You will have a chance to break free from the habit of addiction. The Apostle Paul wrote about the importance of renewing your mind in the following quote from Romans:

> Therefore, I urge you, brothers, in view of God's mercy, to offer your bodies as living sacrifices, holy and pleasing to God—this is your spiritual act of worship. Do not conform any longer to the pattern of this world, but be transformed by the *renewing of your mind*. Then you will be able to test and approve what God's will is—his good, pleasing and perfect will.
>
> (Romans 12:1, 2, NIV, emphasis added)

Television and Movies

Two of Satan's most deceptive tools are television and the movies. In America, we are practically born watching television and movies. I think we spend more time in front of the boob tube than any other nation on earth. Aldous Huxley's *Brave New World* prediction about a future society that is too busy being entertained and amused to care about anything has come to fruition right here in twenty-first century America.

We blindly and passively allow ourselves to be brainwashed by the television, commercials, and the movies. Huxley called it "hypnopædia." This reprogramming of the human mind took place voluntarily via recordings while the subject was asleep. Not only does this compare to today's consumerism, which is the theory and practice of making us buy things that we don't really need, but it also applies to our moral values.

We willingly allow our eyes and minds to be desensitized to immorality, fornication, nudity, bad language, and a host of other objectionable things too numerous to mention. Sadly, like the inhabitants of Huxley's *Brave New World*, our senses have become dulled. We are being programmed to accept the economic, spiritual, and moral values of this world, and we don't even realize it.

In order to truly break free from pornography addiction, you must change your television and movie viewing habits. Today's television programs, commercials, and movies would have been considered pornographic only a few decades ago. With the decline in our morals and the lack of any absolute standard, television, movies, and print media have all resorted to selling by using sexual imagery as a first resort. Why not? Sex sells, right? We hear this all the time. Madison Avenue has known this for a very, very long time, and they have taken full advantage of it.

Don't be taken in. Guard your eyes, your mind, and your heart. If you have to sit there and only *listen* to your favorite shows, by all means do it. I have had to sit through parts of many movies with my eyes closed so that I don't inadvertently expose myself to erotic imagery. Of course, the safest way to insure that you don't see nudity or scantily dressed women is to abstain from watching R-rated movies. You may even have to abstain from PG-13 or television altogether these days.

I try not to watch television, but when I do, I watch in the same manner as I watch movies. I am quick to turn my head or close my eyes should some objectionable material be presented either in a television show or a commercial. Your best bet is to stick with sports or news if you don't wish to be exposed to sexual material. But be careful, as even sports programming is not as safe as you might think. The NFL has chosen to dress its cheerleaders like prostitutes for decades now. No, it's much safer just to turn the thing off or put it out for the trash.

If you really want to hold on to your sin, you will find a way around this and anything else that stands in the way of your fix. I did. At times, during my recovery, I would give in to temptation and find alternate ways to get my fix.

To minimize the risk of being caught looking at porn on your home computer or cable television system, you can always rent porn movies from an adult bookstore.

Make sure you pay cash to hide your sin. Or, you can purchase a magazine while on a business trip and use it when no one is around. Of course, you'll pay with cash again. There are strip clubs you can go to while you're supposed to be at a meeting. All of these activities are easily covered up by a good lie.

The unrepentant addict will always find a way to satisfy his craving if he hasn't totally surrendered his sin to God. Of course, after using and covering up, he will feel the same old filthy, disgusted, worthless feelings about himself that he's felt since the day he became addicted. So why hold onto it? Surrender to God and see how good it feels to be clean and free.

Accepting God's Forgiveness

> In him we have redemption through his blood, the forgiveness of sins, in accordance with the riches of God's grace that he lavished on us with all wisdom and understanding.
>
> (Ephesians 1:7, 8, NIV)

The nature of God's love and forgiveness are two subjects that are joined at the hip. They really are one subject: God's love. In our post-modern, post-Christian society, we have heard much about God's love. We have heard over and over that "God is love." This is very true and a biblical statement at that. However, God is more than just love. Love is only one of his many attributes. God is also just. God is holy. God is omnipotent, omniscient, and omnipresent—just to name a few. To overemphasize one of God's attributes is a slippery slope that can lead to a great misunderstanding about the nature of God. Because we have overemphasized God's love, we have come to believe that he could never sentence anyone to hell. Because we have overemphasized God's love, when something bad happens to a good person, we blame it on God and say things like, "How can an all-loving God allow something like this to happen? Either he doesn't exist or he can't be the loving God we thought he was."

We hear this sort of thing every day in our hospitals, funeral homes, workplaces, and schools. We even hear this in our churches. The problem is that we don't have a sound, doctrinal foundation about the very nature of God, or its technical name, "Theology Proper." To be a sound doctrinal viewpoint on the nature of God, this doctrine must include biblical revelation. It is from this revelation that we know most of what we know about God. He has chosen to reveal himself to us through the pages of the Bible. Yes, you can learn something about God from nature. But nothing can even come close to the information the Bible has given us about the very nature of God and his attributes. You can observe the cosmos. You can look at microscopic organisms under an electron microscope and see the incredible detail that God employed when he created all things. The scripture tells us that "the heavens declare the glory of God and the firmament showeth His handiwork" (Psalm 19:1, KJV).

The evolutionist would have you believe that all of this incredible detail observed in every living thing happened by accident over millions of years, even though the scientific, geologic, paleontologic, and all other observable evidence points to a creator, or "intelligent design." Why is this so? Why has man chosen to willfully deny the existence of God and turned to lies instead? You have to go all the way back to the garden of Eden to find the answer.

Just like Satan, Adam made a choice as to who was going to be his god. Satan chose himself. He rebelled against God, which resulted in his expulsion from heaven with a full third of the angels in tow. John Eldredge does a masterful job illustrating this in his book entitled *Wild at Heart*. Adam made a very similar choice when Eve was deceived by the serpent. From the text in Genesis, it is clear Eve was first to fall for the serpent's deceptive lie and eat from the fruit of the tree of the knowledge of good and evil. Where was Adam while this was happening? Well, evidently he was standing right there beside her. He did nothing to stop her. He just stood there and watched.

What was Adam really doing by not stopping Eve? Adam had made a choice. He let his wife commit the sin against God and then he made the decision to follow her. Adam chose Eve over God. When you think about it, Adam really chose himself over God. He wanted and needed Eve for his own selfish reasons, and he completely abandoned his God so that he could have his pleasure. Unfortunately, man has been making this same wrong choice generation after generation since that very day. We have chosen to worship the creation instead of the creator (see Romans 1) with disastrous consequences. This, my friend, is pure, unadulterated idolatry.

We have been commanded to "have no other gods before" God (Exodus 20:3, NIV). When we elevate anything—including ourselves—to the rightful position that God should play in our lives, we have just committed the sin of idolatry. If we are honest with ourselves, we see that this is exactly what has happened to us when it comes to addiction.

If there is anything in our lives that comes before our relationship with God, be it alcohol, drugs, love, sex, pornography—it doesn't matter what it is—then we are guilty of idolatry. This is why addiction is so powerful and so difficult to overcome. The object of our addiction has become our god. To have it taken away from us is a frightening thought. How will we ever survive without it? How will I ease the pain without a drink or a smoke? How can I live without shooting up? How will I ever be able to take a chance on love if I don't have my safe paper and videotaped women? That was my addiction. Paper women can't hurt you. At least that's what I thought. I was wrong.

When we are hurt, we sometimes intentionally search for something to dull the pain. Sometimes we don't even realize what we're doing is hurting us. I'm not so sure that this happens accidentally.

When I traced the source of my addiction back to its roots, I discovered it was no accident at all. It was all a diabolical plot to trip me up time and time again. The plan was to destroy my ministry, my testimony, my marriage, and my life. And it worked. The plan was too perfect to be accidental. No, my friend, our enemy knows our weaknesses, and he is ready to pounce and take full advantage of them at every turn. Make no mistake. We're told that

Satan "prowls around like a roaring lion, seeking whom he may devour" (1 Peter 5:8, NIV).

So we sin. We sin and we sin and we sin. We make wrong decisions. We fall prey to Satan's deceit. What happens when we do this? Well, for the believer, we feel convicted by the Holy Spirit because we have sinned against God, ourselves, and others. We are told in 1 John 1:9 that "if we confess our sins He is faithful and just to forgive us our sins and to cleanse us from all unrighteousness." The problem is that we don't believe this. We don't believe it, and so we don't confess our sins to God, and we don't accept His forgiveness. Why? *Because we can't forgive ourselves.* Instead, we believe the lies: "I'm a terrible person." "If people knew the real me, they wouldn't like me." "How could God love someone like me?" "You call yourself a Christian?" "You haven't changed a bit."

In not forgiving ourselves, we perpetuate the cycle of hurt and shame. It becomes a self-fulfilling prophecy. It's another vicious cycle. We hurt so we feel pain. Instead of turning to God for healing, we turn to something else. When we turn away from God and to that something else, we feel guilty. So the cycle just keeps repeating itself over and over again.

If we keep turning to something other than God to ease the pain one too many times, we can become dependent on that something, and that, my friend, is how addiction is born. We become attached to something through the overuse of its numbing effects. Once we become attached, we return to the source over and over for more relief from the pain. After a while, we build up a tolerance to the substance that we have turned to so many times. We now require more and more of the substance to get the desired effect. The more we use, the more we need. The more we need, the more we want. It's a never-ending spiral into the depths of addiction that, if left unchecked, leads to certain death.

Why is it so hard for us to accept God's forgiveness and to forgive ourselves? Many times it comes right back to believing a lie. Let me give you an example. A woman marries at a very young age due to an unplanned pregnancy. Before she turns twenty-two years old, she has given birth to three children. Obviously, she is not mentally or emotionally mature enough to handle this situation. Her husband isn't ready mentally or emotionally to handle a wife and three children yet either. He deals with this situation by running from it. He stays away from home, preferring to hang out with his friends, cars, and motorcycles—whatever.

Without her husband around to help her, the woman falls into a deep depression that has been brought on by stress. She tries to tell her husband she needs his help, but he doesn't seem to take her seriously. One day, while he is at work, she does the only thing she can do to survive— she leaves her husband and children. In a very short time she is admitted into a psychiatric institution for evaluation and to protect herself from committing suicide.

Fast-forward forty years and this woman still hasn't forgiven herself for abandoning her children. From being unable to forgive herself and to accept God's forgiveness, she has now become a bitter, judgmental, unforgiving person. She has alienated friends and family due to her inability to forgive. Since she can't forgive herself, she must be the terrible mother and person she has been telling herself she is for all these years. But is this really true? Is she really a terrible mother? No. There were extenuating circumstances that led her to depression.

After leaving her children and eventually divorcing her husband, she was a loving mother to her children. She saw them every weekend. She provided love, food, clothing, and shelter as often as she could with her limited resources and visitation time. She was a very good and loving mother. She continues to be a very good mother to her children to this very day. But all she can focus on is the fact that she left her children all those years ago.

She has completely bought into the lie that she is a horrible person and a horrible mother. She evidently believes that she is not deserving of God's forgiveness. This lie has become a self-fulfilling prophecy as she becomes more and more bitter and resentful of anyone who hurts her. Over the years this woman has attempted suicide a total of four times. No wonder. She has hardened her heart, locked herself in a dungeon, and thrown away the key. All this has happened even though her children have all told her that they forgave her years ago and that they love her unconditionally. Even her first husband has told her that he forgave her years ago.

You ask yourself, "How can this happen to a Christian woman?" Well, I think some of it comes right back to our misunderstanding about God and his character. The Bible tells us that God loves each and every one of us unconditionally. In *What's So Amazing About Grace?* Philip Yancey wrote, "There is nothing you can do make God love you more and there is nothing you can do to make God love you less."⁹ This is such a profound statement. Think about that. God loves you just the way you are. God knows you. He sees what you do when no one else sees. And he still loves you. That can be a life-changing revelation if we actually let it sink into our consciousness. The problem is that we don't believe it.

Like the woman in the previous illustration, we believe the lie instead. We believe we're somehow an exception to God's rules on love and forgiveness. We believe we are unlovable and unforgivable. So, with that attitude firmly entrenched in our heart and mind, we can't accept God's forgiveness. Additionally, we can't forgive ourselves. Eventually, we won't be able to forgive others either.

John 3:16 is probably the best illustration of the way God loves all mankind: "For God so loved the world that He gave His only begotten Son that whosoever believes in Him should not perish but have eternal life."

The Greek word that is used for love here is *agape*. This is one of four different words for love that appear in the New Testament. The others are *eros*, or sensual love; *philéo*, or brotherly love; and *storge*, or affection. *Agape* love means unconditional love. It is love that loves no matter what. It's the kind of love that a husband is supposed to have for his wife (see Ephesians 5:25; Colossians 3:19). That's why the wedding vows say, "For better or worse; for richer or poorer; in sickness and in health." Unconditional love doesn't go away when things get tough. Unconditional love never changes. Unconditional love never dies.

Unconditional love is the kind of love that God has for you and me. He loves us no matter what we have done. In fact, he loved us so much that even though we didn't deserve it, he sent his only Son to die for our sins (see Romans 5:8). He didn't have to do that. He could have chosen to let us all die in our sins and spend eternity separated from him and his love. But he didn't do that. He decided to love us unconditionally and to forgive us. Rather than sentence us to an eternity of punishment, he paid the penalty for sin that was required by his just nature. He provided us with complete forgiveness and salvation for all of eternity. So we see in Christ's vicarious atonement the balancing of God's love and his justice.

When we truly accept God's forgiveness, this should make it possible for us to finally forgive ourselves and to stop believing the lie. I say "should make it possible" because some of us just can't seem to do it. Maybe we accepted God's forgiveness at the hour we first believed, but somewhere along the way we stopped believing it. This could be the result of repeated sin against God in some sort of addictive or near-addictive behavior pattern. This is what happened in my experience.

My inability to conquer my porn addiction wore me down to the point where I just stopped trying altogether. I finally quit going to church. I basically gave up on myself and on the hope of ever being free.

I wanted to die, so I thought about taking my life a few times. That failing due to lack of courage, I let myself go in every way possible: mentally, physically, and spiritually. I gained nearly a hundred pounds over the course of my addiction. Why? Because overeating is just a slow form of suicide. I wanted to die, but I was too chicken to do it. As you would imagine, gaining all that weight brought all on kinds of health problems, but I really didn't care. If it not for my wife making me go to the doctor and take all those pills, I probably wouldn't have done it. All this medical attention was delaying what I really wanted: freedom. Everyone was so amazed at how well I took the news that I had terminal cancer. Well, no wonder I took it so well. This was the out I had been looking for all along.

Thankfully, I discovered that there is a way to be free from addiction without resorting to suicide. As in all things, it starts with God. The first sentence in Rick Warren's *The Purpose Driven Life* reads, "It's not about you." Never has a truer statement been written. How selfish are we? How arrogant are we to think that this life is all about us? It's not about you. It's not about me. It's all about God. We were created by him and for him. We were created to bring honor and glory to him. Makes God seem a bit selfish, doesn't it? Too bad. He's God. Take it up with him. Me? I've come to terms with it. I've finally surrendered my life to him.

What happened to the addictions that I held to so tightly for all of these years? I laid them down at the foot of the cross. An amazing thing happened. My desire to look at porn, to look at a woman with lust, was gone. Flat out gone. It's a miracle! I never would've believed it if it hadn't happened to me.

I've been reading books about freedom from porn addiction for years now. I've read all this stuff before. I've read how this guy and that guy were set free, but I never believed it could happen to me. I used to argue with men in my accountability group about this. One of my friends swore I could be freed from my addiction. He showed me in the pages of scripture how I was a new creation in Christ, how I was a child of the King, that I'd been set free from sin. I argued with him until I was blue in the face. You see, I just didn't get it—at least not at that time anyway.

In not fully surrendering my life and everything in it to God, I deprived myself of the possibility of true freedom from addiction. There were idols in my life, some of which I didn't even know were there. Once the proverbial light went on and these idols were revealed to me, I was able to deal with them and get them out of my life. I was able to ask God for forgiveness and to lay the idols down at his feet once and for all. The peace that came over me was just incredible. I think that I was filled with the Holy Spirit for the first time in my Christian life. Up to this point, I had been saved, but I had not surrendered.

Some would teach that in order to be saved you have to surrender. I promised not to make this a book about lordship salvation, but I feel like a short summary of the doctrine and the opposing position would be helpful here. Lordship salvation is championed by Dr. John MacArthur in his book *The Gospel According to Jesus*, while the *sola fide*, or faith alone, position is defended by Dr. Zane Hodges in his book entitled *Absolutely Free!* Both are best-selling books on the subject that have become required reading for any theological student.

Basically, lordship salvation teaches that for one to be saved, he must first repent. Then once repentance has taken place, he must accept Jesus Christ as Lord *and* Savior. As Tozer put it, "We take Him for what He is— the anointed Savior and Lord who is King of kings and Lord of lords! He would not be who He is if He saved us and called us and chose us without the understanding that He can also guide and control our lives."[10] This, according to lordship supporters, is a distinct variant from their *sola fide* brothers who apparently accept Jesus as Savior only.

Lordship salvation also teaches that if a person has been genuinely saved, he will *always* bear spiritual fruit. The position does not allow for carnal Christians. Rather, lordship teachers would insist that a conversion that doesn't result in a changed life is an indication that no genuine conversion has ever taken place. Even in his preface, MacArthur is clear on this: "Salvation thus establishes the root that will surely produce the fruit."[11] Hodges's view on salvation as established in his book, *Absolutely Free!*, is much more familiar to the bulk of modern-day evangelicals. To summarize the position, Hodges teaches that salvation is by faith alone. There is nothing that a person must do to be saved other than to believe. There is no human work involved in salvation whatsoever. This is the orthodox viewpoint that has been held by the Reformers and most evangelical Christians for the last several hundred years. Hodges and his supporters would accuse lordship supporters of a "faith plus works" gospel.

I'll make no definitive choice here. I urge you to study the matter for yourself and to make an informed decision based upon the Scriptures. I will tip my hand by quoting from my good friend Dr. Gary Steven Shogren. "How then, can sin dominate a person in Christ? By voluntarily surrendering, we can allow ourselves in practice to become slaves."Dr. Shogren goes on to outline the truth about sin, salvation and surrender:

1.   Outside of Christ, men and women live as slaves to sin. Some people may be addicts, and others upstanding citizens, but they are all in bondage.

2.   At the point of conversion, people are instantaneously released from sin's decisive control.

3.   In Christ, they are subject to his kingdom, but they may become enmeshed again in slavery. They need to surrender those specific parts that keep sliding into trouble.[12]

Have you surrendered to God? Or have you become enmeshed again in slavery? Do you have some idols in your life? Have you been holding something back from God? You can't win. You can't beat God at this game. He loves you so much that he will do whatever it takes to get your attention and to transform you into the likeness of his son. You may not be feeling it now but, believe me, if you're a believer, you are heading for a major wake-up call. It will come. No doubt about it. It's just a matter of time.

Sanctification is a process. We're saved in an instant the moment we first believe. But sanctification is a lifelong process that God does in our lives to prepare us for the next life. He uses all kinds of things to teach us. Most times it's a painful lesson to learn, but he loves us so much and he's so wise that he will hurt us if that's what it takes to turn us around.

John Eldredge wrote in *Wild at Heart* that God sometimes "wounds us in our wound."[13] Sounds cruel, doesn't it? But that's exactly what God does. Why? Well, the wound is why we turned to something else instead of him in the first place. This wound and the resulting addiction only exacerbated the pain. By hurting us again right in the very same wound, he is trying to give us an opportunity to get it right this time. He knows that nothing else we turn to can ever truly satisfy us and heal that wound. We're the only ones who don't know this.

In his matchless wisdom, he hurts us again and again until we turn to him like we should've in the first place. What an incredible God we have. This is the kind of love that only a loving father can display for his children. Because he loves us, he disciplines us. He uses the pain to draw us back into a right relationship with himself.

The worst pain that the addict feels is typically from the many broken relationships that lie strewn about his life like so much broken glass. In pursuing addiction, the addict has made relationships with parents, siblings, spouses, and children minor annoyances at best. The addict only cares about getting his next fix. Nothing, not even love, can stand in the way of the next fix.

Many addicts are homeless, divorced, broken people. The relationships that were once so important to the addict have been completely destroyed by the repercussions of addiction. Once an addict comes to the end of himself, or to rock bottom, he can see the damage he has done—the pain he has inflicted on those who love him and care about him. It is at this point that God really uses the wound to bring the addict back to Himself and to his loved ones.

Living According to His Grace

For sin shall not be your master, because you are not under law, but under grace.

Romans 6:14 (NIV)

One of the most difficult things to do as a Christian is to forgive ourselves. Sure, we hear and read how God has forgiven us, but we don't really believe it in our hearts. Because we don't really believe it in our hearts, we can't really live it. Instead, we punish ourselves unnecessarily by not accepting God's forgiveness and, in turn, forgiving ourselves.

When we reject God's forgiveness we produce a Christian life that is void of God's grace. It's a Christian life that has no power to overcome sin and temptation in our lives. Because we have underestimated the depth of his love for us, we think that God can't forgive us. We see him as a punishing God. He's just standing there with a big stick waiting to smack us upside the head when we do something wrong. You laugh, but I know many Christians who actually think this way about God. To these people, he is anything but a loving, gracious, and merciful God. Instead, he's a vindictive, judgmental, merciless God who delights in punishing his children. Nothing could be farther from the truth when it comes to describing God's attitude toward his children.

The Scriptures describe in vivid detail a God of vengeance and judgment. This seems to be especially true in the Old Testament. But a closer look reveals that his anger and vengeance was directed almost exclusively at the *enemies* of Israel. Toward Israel, his chosen people, he had nothing but love even though they rejected him time and time again. As any loving father would do, God had to eventually chasten Israel in an effort to make them see the error of their ways and to get them to return to him. He didn't delight in disciplining Israel, but, as a loving father, he had to do it for the good of his children. Remember when your father was about to spank you with the leather belt or the paddle? What did he say before he spanked you? He said, "This is going to hurt me more than it hurts you." You thought, *Yeah, sure it is. Then why don't we just skip the spanking and play catch in the backyard?* God wouldn't be a good or loving father if he let his children go unpunished. We would do well to remember this as we raise our children in the nurture and admonition of the Lord.

What kind of behavior is produced by seeing God in this unloving, uncaring and punishing persona? Seeing

God in this manner could produce a very legalistic Christian life. We could try to follow the rules. But the rules—or Mosaic Law—was given by God to show that it's impossible to keep it. The Apostle Paul made this abundantly clear in Romans 3:19–21 (NIV):

> Now we know that whatever the law says, it says to those who are under the law, so that every mouth may be silenced and the whole world held account-able to God. Therefore no one will be declared righteous in his sight by observing the law; rather, through the law we become conscious of sin.
>
> But now a righteousness from God, apart from law, has been made known, to which the Law and the Prophets testify.

Jesus also demonstrated that the Law was impossible to keep, the most notable of which was His confrontation with the rich young ruler in Luke 18:18–27. This wealthy young man asked Jesus what he needed to do to inherit eternal life. This young man insisted that he had kept all of the commandments since the time of his youth. Jesus then asked him to sell all of his possessions and to follow him as one of his disciples. The rich young ruler went away sad and dejected. He had broken the very first com-mandment: "You shall have no other gods before me." He had committed the sin of idolatry. His god was his wealth.

An inability to keep the commandments produces dis-couragement, just as it did with the rich young ruler. Over the course of time, discouragement can lead us to the point where we give up—we just quit trying. Actually, this is a good place to be, for now we can begin to understand the true meaning of God's grace. You see, God doesn't expect us to be perfect. He knows that we're human—that we're prone to wandering and mistakes. He still loves us, and he forgives us when we sin. All we have to do is confess our sin and he "is faithful and just to forgive us our sin and to cleanse us from all unrighteousness" (1 John 1:9).

Caution: This doesn't mean that we can go on willfully sinning against God. Please read Romans 6. God wants us to be dependent upon him to live the Christian life and not rely on our own efforts. Left to our own efforts, we will fail every time. It is only when we fully surrender everything in our lives to God that we can experience victory over temptation, sin, and addiction. Sounds easy. It's not. I'm fifty years old and I've just learned the secret of complete surrender.

I wish I had surrendered everything in my life to God many, many years ago. Oh, the pain I could've spared myself and my loved ones. But I didn't completely surrender everything all those years ago. I held onto and hid my sin from everyone. I was terrified that if anyone ever knew what I was doing that he or she wouldn't like me or accept me. I felt dirty. I felt different. I felt alone. So I hid my sin and lived a double life until I just quit trying.

We've been talking about what could be termed "sanctification." Sanctification could be defined as the lifelong process whereby God conforms us to the image of his Son. Now, let's look at justification. I have purposely put sanctification before justification here to make a point. Obviously, no one can be sanctified until he or she has been justified. But understand this: No one has ever been justified or saved by keeping the Ten Commandments or any other part of the law.

It's also important to understand that God is the one who justifies sinful men. It is an attribute that is bestowed on us. We are still sinful even after we have been justified. God declares us justified based upon Christ's righteousness and his payment for sin on the cross. Man plays no part in justification. For greater study in this area, read chapters three and four of Paul's Epistle to the Romans. Here, Paul builds a solid case that Abraham was not justified by keeping the law, nor was he justified because he was circumcised. Rather, Abraham was justified by God *before* he was circumcised and *before* the Mosaic Law had ever been given. Abraham was justified by faith and so has every person who has ever been justified.

One of my former professors at Philadelphia College of Bible was the late Dr. John McGahey. He had a great way of explaining justification prior to Christ's crucifixion and resurrection. He taught us that Old Testament saints were saved on credit, looking forward to the payment to be made later through Christ's vicarious atonement. What a great illustration. We have an all too clear understanding of credit in twenty-first century America. Buy now, pay later. It sounds good on paper. Unfortunately it doesn't always work out well in the end as we are discovering in present-day America.

Prior to and following Christ's crucifixion and resurrection, all men have been justified in exactly the same manner: by faith. Genesis 20 and Romans 4 tell us

"Abraham believed God and it was credited to him as righteousness." So salvation is by faith alone not by works (Ephesians 2:8, 9). Much more could be said about salvation by faith alone, but that is not the purpose of this book. If you have any doubts about your eternal destiny, I would encourage you to study the book of Romans and form your own opinion about the mode of salvation.

Is salvation by faith or by works? If salvation is by faith, then why do we work so hard to try to please God? We work so hard to please God because we are confused about the mode of salvation. We have believed the false teaching that salvation is by works. The Protestant Reformation was a direct refutation of this false premise. When Martin Luther nailed his "95 Theses" to the door at the Church at Wittenberg, he was calling out the established church of the day on this very point. Martin Luther was a Roman Catholic priest. As such, he had always been taught and believed that salvation had to be earned, that keeping church tradition was equal, if not superior, to biblical authority. The more Luther studied the Scriptures, the more it became clear to him that salvation was not by works of human effort but by faith alone.

From the very first chapter of Romans, Luther noted a common thread in Paul's writing: salvation by faith apart from law. "For in the gospel a righteousness from God is revealed, a righteousness that is by faith from first to last, just as it is written, 'The righteous shall live by faith'" (Romans 1:17).

Romans 3 says that there is nothing that we could ever do to please God. As a matter of fact, we're told "all of our righteousness is as filthy rags." (See Isaiah 64:6.) The message is crystal clear: Stop trying to earn God's favor and accept the free gift that he has offered you. (See Romans 6:23.)

Until you have accepted the free gift of salvation and you surrender completely to Jesus Christ as Lord of your life, there is no way that you can be truly free from addiction. As a believer, you may have accepted Christ as your Savior, but you have not fully surrendered everything in your life to him. This is the mistake that I made so many years ago. I accepted Christ in 1973, but it wasn't until 2009 that I finally surrendered everything in my life to him without holding anything back.

For many of those years I lived in complete submission to my sinful master. I lived apart from God's grace. I was in chains, and I had no choice but to obey my addiction. This is because I did not completely surrender this sin in my life when I became a Christian. Sure, I was saved, but deep down there was really one thing that I wanted even more than Jesus Christ. That one thing was sex. I wanted sex.

I wanted as much sex as I could get any way that I could get it. I used sex as a drug. I got what I wanted without having to give anything of myself. This is one of the most selfish sins a man can commit. Rather than pleasing my wife, I chose to please myself. In so doing, I also chose sex over God. Sex *was* my god. I worshipped at the altar of sex.

It's no wonder I quit the ministry after a few short years. It's no wonder I finally quit going to church for a ten-year period. It's no wonder I didn't want anything to do with Christian friends or Christian family members. I was living a double life. I was a fraud. I hid my sin until it totally controlled me and destroyed my life.

The problem with addiction is that it is unmanageable. Ask any recovered addict and he or she will tell you without hesitation that if his or her addiction had not gotten out of control—if it could have been managed—he or she would still be using today. We all know this about ourselves. Thank God our addictions were so unmanageable that they finally brought us to rock bottom. It was there that we turned back to the God who loves us and forgives us unconditionally.

Some Encouragement

> Now if I do what I do not want to do, it is no longer I who do it, but it is sin living in me that does it. So I find this law at work: When I want to do good, evil is right there with me. For in my inner being I delight in God's law.
>
> Romans 7:20–22 (NIV)

As a part-time pastor, I don't get to preach very often. But when I do, some have noticed a common theme in my preaching. I tend to preach about sin an awful lot. Even when the message isn't particularly about sin, somehow the subject of sin seems to work its way into the message. I offer no apology for this. But I did ask myself the question, "Why do I preach on sin so much?" Well, there are a few very good reasons for it.

First of all, the Bible is a book about sin. From Adam and Eve's fall in the garden of Eden to sin and death being cast into the lake of fire in Revelation, the Bible talks about sin a lot. Fortunately, it's also a book about salvation. The two go hand in hand: sin and salvation. If it weren't for sin, we wouldn't need salvation. Without salvation, we'd be lost in our sin. So you see, the overarching theme of Scripture is the story of sin and salvation, the story of man's fall and redemption.

The second reason is simple. I hate sin. Sin has played far too prominent a role in my life. Sin nearly destroyed my life. Sin destroyed any chance I had at ministry for many, many years. Sin destroyed my first marriage. Sin hurt my children so badly that they bear scars that may never fully heal. And sin continues to attempt to destroy me at every chance it gets. Yes, I hate sin. I hate sin with a passion. So please bear with me. I'm going to talk about sin a little bit more.

Specifically, I'm going to talk about the Apostle Paul's sin as outlined in Romans 7. I hope you'll be encouraged by what I have to say about Romans 7. *I'm* encouraged when I read Romans 7. You say, "Brent, how can you be encouraged when you read about Paul's struggles with sin in Romans 7?" Well, the answer is really quite simple. If the Apostle Paul, who was the single greatest Christian missionary of all time, the author of most of the New Testament, the man who Christ single-handedly pursued and chose to be his apostle to the Gentiles, if this Paul struggled with sin in the manner he describes here in Romans 7 and was still used so mightily by God, well, then there's still hope for me. That's why I'm so encouraged by this passage.

I've struggled with sin every day of my Christian life. The struggle will never end until I am home with our Lord someday. We all struggle with sin. This is because we are human. To sin is human.

Please open your Bible to Romans 7 and see what the Apostle Paul has to say about his struggle with sin and how it applies to you and me in our Christian lives today. In verse 7, Paul is referring back to the previous context in chapter seven where he makes a comparison between the law of marriage and the law of sin. It is extremely important to consider the immediate context of Scripture when attempting to interpret and apply it to our lives. If we do not interpret Scripture according to its immediate context, and to Scripture as a whole, we can make Scripture say just about anything we want it to say. This is a dangerous practice and has led to many misinterpretations and heresies that exist to this day.

In that previous context, Paul concludes that the believer is no longer under the law of sin. He writes we have "died to sin." Just as the married woman is freed from the law of marriage upon the death of her husband, the believer is no longer bound to the law of sin. We "have been released from the law so that we serve in the new way of the Spirit, and not in the old way of the written code" (Romans 7:6). Before moving on, I would be remiss if I neglected to emphasize one of the points Paul is making here. We have "died to sin." Do you realize the magnitude of that statement? If you're a Christian, *you are dead to sin.* Just like the married woman is not held to law of marriage once her husband dies, so we are free from bondage to sin. We don't have to sin. We don't have to sin. This is incredibly joyous news. We don't have to sin. So why do we? Stay with me now. Paul is going to make it very clear in the next few verses.

Having established that we are free from sin, Paul now goes on to a passage of Scripture that is both confusing and encouraging all at the same time. Some believe that Paul could not have been describing his Christian life in verses 7 through 12. Conversely, some believe Paul was certainly describing his Christian life and the constant battle he waged against sin in these very same verses—two very different viewpoints. It will be very important for us to come to a conclusion on one of these points to fully understand this passage. Both viewpoints cannot be true at the same time. So was Paul describing his pre-Christian life or his Christian life here in these verses? The answer is right here in Romans 7.

If we look at the preceding context, we find that Paul has clearly given us the answer to the question. Let's look at verses 4 through 6. In verse 4, Paul refers to his readers as "brothers." He goes on to say that "they (you) also died to the law through the body of Christ." Now I ask you, why would Paul refer to his readers as brothers and remind them that "they also died to the law through the body of Christ" if he himself was not a brother and had also experienced death through the body of Christ?

Another clear indication that Paul was definitely writing about his condition as a believer is that he writes in the first person singular (used forty-six times from verses 7 through 25). From verse 14 on, Paul also writes in the present tense. If Paul were trying to convey that he was writing about his past struggles with sin while he was yet an unbeliever, he would have written in the past tense. If he were describing someone else, he would not have used the first person singular. John MacArthur writes on this passage:

> It seems rather that Paul is here describing the most spiritual and mature of Christians, who, the more they honestly measure themselves against God's standards of righteousness the more they realize how much they fall short. The closer we get to God, the more we see our own sin. Thus it is immature, fleshly, and legalistic persons who tend to live under the illusion that they are spiritual and that they measure up well by God's standards. The level of spiritual insight, brokenness, contrition, and humility that characterize the person depicted in Romans 7 are marks of a spiritual and mature believer, who before God has no trust in his own goodness and achievements.[14]

There's another pretty accurate indicator that Paul was describing his Christian life here in Romans 7. It's not indicated here in the text but it's an indicator that comes from our own Christian and non-Christian experience. Paul describes himself as "wretched." How many non-Christians do you know who are so wrecked about the sin they are enjoying that they would call themselves "wretched?" I mean, hey, let's face it—sin can be very attractive. If it weren't attractive, we wouldn't sin. Sin can be fun to the unsaved individual. It sure looks fun on TV and in the movies, doesn't it? But to the believer, sin is anything but fun. If a believer willfully continues in his sin in spite of the fact that he has been bought with the price of Christ's precious blood, it is only a matter of time before this individual will describe himself in the same manner which Paul describes himself: wretched.

It is clear from these preceding verses that Paul was indeed a Christian. He was describing something that is completely unique to the experience of the regenerated believer in Jesus Christ. We will refer to this as "The Divided Man."

"The Divided Man" is a phenomenon that the Christian experiences every day of his life. The Christian has not one, but two, natures. The first nature is the old sin nature, the nature that we were born with as human beings. The second nature is the new nature, the nature that we were given when we were born again. We will explore both of these natures, but we'll begin with the old sin nature.

Paul gets very personal here as he describes in vivid detail the effect the old sin nature has had on his life. The struggle he describes here is nothing short of Herculean, especially from verse 14 to the end of the chapter.

> We know that the law is spiritual; but I am un-spiritual, sold as a slave to sin. I do not understand what I do. For what I want to do I do not do, but what I hate I do. And if I do what I do not want to do, I agree that the law is good. As it is, it is no longer I myself who do it, but it is sin living in me. I know that nothing good lives in me, that is, in my sinful nature. For I have the desire to do

what is good, but I cannot carry it out. For what I do is not the good I want to do; no, the evil I do not want to do—this I keep on doing. Now if I do what I do not want to do, it is no longer I who do it, but it is sin living in me that does it.

So I find this law at work: When I want to do good, evil is right there with me. For in my inner being I delight in God's law; but I see another law at work in the members of my body, waging war against the law of my mind and making me a prisoner of the law of sin at work within my members. What a wretched man I am. Who will rescue me from this body of death? Thanks be to God—through Jesus Christ our Lord.

So then, I myself in my mind am a slave to God's law, but in the sinful nature a slave to the law of sin.

Romans 7:14–25 (NIV)

Does this sound familiar? Can you relate to what the Apostle Paul has just written here about himself? Good. I'm not the only one.

When I read these verses, I am amazed that Paul could have gone through the same struggles that I go through. As I said at the beginning of this chapter, this has been encouraging to me, in a sick sort of way, I suppose. Maybe it's encouraging to you as well. It should encourage you. This passage makes it clear that we are all the same. Remember, one of Satan's most devious ploys is the "divide and conquer" strategy. He wants you and me to believe we're the only ones who are struggling with sin in our lives. He knows that if he can get you and me to believe this lie, then he can easily defeat and eventually destroy us. And you can be sure of this: if you believe this lie, you and your Christian life will be destroyed. No, you won't lose your salvation, but you'll have very little joy or impact for God in your lifetime, and this is exactly what Satan is hoping for in the first place.

Don't believe the lie. You are not alone. We all struggle with sin. Sure, we come to church on Sunday morning and we put on our shiny, happy people faces. We try to make everyone think that everything is just peachy in our marriages and, of course, in our shiny, happy Christian lives. Inside we are terrified that if anyone ever found out what is really going on in our lives, he or she would probably bar us from attending church here anymore. What a lie we have bought into. Talk about deception. We make Adam and Eve look like trainees.

Transparency, honesty, and public confession are so important for this very reason. Unfortunately, these are missing components in our twenty-first century churches. Lucius Anneaus Seneca said, "Why does no one confess his sins? Because he is yet in them. It is for a man who has awoke from sleep to tell his dreams." I believe that as long as we continue to make-believe and portray this false persona in our churches, real life change will be difficult if not impossible. This is why I am drawn to addiction recovery ministry.

Forgiven, transformed addicts are dead-honest about their past and present condition. At addiction recovery meetings, we get down and dirty about ourselves. There is no faking it, no pretending that everything is okay, that everything has always been perfect in our lives. No, on the contrary, we confess our sins and failures to each other in a group format. In doing this, we forgive one another and encourage one another to get up and try again.

I wish our churches would get this. Not only would this make a huge difference in how we see ourselves as Christians—what a difference this would make in the way the world sees us. Instead of the masks we wear and masquerades that we play, if the world saw us as we really are—flawed but forgiven human beings—they might actually be attracted to Christianity. As it is, we appear far too perfect for them. They could never measure up. How sad that through our own hypocrisy we are pushing away the very people we hope to reach.

Now let's get back to Romans 7: Paul writes in verse 14 that he was "sold as a slave to sin." What does this mean? Well, put yourself in the position of the slave. Did he have any rights? Did he have any say in his life, his conditions, or his fate? No. The slave has no choice but to obey his master. Likewise, without the Holy Spirit's control in your life, you have no choice but to obey your master as well. You ask, "Who is my master?" According to the Bible, your master from the day that you were born has been sin. You were born a slave to sin (Romans 7:14). You were sold as a slave to sin.

How can a slave gain his freedom? Well, he can escape on his own, but this risks a punishment of death. Or a slave could be redeemed and set free by another master. Skipping down to verse 24, Paul asks this very question: "Who will rescue me from this body of death?" His answer: "Thanks be to God—through Jesus Christ our

Lord." Only Christ and the debt he paid on the cross for our sin can redeem us, rescue us, from the law of sin. If you have accepted Jesus Christ as your Lord and Savior, you have been freed from the law of sin.

If Paul had been rescued from the law of sin through Jesus Christ, why does he say of himself, "What a wretched man I am"? This doesn't seem to make sense, right? Yet every one of us who considers him or herself a believer knows exactly what Paul is talking about here. We can relate. Can we not? Of course we can, because we are human.

When you accept Christ as your Savior, you are given a new nature. This is the good news. The bad news is that the old nature is still hanging around as well. The two natures are diametrically opposed to one another. They are at constant war with one another. This is the phenomenon of "The Divided Man." We have *two* natures. As if it's not complicated enough to live with *one* nature. How in the world are we supposed to live with *two different natures* at the same time? Maybe now you understand why Paul called himself a "wretched man."

Notice what Paul says in verses 16–17: "And if I do what I do not want to do, I agree that the law is good. As it is, it is no longer I myself who do it, but it is sin living in me." Did you catch that? *We're* not the ones sinning— it's our old sin nature. We have been given a new nature. Eldredge points this out in *Wild at Heart*. He calls this old sin nature "The Traitor Within." Listen to what he writes: "To put it bluntly, your flesh is a weasel, a poser, and a selfish pig. And your flesh is *not you*. Did you know that? Your flesh is not the real you."[15]

Eldredge goes on to clarify that this old sin nature is not "our true self." This is a critical belief that can change your life. Instead of believing that we are nothing but wretched sinners, we find instead that our true self is good. God created man good. He created everything good. It's sin that's bad, not mankind.

Ezekiel 36:26 says, "I will give you a new heart and put a new spirit in you." Now, I realize this verse was written with Israel in mind, but this is also true for the believer. When you were born again, you were given a new heart and a new spirit. We are indeed a "new creation in Christ." The problem is that we don't know it or we don't believe it. But be encouraged by Paul's own struggle and the fact that sin is the bad guy here—not you.

Romans 7:14–25 is encouraging because it tells us that we're not alone and that Christ has set us free. But it doesn't tell us how we can live with these two separate natures and not feel the way that Paul felt. I mean, who wants to be wretched? For the solution to this problem, you have to keep reading Paul's letter where the secret is revealed in chapter eight. I'll give you a hint: it has something to do with surrender and the Holy Spirit.

Make no mistake about it, my friends. We are in a battle. The battle isn't for your soul because, if you are a believer, that battle has already been won. Your soul is safe in the hands of God the father. You didn't do anything to gain your salvation; therefore, you can't do anything to lose your salvation.

The battle is for your life. The battle is for whatever influence you can have for Christ. Satan and his henchmen want to destroy any chance you have of influencing your family, neighbors, friends, and co-workers for Christ. He will use every trick in his bag to get you. Genesis 4 tells us "sin is crouching at your door. It desires to have you but you must master it." Did you notice the personification of sin there? Sin is an active, animated, and powerful enemy.

Our own sin nature is constantly at war with our new nature on the very same turf. Throw in the temptations that the world and the devil put in front of us and it's no wonder we struggle. We are being attacked on three fronts. The only way that we can win this battle is to surrender. Yes, you heard me correctly. I said surrender. But we don't surrender to the enemy—we surrender to God. Unless your heart and mind are completely surrendered to God—unless he is in his rightful place in your life—unless you surrender everything to Christ, you will be defeated. Oh, you might not end up wretched like Paul. Oh, you might not end up quitting the ministry like I did some thirty years ago, but you will never reach your full potential in Christ. You will never be truly victorious. And isn't that what fighting a battle is really about anyway—winning?

Instead of enjoying victory over sin in our lives and the blessings that come from that victory, we are content to just win a battle here and there. You win some; you lose some. Oh well. What can you do? Nobody's perfect, right?

That's no way to live.

Can you relate to Paul's description of his Christian life? Have you been feeling wretched? Has sin taken a hold of you and you just can't seem to break free?

Well, I've got some good news for you. You're not alone and you can be free. Just like that slave who was set free by a kind emancipator, you can live a life free from slavery to sin. All you have to do is surrender to God. Give up the sin that has you in bondage. Lay it at the foot of the cross. Give up the fight. Surrender your heart, mind, and life to God and he will fight the battle for you from this moment on. Why live like a slave any longer? You have been set free. You are a child of the King!

Endnotes

1. Shogren, Gary Steven, Edward T. Welch. *Running in Circles: How to Find Freedom from Addictive Behavior.* Grand Rapids: Baker Books, 1995, 22.

2. May, M.D., Gerald G. *Addiction and Grace.* New York: HarperCollins, 1988, 39.

3. Felitti, Vincent J., *The Origins of Addiction: Evidence from the Adverse Childhood Experience Study.* English version of the article published in Germany as: Felitti VJ. Ursprünge des Suchtverhaltens–Evidenzen aus einer Studie zu belastenden Kindheitserfahrungen. Praxis der Kinderpsychologie und Kinderpsychiatrie, 2003. 52:547–559.

4. Burns, M.D., David. *Feeling Good: The New Mood Therapy.* New York: Signet Publishing, 1980, 184.

5. Johannes P. Louw and Eugene Albert Nida, *Greek-English Lexicon of the New Testament: Based on Semantic Domains*, electronic ed. of the 2nd edition. (New York: United Bible societies, 1996, c. 1989). 1:770.

6. Johannes P. Louw and Eugene Albert Nida, *Greek-English Lexicon of the New Testament: Based on Semantic Domains*, electronic ed. of the 2nd edition. (New York: United Bible societies, 1996, c. 1989). 1:770.

7. Excerpt from "Strongholds." Words and music by Rick Sawyer. Freewind Music.

8. Robert S. McGee, Pat Springle and Susan Joiner. *Rapha's Twelve-Step Program for Overcoming Chemical Dependency*. Merritt Island, FL: Rapha Resources, 1990.

9. Yancey, Philip D. *What's So Amazing About Grace?* Grand Rapids: Zondervan,1997, 70.

10. Tozer, A.W., *I Call It Heresy*. Gerald R. Smith, ed., Camp Hill: Christian Publications, 1991, 13.

11. MacArthur, *The Gospel According to Jesus*. Grand Rapids; Zondervan, 1998, xiii.

12. Shogren, Gary Steven, Edward T. Welch. *Running in Circles: How to Find Freedom from Addictive Behavior*. Grand Rapids: Baker Books, 1995, 45, 46.

13. Eldredge, John. *Wild at Heart*. Nashville: Thomas Nelson Publishers, 2001, 106.

14. MacArthur, John. *MacArthur's New Testament Commentary: Romans* 1–8. (Electronic Version) Chicago: Moody Bible Institute,1991. Chapter 28.

A GUIDE TO
RESEARCH FOR EDUCATORS
AND
TRAINERS OF ADULTS
(UPDATED EDITION)

by

Sharan B. Merriam
University of Georgia

and

Edwin L. Simpson
Northern Illinois University

KRIEGER PUBLISHING COMPANY
MALABAR, FLORIDA

Original Edition 1984
Reissue with updates 1989

Printed and Published by
ROBERT E. KRIEGER PUBLISHING COMPANY, INC.
KRIEGER DRIVE
MALABAR, FLORIDA 32950

Copyright © 1984 by
ROBERT E. KRIEGER PUBLISHING COMPANY, INC.

Library of Congress Cataloging-In-Publication Data

Merriam, Sharan B.
    A guide to research for educators and trainers of adults / by
Sharan B. Merriam and Edwin L. Simpson. -- Reissue with updates.
        p.   cm.
    Includes index.
    ISBN 0-89464-410-6 (alk. paper)
    1. Adult education--Research. I. Simpson, Edwin L. II. Title.
LC5225.R47M47 1989
374'.0072--dc20   89-15239
                                                            CIP

10   9   8   7   6   5

PREFACE

As the demand for educational and training opportunities for adults has accelerated within the last decade, so too has the need for competent teachers, administrators, trainers, and counselors of adults. In addition to the fields of adult education and human resource development which have traditionally dealt with adults, other areas of social practice--vocational education, allied health, social work, and counseling--have begun preparing people to attend to the needs of a growing adult clientele. Within the last decade, the number of graduate programs in adult education and human resource development and the number of adult-focused courses in other social science programs have increased dramatically.

Academic programs that train practitioners to work with adults also strive to produce graduates who not only understand but will perhaps contribute to the theory and knowledge base of their field. In order to realize this goal, those involved in the education and training of adults must know something about research, for it is through research, or systematic inquiry, that the knowledge base of a field expands. The development of research skills in most graduate programs has the two-fold purpose of training persons (1) to be consumers of research-- that is, to be able to understand, interpret, and apply research findings to their practice, and (2) to be researchers themselves, to initiate and implement investigations.

There are, of course, numerous books available on research design and statistical procedures. However, most texts on educational research methods present only the most commonly used research designs and draw supporting material from school-related studies. The authors of this book have attempted to address the shortcomings of other educational research texts by presenting a full range of methodology for doing research, and by supporting points with examples from research studies done with adults in adult settings. The traditional experimental, descriptive, and historical research methods are presented in Chapters 4 and 5. A discussion of ethnography, case study, and grounded theory can be found in Chapter 6. Also presented are philosophical inquiry (Chapter 5), interactive, ecological, and futures research (Chapter 7).

To provide an organizing framework for discussing these methodologies, the common processes found in all research approaches are used as a guide: (1) types of research problems, (2) assumptions underlying methodology, (3) ways the research phenomenon is delineated, and (4) use of data gathering procedures and techniques. Throughout the discussion, examples of actual research studies will be used and strengths and limitations of each method pointed out.

The text also contains two chapters not commonly found in other research texts. Chapter 3 explains the purposes and functions of a literature review and offers a step-by-step procedure for conducting and writing a review of the literature. And since much of the research in applied fields dealing with the education and training of adults is done by graduate students, Chapter 10 is devoted to the process of graduate research and the procedures unique to that process.

The authors hope this text will be a helpful resource for conducting and understanding research. Decisions about what to include and what to leave out were guided by our overall purpose of providing an overview of the research process and the alternative methodologies one might choose from in conducting a research study.

Many of our colleagues have contributed in different ways to the development of this book. We would like to give special thanks to two people--William Russell, author, doctoral student, and a former editor who put in long hours editing and critiquing the entire manuscript, and Dorothy Jossendal, who deftly typed numerous drafts and finally the entire manuscript. We would also like to acknowledge help from colleagues Peter Abrams, Ronald Cervero, Sean Courtney, Suzanne Davenport, John Niemi, Jeffry Simpson, and Harold Stubblefield who read and critiqued individual chapters. Finally, we want to thank our families and the Adult Continuing Education Program at Northern Illinois University who provided support throughout the project.

TABLE OF CONTENTS

LIST OF FIGURES

LIST OF TABLES

A GUIDE TO
RESEARCH FOR EDUCATORS
AND
TRAINERS OF ADULTS

CHAPTER 1

THE NATURE OF SYSTEMATIC INQUIRY

Research is central to the development of any field of study. Research activity is largely dependent upon the curiosity and energies of individuals who are attracted to practice and study in the field. Some people imagine research as the job for a well-trained scientist engaged in an important but somewhat mysterious activity in a laboratory. Though this perception may have been accurate at one time, it no longer is true. Today research is conducted by many people in many settings. All fields, including applied areas of social sciences (e.g., education, counseling, social work, human resource development), recognize the need for and the value of research. It is the means by which a discipline expands its knowledge base; and in applied fields, it informs and enhances practice. This text is intended for those persons engaged in an applied field of social practice and, in particular, areas of practice dealing with adults.

Because the practice of educating and training adults is diverse, research interests and pursuits of researchers in the field also are diverse. Such fields as business, political science, health, religion, industry, and vocational education all deal with educating and training adults. The daily work lives of persons engaged in any one of the above-mentioned fields entail problem solving, decision making, planning, instructing, and evaluating. As additional experience is gained in doing these tasks in our work, knowledge accumulates, decisions improve, better planning results, and so on. Hence, more experience and knowledge lead to more "professional" practice.

How do practitioners get the experience and knowledge to handle problems and make decisions? There are both informal and formal ways of enhancing practice. For instance, if you are the one who determines what training courses to offer company employees, informally you could ask your friend in another company what has been successful there, or you could ask for some suggestions from the employees themselves. You could do some casual reading in the latest issues of *Training and Development Journal*. You could also use your common sense and guess what might be relevant to the employees, given the particular business. Finally, you might employ a trial and error approach, offering some courses and seeing which ones the employees select.

However, more systematic ways exist for approaching the same problem -- ways that are more effective and more efficient in the long run. First, you could read in an organized fashion, using indexes to pinpoint specific articles that are relevant to the problem. Second, rather than asking a friend, you could consult with an expert or authority on the topic. You could also take a course in program development or attend a workshop on how to assess needs. Finally, you could conduct a systematic investigation to determine what is needed and when and how it should be offered. This systematic investigation might entail interviewing certain employees, administering a paper and pencil survey, searching company records of course offerings, and so on. In using this last method to handle the problem you would be engaging in "research." The purpose of this book is to acquaint those in applied fields with this particular systematic approach to enhancing practice -- that of doing research. We especially hope that those who deal with adults will not only discover the importance of conducting research in their field, but will also consider the ways in which they themselves can engage in the process.

The Meaning of Research

As many definitions of research exist as there are books on the topic. Some see research as "structured problem solving" (Helmstadter, 1970, p. 4), as "disciplined inquiry" (Good, 1973, p. 494) or as "the discovery, reinforcement, or refinement of knowledge" (Dreighton et al., 1971, p. 511). All of these conceptualizations have one idea in common -- research is a systematic process by which we know more about something than we did before engaging in the process. Two questions are important to the understanding of research: first, where does knowledge come from and second, what is meant by *systematically* searching for this knowledge?

Knowledge can be accessed through the four human processes of believing, thinking, sensing, and feeling (Royce, 1964). If we are told something by some trusted individual, or if we have always found something to be true in the past, we say that we *believe* it to be true. If reason is what we use to sort out the truth, our claim is that we *think* it is true. Experiencing truth through one or more of the five senses -- seeing, hearing, tasting, touching, smelling -- is how we *sense* knowledge to be true. Also, knowledge is interpreted as true if we have a positive, affective response to the knowledge; if we "*feel* good" about what is true or have insight as to the correctness of knowledge. Individuals accept or reject what they interpret to be true through the use of these four ways of knowing.

The type of knowledge is determined by which one of the four processes is used for accessing knowledge. For example, when personal belief is the source, the result is referred to as *authoritative* knowledge. In this instance, knowledge is based upon the acceptance of an ideology. Knowledge based upon thinking is termed *rational* knowledge. Logical, as opposed to illogical, reason is the test of thinking as the source of knowledge. Use of the five senses is referred to as *empirical*. Here, sensory perception is trusted to reveal truth. Feeling is cast as *intuitive* knowledge. Intuition is judged by the degree of insight or revelation an individual possesses.

Although all sources of knowledge have been used throughout human existence to help explain and adapt to life, certain sources have been used more at particular times than others. In pre-literate societies effective patterns for adapting to life were learned by watching other people and passing on traditions from one generation to the next.

Authoritative knowledge greatly influenced the interpretation of truth and reality. Truth was often accepted by virtue of the role assumed by appointed individuals, such as priests, witchdoctors, or soothsayers, who espoused certain special abilities. Belief, usually conveyed through cultural or religious tradition, is still a principal conveyor of truth. Documents such as the Bible or the Koran represent knowledge that is authoritative. Individuals representing cultural or religious traditions, such as Jesus Christ or Mohammed, are used as authoritative sources of knowledge. In a contemporary sense, dictionaries and legal documents are authoritative sources, as well as Supreme Court judges and religious leaders such as the Pope.

Rational thinking gained acceptance as a pathway to knowledge during early Greek civilization and again in seventeenth and eighteenth century Europe. Emphasis was placed upon logic and the elements of the rational process. Use of deductive Aristotelian logic and inductive thought, proposed by Francis Bacon in the seventeenth century, helped develop thinking as a way to knowledge. Deductive reasoning -- moving from general observations to specific cases -- and inductive reasoning -- observing individual cases in moving to generalizations -- have greatly influenced research methodology.

Two approaches commonly used to solve the problems of everyday life involve gaining access to knowledge through sensory experience and through intuition. In using our five senses we are trusting our sensory experience above other sources of truth.

An example of sensory-based knowledge is the way we know the sun rises and sets. If a resident of the United States were asked about the regularity of the sun each day, the response probably would be that the sun rises each morning and sets every evening. This, of course, would not be the same experience as a Finnish Laplander living in the land of the midnight sun where the regularity of the sun is in terms of months.

Knowledge resulting from the use of feeling, or a prior knowledge, as explained by Kerlinger (1986), is intuitive knowledge. Intuition is a self-evident way of determining truth. By using feelings as the pathway to knowledge, the researcher jumps from the known to the unknown, and the responsibility for the validity of that knowledge belongs to the individual. Some researchers refer to intuition as the pursuit of hunches, while others, such as Bruner (1967), identify this source as an "educated leap." Artistic or creative expression is an example of intuitive knowledge. By blending contrasting colors from the palette into a provocative synthesis on the canvas, the artist is demonstrating a way of knowing. Likewise, the novelist's woven tale of fiction, or the jazz musicians's improvisation on a Dixie-land tune, is a form of knowledge.

The defining characteristic of research is that it is a systematic, structured, purposeful, and disciplined process of discovering reality. Research is a matter of process, not of outcomes. Whether or not an investigation leads to uncovering truth is only of immediate concern. For example, the alchemists of the Middle Ages seriously undertook the task of determining what sort of matter made up the world. While they failed to find an answer to their question, alchemy was a scholarly process of inquiry. And through alchemy "hard facts were learned about the behavior of metals and their alloys; the properties of acids, bases, and salts were recognized; the mathematics of thermodynamics was worked out; and, with just a few jumps through centuries, the helical molecule of DNA was revealed in all its mystery" (Thomas, 1982, p. 35).

Since each type of knowledge is unique, different "systems" or methods have been developed to access different types of knowledge. For example, logic has been developed to help access rational knowledge and the scientific method structures an investigation of empirical knowledge. Historical methods are in part used to investigate authoritative knowledge, and intuitive knowledge can be accessed by methods of naturalistic inquiry.

no pursuit of a hunch

Until recently researchers have made more use of rational and empirical knowledge bases than those of authority or intuition. During the Renaissance there was a great desire to interpret the so-called laws of nature. Experiments were conducted, for example, on the speed of objects falling through space in relation to their weight and the density of air (Santillana, 1953). Systematic though these early experiments were, it was not until Charles Darwin combined inductive and deductive reasoning with observations that research became "scientific." Realizing that direct observation of various species of animals alone was not leading to productive ends, Darwin formulated a tentative explanation about the extinction and continuation of animals. In so doing he posed a hypothesis of natural selection which he could then test through additional observation and data collection.

Darwin's approach, which was considered "scientific," came to characterize much of the research that was done after the mid-nineteenth century. The term "science" itself came to mean "a body of knowledge which is accurate, verifiable, and organized in a definite manner" (Helmstadter, 1970, p. 7). It no longer only referred to specific subjects such as physics, chemistry, or biology. The scientific method in research involves inductive and deductive reasoning, testing hypotheses, and observing empirical phenomena. It is a highly refined, systematic approach to rational and empirical sources of knowledge.

It was not until the mid-twentieth century that a source other than rational and empirical knowledge was thought suitable for systematic inquiry. In contrast to the objective, rational approach of the scientific method, humanists make the point that all science is grounded in the subjectivity of human experience (Kockelmans and Kisiel, 1970). Based in phenomenological philosophy, this approach added an intuitive or inner perspective to social research and theory (Bruyn, 1966). That is, research in this mode involved "direct investigation and description of phenomena as consciously experienced, without theories about causal explanation and as free as possible from unexamined preconceptions and presuppositions" (Encyclopedia Britannica, 1967, p. 810). The influence of phenomenology and humanism has resulted in a different emphasis in the research process. "Qualitative" or "naturalistic" research, as this approach has come to be labeled, rests upon different assumptions about knowledge and the nature of reality (Lincoln and Guba, 1985). Consequently, research techniques other than the scientific method have also been developed with which to access this type of knowledge.

Purpose and Types of Research

Typically, persons in applied fields of practice are overworked and underpaid. Taking the time to learn about the research process and to carry out a study requires a commitment that not many are able to make. Many professionals, however, realize the value of research to the field and are able to involve themselves in various ways. In addition to actually conducting research, they are in positions to utilize research results and to identify problems needing study.

Ultimately the value or purpose of research in an applied field is to improve the quality of practice of that discipline. The improvement of practice can come from either of two types of research endeavors. *Basic* or pure research is motivated by intellectual interest and has as its goal the extension of knowledge. *Applied* research is directed toward solving an immediate practical problem. Selltiz, et al. (1959) comment on the role of basic and applied research in the social sciences:

> Historically, the scientific enterprise has been concerned both with knowledge for its own sake and with knowledge for what it can contribute to practical concerns. This double emphasis is perhaps especially appropriate in the case of social science. On the one hand, its responsibility as a *science* is to develop a body of principles that make possible the understanding and prediction of the whole range of human interactions. On the other hand, because of its social orientation, it is increasingly being looked to for practical guidance in solving immediate problems of human relations. (p. 4)

While more applied research is carried out in fields dealing with the education and training of adults, both basic and applied research can have an impact upon practice. The results of basic research may have very practical applications, and applied research may lead to the building or testing of theory. For example, applying Piaget's theory of cognitive functioning could lead to very specific curriculum materials and instructional practices when working with learners at various levels of cognitive functioning. On the other hand, if one were to test the levels of cognitive functioning of adults and find that many have not achieved formal operations (said by Piaget to develop at adolescence), then Piaget's theory would be challenged.

A form of applied research widely used in fields of social practice is evaluation studies. The difference between evaluation and research, which are both forms of systematic inquiry, lies in the questions asked, not in the methods used, for the methods in each are essentially the same. Evaluation research collects data or evidence on the worth or value of a program, process, or technique. Its main purpose is to establish a basis for decision making. "Such decisions might pertain to selecting the most effective procedure, material, or organizational structure. Evaluation studies may also address such questions as 'Does this technique (material, treatment) work?' " (Drew, 1985, pp. 16-17). Evaluation is considered a type of applied research because it is involved in immediate problems and is likely to have an immediate impact upon practice. Selltiz *et al.* (1976) in fact notes the prevalence of evaluation studies being done by federally funded agencies and the impact this research has upon social policy.

In business and industry, applied research often deals with the development of a product and is thus referred to as "developmental" or "product" research. Companies may have research development (R&D) divisions devoted exclusively to product development. Borg (1981) discusses the relationship of R&D to applied and basic modes of research. Too often, he feels, basic and applied research studies have little effect upon practice.

> R&D takes the findings generated by basic and applied research and uses them to build tested products that are ready for operational use....R&D is not a substitute for basic or applied research. All three research strategies -- basic, applied, and R&D -- are required to bring about...change. In fact, R&D increases the potential impact of basic and applied research findings upon... practice by translating them into usable...products. (p. 222)

Thus, practitioners have many options open to them if they choose to make an active contribution to their field through research. Searching for new knowledge for its own sake or refining available knowledge may prove as important in the long run as using research to solve an immediate practical problem, evalute a program, or develop a new product. The type of research done will be determined by the questions raised as a result of being engaged in a particular field of practice. Whether one's motivation is primarily intellectual or practical, however, the process of research is essentially the same.

The Research Process

The process of planning and conducting research can be divided into the tasks of (1) identifying a problem, (2) establishing a conceptual framework, (3) delineating the research phenomenon, (4) selecting a research methodology and using data gathering procedures and techniques, and (5) analyzing data. As authors of this book, we have chosen this research process as the organizing structure. We realize, however, that the *process* is not always sequential and that variations in the sequence are not only possible, but appropriate at times. The reader is advised to treat the book as a reference, using those portions that fit the need for assistance in planning and conducting research as it arises.

Problem identification occurs at the very beginning of most research. Development of a problem statement identifies the particular concern of the researcher. At this point in the process, the researcher considers such things as the applied or basic nature of the research. Problems in applied fields such as adult education and training are usually taken from practice. Problems of a conceptual nature, on the other hand, typically guide basic or fundamental research. The research problem statement describes variables and/or concepts around which research activity will focus. The problem statement is a paragraph that identifies the research topic area and ends in a broad general question, such as "What is the influence of training on adult performance on the job?" or concludes in a hypothetical statement such as "There is a difference in patient wellness after leaving a hospital that provides programs of patient education." Some statement of a problem, no matter how general in description, is established in order to guide further activity. The research problem is discussed in more depth in Chapter 2.

A second task in the process of research is establishing a conceptual framework. Recognizing and discussing theories, concepts, and factors that are part of the study are essential to developing a useful problem statement. Developing a conceptual framework involves the progressive discovery of the exact problem to be studied. As the problem becomes clearer, related theories and concepts are clarified. In a reciprocal way, delineation of the problem statement also assists in identifying and clarifying important concepts and factors to be studied. A review of research literature is frequently used to assist the researcher in developing a framework. Once the research problem has been identified, it is helpful to discover what concepts and procedures other researchers have used in pursuing the same or similar lines of inquiry. Knowing the variables and methods that others have identified in their research also gives direction and warns against pitfalls in planning research. These functions and other aspects of the literature review are discussed in Chapter 3.

After describing the problem and reviewing literature to develop a conceptual background for the study, the researcher begins the third task of identifying the specific research phenomena -- that is, the variables that will be investigated. Careful identification of phenomena to be studied is accomplished by (1) defining terms, (2) delimiting the scope of the study, and (3) specifying the assumptions upon which the study is based. For example, if a researcher planned to study training as it influences job performance, terms such as "method," "influence," and "performance" would require definition. Also, characteristics of the adults participating in the study would need to be described (e.g., age range, sex, and socioeconomic status). Defining and delimiting the study help establish boundaries of the inquiry and bring into focus the particular variables and interrelationships that are important in the investigation. Assumptions the researcher is making about training, as it is related to performance, would be another consideration in developing an adequate conceptual framework.

As the conceptual framework for the particular problem is being developed, one becomes aware of the research methodology that would be most appropriate in conducting the study. The selection of a methodology depends upon the source of knowledge being accessed and the assumptions underlying the nature of research. Testing theory or describing phenomena involves sampling, hypothesis testing, and so on, which are common to experimental, ex post facto, and descriptive research designs. Building theory or interpreting phenomenon will most likely involve qualitative or naturalistic approaches such as those found in ethnography, grounded theory, historical or philosophical inquiry. Chapters 4, 5, 6, and 7 are devoted to explaining various research methodologies that one might use in conducting a study.

As part of the fourth task of settling upon an overall methodological approach, one must also select the appropriate data collection techniques. Using the training study as an example, the researcher might use a questionnaire or interview protocol in collecting data. Or, if observation is to be used, a rating scale might be incorporated. Specific data collection techniques are discussed in Chapter 8.

The fifth part of the process that all research has in common is data analysis. If research is carefully planned and conducted, an analysis of data will produce descriptions and inferences about the phenomenon being studied. Research findings eventually lead to conclusions pertaining to the original problem, or they serve as a guide to reconceptualize the problem in the event conclusions cannot be drawn. Analyzing data depends to a large extent upon the particular methodology being used. Therefore, general considerations in the handling of data according to the type of methodology being employed are found in Chapters 4 through 7.

Once the research investigation is completed, it is important to report the results. Only through the reporting and disseminating of findings can research contribute to the knowledge base of a field and enhance practice. Chapter 9 offers suggestions on how to report and disseminate research.

In the experiences of the authors of this text, much of the research in an applied field is done by graduate students employed in the field who are also pursuing (usually part-time) a master's or doctoral degree. While the actual research process is the same regardless of the role one is in, there are some formalized procedures characteristic of graduate research. Writing a proposal, forming a committee, and holding an oral defense are three procedures most students need to deal with as part of their graduate research experience. Chapter 10 deals with the practical aspects of doing graduate research.

Finally, at the end of the book, readers will find a comprehensive glossary of commonly used research terms. It is our hope that all parts of the book will assist researchers in meeting the challenges of conducting research effectively -- to achieve both efficiency in use of limited research time and personal satisfaction in the quality of research results.

REFERENCES

Borg, W. R. (1981). *Applying Educational Research*. New York: Longman.
Bruner, Jerome S. (1967). *A Study of Thinking*. New York: John Wiley and Sons.
Bruyn, Severyn T. (1966). *The Human Perspective in Sociology*. Englewood Cliffs, New Jersey: Prentice-Hall, Inc.
Dreighton, Lee C. (1971). *Encyclopedia of Education* (ed.). New York: the Macmillan Company, Vol. 7
Drew, C. J. (1985). *Introduction to Designing and Conducting Research*. St. Louis: The C. V. Mosby Co.
Encyclopedia Britannica. (1961). Chicago: Encyclopedia Britannica Inc.
Good, Carter V. (1973). *Dictionary of Education*, (ed.). (3rd ed.), Chicago: MacGraw-Hill.
Helmstadter, C. C. (1970). *Research Concepts in Human Behavior*. New York: Appleton-Century-Crofts, Inc.
Kerlinger, F. N. (1986). *Foundations of Behavioral Research*. New York: Holt, Rinehart and Winston. (3rd ed.)
Kockelmans, Joseph J. and Theodore J. Kisiel. (1970). *Phenomenology and Natural Sciences: Essays and Translation*. Evanston, Illinois: Northwestern University Press.
Lincoln, Yvonne and Egon Guba. (1985). *Naturalistic Inquiry*. London: Sage Publishers.
Royce, Joseph R. (1964). *The Encapsulated Man*. Princeton: VanNostrand Company.

Santillana, G. de. (1953). *Dialogue of the Great World Systems*, (ed.). Chicago: The University of Chicago Press.

Selltiz, Claire et al. (1959). *Research Methods in Social Relations*. New York: Holt, Rinehart and Winston.

Selltiz, Claire, et al. (1976). *Research Methods in Social Relations*. New York: Holt, Rinehart and Winston.

Thomas, Lewis. (1982). "On Alchemy." *Discover*. 3:34-35.

CHAPTER 2

FOCUSING THE RESEARCH

In any research endeavor, the careful delineation of the problem to be studied saves time in the long run and results in a more satisfactory experience overall. The process of identifying a researchable problem begins with being interested in a particular topic or area of concern. For most people, determining an area of interest is easy. The difficult step is to perceive a problem within the area of interest that is significant, of manageable size, and is systematically approachable.

Once a problem has been identified, it must be shaped in order to guide the study. "Shaping" is done by delineating its relationship to theory and previous research, by defining terms and concepts, and by developing research questions or hypotheses. The purpose of this chapter is to present the considerations involved in identifying and shaping a research problem. Specifically, the selection of a topic, the nature and significance of the problem, and the place of theory in the research process will be covered. Also discussed are how to formulate a problem statement, arrive at definitions, and write questions and hypotheses.

Topic Selection

Research topics come from either practical situations or intellectual curiosity (Selltiz, et al. 1976). Topics of practical concern stem from day-to-day experiences. What causes certain events to happen or how particular sets of events are related might be questioned. For example, a classroom teacher has the opportunity to use various instructional techniques. A practical concern would be to determine which method is most effective in helping adults achieve more rapidly or learn in greater depth in a given set of circumstances. A topic that evolves from practical concerns tends to be quite focused and specific.

Intellectually motivated topics lead to broader, more conceptual questions that deal with general rather than specific classes of phenomena. The researcher who chooses such a topic may end up exploring areas about which very little is currently known. Often, an area of general conceptual interest may have many components, any one of which could be pursued. For example, curiosity about midlife career change may lead the researcher to study a number of related topics such as job burnout, career decision making, perspective transformation, or stress management.

An important consideration in selecting the research topic is the part that values play in the process (Selltiz, et al. 1976). The topic a researcher selects is dictated, to a large extent, by what one considers worth pursuing. Selltiz (1976, et al. p.53) point out that while values aid in selection of a topic, care must be taken that they "not be allowed to influence the *outcome* of research." Self-awareness of motives and biases on the part of the researcher will help ensure the appropriate planning and execution of a quality research study.

The Research Problem

No simple formula exists for extracting a researchable problem out of a topic of interest. As Guba (1978, p. 45) observes, "problems do not exist in nature, but in the *minds of people*." What becomes identified as a problem depends upon an individual researcher's notion of the nature of a problem. Some have defined it as a situation demanding a solution. Others, like Kerlinger (1986, p. 16), define it as "an interrogative sentence or statement that asks: 'What relationship exists between two or more variables?' " Not everyone defines a problem as a specific situation needing a solution or as a question needing an answer. The growth of social science and applied fields of study has led some researchers to accept a more heuristic or dynamic view. John Dewey (1933), for example, observed that a problem arises out of some felt difficulty; a person is puzzled, dissatisfied, unsure about something. Dewey points out that "there is a genuine problem or question if we are willing to extend the meaning of the word...to whatever...perplexes and challenges the mind so that it makes belief...uncertain" (Dewey, 1933, pp. 12-13).

A problem, then, might be best defined as something that "perlexes and challenges the mind." Just how something might be perplexing is addressed by Guba (1978):

> A problem is a situation resulting from the interaction or juxta-position of *two or more factors* (e.g., givens, constraints, conditions, desires, etc.) which yields: (1) a perplexing or enigmatic state (a *conceptual* problem); (2) a conflict which renders the choice from among alternative courses of action moot (an *action*

problem); or (3) an undesirable consequence (a *value* problem). (pp. 44-45)

Conceptual problems stem from "two juxtaposed elements that are conceptually, or theoretically inconsistent" (Guba, 1978, p. 45). The concept "intelligence," for example, is often defined for research purposes in a way that is inconsistent with its functional use in everyday life. Action problems result from a conflict that seems to provide no clear choice of alternative courses of action. Wanting to know which teaching method produces the best results is an action problem. Value problems come from "undesirable consequences" according to some expected or set standard; for example, questioning the effect that handicapped adult students who have been placed in a learning group have upon the learning of other adults in that group.

The process of identifying a research problem can be facilitated through such activities as reading widely on the topic of interest, talking with other people, especially those who are familiar with the area, observing closely situations pertinent to the problem, taking notes as thoughts on the topic occur, and, most importantly, adopting a critical stance that permeates all the above activities.

The research problem is a catalyst for transferring one's general curiosities into a workable tool for planning and guiding research. The process of problem identification involves refining and narrowing the focus of research. The process may start with a general notion or idea that the researcher has; no significant event or pronouncement is necessary. The researcher is constantly aware of relationships and inconsistencies that exist in day-to-day experience, and so, in a sense, the researcher is always entertaining problems for research.

Significance of the Research Problem

At least three levels of reasoning are involved in the decision to pursue a piece of research (Manheim, 1977). First, there are personal reasons, which typically involve asking such questions as, Why am I interested in the topic? How can I justify doing the study? What personal satisfaction do I hope to gain from the study?

Second, the researcher judges the value of a study by its importance to the field of study it represents. Of what professional value will the research be? How will it contribute to knowledge about adult education and training? How will results of the study be used? How does the study relate to the development or refinement of theory? What generalizations can be made from the study? Fox (1969, p. 107) lists the several ways a study can make a contribution--it can "look at some new aspect of a problem, seek to clarify an ambiguous point of theory, (and) seek to test some new interpretation of data from other studies." The problem itself need not be "new" for the research to be important. For example, the accurate assessment of the educational needs of older learners has been a continuing concern in adult education. Green and Enderline (1980) supported through research their hypothesis that older adult learning needs are a function of socioeconomic class and age (the very old having different needs than newly retired people). Their new way of looking at an old problem has added to our knowledge of the older adult.

A research study can also be a contribution if it leads to new problems and questions. Not finding what is expected may raise additional questions and may prove more productive than simply supporting a hypothesis or answering a question. Likewise, those studies that lead to hypotheses or that build theory (rather than test it) also stimulate further research.

A third but less important reason for investigating a particular topic might be the availability of financial and other forms of support. Quite often research activity is supported by outside agencies, such as the government or private foundations. In considering the importance of research from this level, the goals of funding sources are helpful guidelines in determining significance. The blend of personal interests, value to the field, and practical conditions of support are all used by the investigator to determine the significance of a research problem.

The selection of a research topic and the identification of a significant problem are not necessarily sequential steps. Problems that one encounters related to practice often are the starting point in the development of a research study. The significance of the problem is considered alongside the establishing of a theoretical framework. Such a framework evolves out of a familiarity with the previous research and thinking that has been done on the topic.

Theory and the Research Process

Establishing the theoretical framework of a problem involves a consideration of the place of theory in the research process. Vagueness as to the role of theory is apparent in the frequent characterization of theories as idealistic generalizations of no practical use. Terms such as "a priori" and "substantive" contribute to the confusion (see Glossary). However, establishing a problem's relationship to theory not only helps to ascertain the problem's significance, but also lends direction to the overall research study.

Research, or the systematic search for knowledge, involves more than collecting information about a particular phenomenon. The facts, observations, experiences -- the "data" that we gather -- have little meaning by themselves. An attempt must be made to show how facts about a phenomenon relate to one another. Theorizing is the ordering and integrating of pieces of information into a whole; it is the way we make sense out of our world; it is finding an underlying pattern or order. A theory, then, summarizes information and offers a general explanation of the phenomenon being studied. The more powerful theories explain more of our world to us and also predict future events. In Kerlinger's words, a theory is a "set of interrelated constructs (concepts), definitions, and propositions that presents a systematic viewpoint of phenomena by specifying relations among variables, with the purpose of explaining and predicting the phenomena" (Kerlinger, 1986, p. 9).

The place of theory in the research process depends to a large extent upon what is known in the particular area of investigation. In some areas of social science research, a considerable amount of data has already been gathered and interpreted by theory. Much is known, for example, about people's behavior in groups, and several theories have been advanced to explain and predict how people will act in various group settings. In other areas of human behavior, less is known and there are few theories. Thus, depending upon the state of knowledge, the research process might be one of *testing* well-developed theory, *clarifying* or *refocusing* tentative theories, or *developing* new theory.

Much of scientific research tests what is called hypothetical-deductive or a priori theory. That is, a theory is proposed from which deductions are made about corresponding behavior or events in the real world. These deductions or hypotheses are tested and, to the extent that they can be verified, the theory becomes more credible. In this mode of inquiry one decides in advance what general principles will be applied to understanding specific phenomena. The theory provides a framework or guide for what is to be observed and which facts are to be collected. Empirical evidence then confirms or refutes the theory. When a theory is being tested, control of extraneous variables is an important consideration; equal concern must also be given to the number and representativeness of the cases used to test the theory. Hence, research in this mode is often labeled "scientific" or "quantitative." Selltiz et al. (1959, p. 490-491) have delineated several advantages to theory-guided research:

- theory provides a means of structuring the inquiry;
- phenomenon other than the theory's referent may be explained by the theory;
- theory increases "the meaningfulness of the findings of a given study by making it possible to perceive them not as isolated bits of empirical information but as a special case of the working out of a set of more abstract propositions";
- theory "provides a more secure ground for prediction than do the findings by themselves."

In some research, the role of theory is not as directive as the above discussion would suggest. There are not as many long-standing, well-established theories in the social sciences as there are in the natural sciences where phenomena are easier to observe and manipulate. Theories about human behavior thus tend to be more tentative than those dealing with physical and biological phenomena. Education and psychology, for example, are also relatively new areas of investigation. Most theories in these and similar areas have evolved within the last century and have not been extensively tested. Much of the research in the social sciences results in the extension, refinement, or enhancement of theory. For example, Jean Piaget studied the intellectual growth of a small group of children, which led to a theory of cognitive development. Piaget identified four stages of cognitive growth: the sensory motor stage, the preoperational stage, the concrete stage, and the stage of formal operations. Subsequent studies testing Piaget's theory have generally supported his observation of the original four stages and have tentatively extended the theory to a fifth stage associated with adulthood -- the problem-finding stage (Arlin, 1975). In this example, inductive investigation of the behavior of children led to theoretical assumptions that have implications for adult development and learning.

Theory may be tested and modified in the research process. In either case, it serves to guide the collection of information and the interpretation of results. Theory may also be the end result of research. It is necessary to develop theory when (1) there is none available, in order to explain a particular phenomenon, or (2) when existing theory fails to provide an adequate or appropriate explanation. The process by which research leads to theory is an inductive one. Theories that evolve from phenomenon are labeled "inductive" in contrast to the hypothetical-deductive mode mentioned earlier. Those studies that have as their goal the discovery of theory rather than verification are often called "qualitative" or "naturalistic" studies. Based in phenomenology, rather than in logical positivism, this type of inquiry differs from theory-testing approaches on two dimensions: (1) "the amount of manipulation of conditions antecedent to the inquiry" and (2) "the degree of constraint imposed on outputs" of the inquiry (Guba, 1978, p. 3). Because there is no theory by which to direct the study and predict the results, there is little or no manipulation of the phenomenon and no predicted outcomes. The phenomenon is merely observed, and an explanatory paradigm or theory is allowed to emerge from the data itself. Once a theory has emerged, it has the status of an a priori or hypothetical-deductive theory and must itself be tested (Guba and Lincoln, 1981).

The role of theory in the research process can be seen in Figure 2.1.

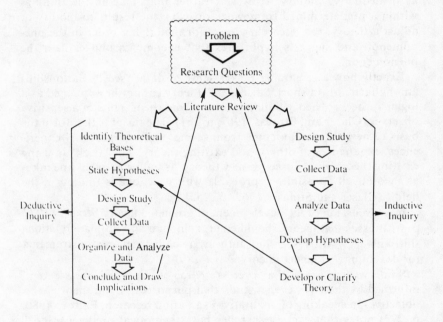

Figure 2.1. The process of systematic inquiry

The process begins with a problem from which questions rise. A review of previous research will reveal the extent of knowledge and theorizing pertinent to the topic. A researcher must then decide whether existing theory can be used as a guide in the investigation, or whether the investigation will focus upon developing a theory to explain the phenomenon.

If there is theory to guide the research, the hypotheses can be deduced from that theory. Hypotheses are tentative explanations that direct our search for order among facts. Once hypotheses are formed, the study can be designed; data is then collected and analyzed, and conclusions and implications are drawn with regard to the theory that originally informed the study.

If a literature review reveals that no theory fits the phenomenon under investigation, then one study goal might be to formulate a theory and/or hypotheses to explain observed events or behavior. In this case the researcher designs a study, collects data, and analyzes data just as in deductive inquiry. However, rather than placing the findings within a predetermined framework or using the results to modify or adjust a theory, the researcher looks for underlying order in the phenomenon and suggests hypotheses that encompass and explain the phenomenon.

Exactly how a researcher makes sense of data, "sees" relationships among facts, or, in short, "discovers" theory cannot be explained as a logical process. Theory building comes from the insights of a sensitive observer (Glaser and Strauss, 1967, p. 281). The insights that form the basis of new theory can come from several sources: personal experiences, experiences of others, and existing theory. The "trick" in using existing theory as a source for new theory "is to line up what one takes as theoretically possible or probable with what one is finding in the field" (Glaser and Strauss, 1967, p. 253).

In a discussion of the development of grounded theory Strauss (1987 p. 6) stresses that theory should emerge through an "intimate relationship with data, with researchers fully aware of themselves as instruments for developing grounded theory."

Some writers argue that every research study is, to some extent, informed by theory -- even a study that purports to build theory as its objective. In speaking of qualitative evaluation research, Patton (1980, p. 277) notes that every researcher has "theoretical predispositions" that affect the focus of a study and, to some extent, observations and analyses may be "distorted by conscious or unconscious predispositions." Researchers have a responsibility to examine and make explicit their theoretical orientation.

In summary, theory is a shorthand account of how some aspect of our world works. If the account is a good one, it will be internally consistent, easy to understand, and applicable to similar situations. The more situations the theory can explain, predict, and control, the more powerful it is.

As the researcher develops the problem and reviews related theory, concepts and terms emerge that are central to a specific statement of the problem. Each key concept and term requires definition if useful guidelines for conducting research are to be achieved. Thus, another task in problem identification is developing a problem statement in which the terms are clearly defined.

Problem Statement and Definitions

The formulation of a research problem statement "involves both a progressive sharpening of concepts and a progressive narrowing of scope" (Selltiz, et al. 1976, p. 55). Just what needs to be determined or solved must be clarified. The problem statement is usually a paragraph within the discussion of the problem that pinpoints the primary question the researcher is asking. Given the vital role the problem statement plays in the research process, the need for precision is evident. A statement that is too broad in scope may not adequately delineate the relationships or concepts to be studied. A problem statement that is too narrowly focused, however, may direct the researcher only toward trivia. The problem statement (which can be stated as a question) identifies the key factors in the study. For example, a research problem dealing with the educational needs of adults over sixty-five years of age might lead to a problem related to how innovations are adopted into practice might lead to asking how a company that has a record of adopting innovative ideas differs from one that does not.
lead to asking how a company that has a record of adopting innovative ideas differs from one that does not.

Defining terms and concepts is an important step in shaping the problem. Concepts represent a constellation of ideas used to explain and describe the phenomena being studied. Concepts are abstractions --such as achievement, intelligence, and chauvinism -- that develop from particular observations of behavior, conditions, or events. They represent phenomena understood to exist but which cannot be observed directly (Kerlinger, 1986). Selltiz (1959) points out that:

> The greater the distance between one's concepts, or constructs, and the empirical facts to which they are intended to refer, the greater the possibility of their being misunderstood or carelessly used, and the greater the care that must be given to defining them. They must be defined both in abstract terms, giving the general meaning they are intended to convey, and in terms of the operations by which they will be represented in the particular

study. The former type of definition is necessary in order to link the study with the body of knowledge using similar concepts or constructs. The latter is an essential step in carrying out any research, since data must be collected in terms of observable facts. (p. 41)

Using the problem statement posed earlier concerning the effectiveness of commuity college classes in meeting the educational needs of adults over sixty-five years of age, the researcher would need to define "effectiveness," "community college," and "educational needs." Additionally, the researcher must indicate how these concepts are going to be observed and measured.

In this example "adults" are defined in terms of age (over sixty-five). In many studies dealing with the education and training of adults, the term "adult" will need clarification. Webster's definition, "a human being after an age specified by law," may be too broad for use in the investigation. An operational definition such as "a person assuming the roles and responsibilities for independent living" may be more helpful in focusing the problem. In addition, the cultural, racial, and socioeconomic makeup of participants may contribute to defining "adult." In the above study, adults over sixty-five living in a certain geographic area or those that have common work or life experiences (government employees, new retirees, for example) might be incorporated into an operational definition to further focus the study.

Not all concepts mentioned or implied in the problem can be defined prior to the study. In fact, the purpose of some inductive lines of inquiry, such as grounded theory and ethnographic research, may be to delineate concepts. The important consideration in the identification of the problem and in the writing of the problem statement is to recognize those terms and concepts that do require definition in order for the research project to be successfully carried out.

Developing a well-constructed problem statement, examining related theory, and defining terms and concepts lead to more specific questions or hypotheses -- the final task in the process of problem identification. Research questions usually guide exploratory, theory-building, or descriptive studies. Hypotheses are used in experimental, theory-testing research designs.

Formulating Research Questions

Two types of questions guide research: (1) questions that address whether certain observed events always follow a pattern, and (2) questions that address whether particular circumstances produce the same or different outcomes. A question that addresses a pattern of events, for example, might direct the researcher to observe how participants in a training setting learn a particular skill in a series of training episodes. A question directed toward outcomes in the same training setting might direct the researcher to discover how effectively participants learn in one training episode as opposed to another. Each type of question could quide research in the same topic area. The choice of which to use is determined by the factors in the problem statement and the researcher's judgment of the most significant factors to study. Common stems of research questions include What happens when...? Which is the most efficient way of doing...? What is the difference between...? Which variables influence the outcome of...? The research question may focus upon filling a gap in knowledge, testing an idea, or assessing whether an accepted proposition is indeed tenable.

Development of Research Hypotheses

Much of what has been said about research questions is also true of research hypotheses. The primary difference between questions and hypotheses is the greater precision and predicted direction of change that is included in many hypotheses. Hypothesis statements assist not only in the gathering of data, but also in the measurement and analysis. For example, one might hypothesize that fewer incidents of absence from work by trainees will occur after the trainees have learned a new technique on the job. Occasionally, positive and negative degrees of relationship between variables are also predicted in the hypothesis statement (a greater positive relationship between worker attitude and work productivity will exist following on-the-job training, for example).

Certain characteristics are present in well-constructed hypotheses (Ary, 1985). Effective hypotheses should:

1. have explanatory power
2. state expected relationships between variables
3. be testable
4. be consistent with the existing body of knowledge
5. be stated concisely

Having explanatory power means that the hypothesis provides a plausible answer to the stated research problem. Incongruence between the problem and the answer supplied in the hypothesis statement is of little or no help in gathering and analyzing data. For example, if one were seeking an answer to the problem "What kind of continuing education is most useful to professionals in carrying out their professional roles?" the hypothesis "There is greater job success among professionals graduating from universities than among those graduating from technical schools" does not provide a plausible answer. Though there may be a relationship between preservice education and job success, the hypothesis does not address the question about continuing education inherent in the problem.

The statement of expected relationships indicates what the researcher anticipates or does not anticipate (null hypotheses) will come from the study. In the previous example, "greater job success" is the expected relationship. Words such as higher, lower, negative, and positive often are used to indicate expected relationships.

A testable hypothesis is one that can be verified. That is, empirical observations can support or not support any deductions, conclusions, or inferences drawn from the hypothesis (Ary, 1985). If a hypothesis is stated in such a way that it can stand scrutiny through empirical observation, it is testable.

Finally, simplicity or conciseness in stating hypotheses is necessary to make them of maximum value in guiding research. Long, wordy statements make identification of variables and expected relationships difficult to sort out. If a hypothesis cannot be expressed concisely, it may contain more than two variables to be investigated; having more than two variables requires making multiple hypotheses. To give the reader a clearer understanding of the overall process of problem identification, two examples are discussed in the next section.

Examples of Problem Identification

The overall process of problem identification can be reviewed by tracing the formulation of two studies, each of which evolved from a similar topic of interest.

The topic for the first study was selected from practical work experience, as well as from the intellectual interest the researcher had in the learning styles of adult students (Walker, 1981). As an instructor in a community college nursing program, Walker observed that student nurses seemed to have definite preferences and patterns of behavior as they approached learning in the nursing program. Some preferred small group instruction, for example, while others opted for individual instruction when it was provided. She also noticed that some nurses seemed to learn more efficiently from classroom experience followed by clinical experience, while others found the reverse to be more effective.

An initial review of learning theory and research literature on learning methods suggested that definite patterns or styles of learning may be related to how successful a nurse is in training. Curiosity about the phenomenon and desire to assist nurses in becoming more effective learners led the researcher to focus upon a particular problem --"the relationship of learning style to learning approaches and success in the nursing program."

A more thorough review of the literature produced only limited sources linking learning style of nurses and achievement. However, a large amount of theory building and related research was found dealing with cognitive style. Also, a well-developed instrument for measuring cognitive field dependence/independence was discovered. Walker chose to use Witkin's theory of cognitive style (Witkin and Goodenough, 1981) to guide the research.

Through the process of examining cognitive field dependence/independence theory and related research based upon the construct, other concepts and factors were defined to help focus the study. The problem statement included the question, "What is the relationship of cognitive style and student characteristics (such as age, experience, and ability) to how student nurses approach learning and achieve in the first course of the program?"

Walker hypothesized from the problem statement that cognitive style is related to the learning effectiveness of nurses in training. Recognizing that a number of factors other than cognitive style are involved with how nurses learn, the researcher further refined the study by developing research hypotheses to test the relationship of each factor to learning approach and achievement. This final task in the problem identification process laid the groundwork for the manner in which the data were collected.

As is often the case, a second study grew out of the first investigation. Results of the first study of learning style and learning outcomes produced some unexpected findings. For example, nurses that were field dependent did not uniformly choose small group methods above independent study as was hypothesized. Desire for answers to questions stemming from the inconsistencies prompted the researchers to pursue the same topic inductively. In the second study (Simpson and Walker, 1983), clearly field-dependent and clearly field-independent nurses who had completed the two-year program were interviewed. The problem in this instance was, "What are the qualitative differences among field dependent and field independent nurses as they approach learning?" Research questions (not hypotheses) such as "What are the resources for learning chosen by field dependent and independent nurses?" and "What contributes to successful learning as a nurse completes the program?" guided the study. From the research questions, an open-ended interview protocol was prepared for gathering data. Thus, in this study learning style differences were induced from the data, rather than data being gathered to confirm learning style differences as hypothesized in the first study.

In summary, the research problem is a mechanism for translating the researcher's curiosity into a workable tool for conducting the study. A number of important tasks are involved in focusing the study. Selecting the topic, stating the problem clearly, and judging its significance are the initial steps in the process. Reviewing related theory associated with the problem, defining terms and concepts, and developing research questions or hypotheses to guide the investigation are the subsequent steps that help shape the study. This process deserves deliberate and thorough attention. Excessive work and frustration in conducting the study can be avoided if adequate time and energy are given to first clearly delineating the research problem.

REFERENCES

Arlin, P. K. (1975). "Cognitive Development in Adulthood: A Fifth Stage." *Development Psychology.* 11:602-606.

Ary, D., Jacobs, L. C., and Ragavich, A. (1985). *Introduction to Research in Education.* (3rd ed.). New York: Holt, Rinehart and Winston.

Dewey, John. (1933). *How We Think.* Boston: D. C. Heath and Company.

Glaser, B. C., and A. Strauss. (1967). *The Discovery of Grounded Theory.* Chicago: Aldine Publishing Company.

Green, Rosalie and Maxine Enderline. (1980). "A New Bottle For Good Wine." *Lifelong Learning: The Adult Years.* 4:12-15

Guba, Egon G. (1978). *Toward a Methodology of Naturalistic Inquiry in Educational Evaluation.* CSE Monograph Series in Evaluation No. 8. Los Angeles: University of California.

Guba, Egon G. and Yvonne S. Lincoln (1981) *Effective Evaluation: Improving the Usefulness of Evaluation Results Through Responsive and Naturalistic Approaches.* San Francisco: Jossey-Bass.

Kerlinger, F. N. (1986). *Foundations of Behavioral Research.* New York: Holt, Rinehart and Winston. (3rd ed.).

Manheim, Henry I. (1977). *Sociological Research: Philosophy and Methods.* Homewood, Illinois: Dorsey Press.

Patton, Michael A. (1980). *Qualitative Evaluation Methods.* Beverly Hills: Sage Publications.

Selltiz, Claire et. al. (1959). *Research Methods in Social Relations.* New York: Holt, Rinehart and Winston.

Selltiz, Claire, Lawrence Wrightsman and Stuart Cook. (1976). *Research Methods in Social Relations.* New York: Holt, Rinehart and Winston.

Simpson, Edwin and Susan Walker. (1983). "Qualitative Differences Between Field Dependent/Independent Nurses' *Adult Education Research Conference Proceedings.* Montreal, Canada.

Strauss, A. L. (1987). *Qualitative Analysis for Social Scientists.* Cambridge University Press.

Walker, Susan. (1981). "The Relationship of Field Dependence/Independence to Learning Approach and Achievement of Associate Degree Nursing Students." Unpublished Doctoral Dissertation, Northern Illinois University.

Webster's New Collegiate Dictionary. (1977). Springfield, Massachusetts: G & C Merriam Company.

Witkin, Herman A. and Donald G. Goodenough. (1981). *Cognitive Styles: Essence and Origins.* Monograph 51. New York: International Universities Press.

CHAPTER 3

THE LITERATURE REVIEW

An important step in the research process is to review the thinking and research relevant to the topic at hand. Only by becoming thoroughly familiar with prior research and theory can you hope to contribute something that others will build upon, thereby extending a discipline's knowledge base. A review of the literature thus safeguards against undertaking a study that may have already been done, that may not be feasible to conduct, or that may be trivial or insignificant when set against the research needs in a particular field.

Essentially, a literature review integrates and synthesizes what has been thought and researched in the area of interest. A review of the literature may be "freestanding"; this type of review presents the state of the art with regard to a particular interest or concern and is not a part of a research study. Such self-contained reviews offer readers a general overview of the problem area and, perhaps, suggestions for future research investigations. Most literature reviews, however, are part of a study. The task of locating, reading, synthesizing, and writing a review of the literature provides the researcher with a foundation from which to explore further.

In social science research, the literature review serves a variety of functions that precede the collecting and analyzing of data. These functions are discussed in detail in the next section. Certain types of research such as historical research, policy studies, literary analyses, and philosophical inquiries use "literature" or documents as the source of data. Nevertheless, these approaches still review what others have written about the topic and how others have interpreted the documents or literature to be used in the study at hand.

Functions of a Literature Review

The purpose of a literature review is to summarize and integrate previous work and to offer suggestions for future inquiries. Freestanding reviews often present interesting insights about a problem area and almost always provide a starting point for researchers who must acquaint themselves with work that was done prior to the setting up of their own study. A freestanding review will rarely focus upon the questions relevant to a particular study, however, and, for this reason, researchers must pull together their own. The following are functions of a literature review conducted prior to a research study:

1. To provide a foundation for building knowledge. No research problem in the social sciences exists alone as an area of human endeavor. There is *always* some related literature, and it is this literature that is reviewed to form the "pedigree" of the problem. In order to add to knowledge in a field, you must have a thorough understanding of the major theoretical points of view and the major research investigations relevant to the topic. A literature review should reveal what has been done or what is being done in a particular problem area. In a sense, the literature review sets the stage on which the study will be presented.

2. To show how a study advances, refines, or revises what is already known. All investigators are concerned that someone, somewhere, might have done or might be doing the very study being proposed. A thorough literature review should alleviate this concern. The review should state, rather precisely, just how the study being proposed deviates from previously conducted studies. A literature review is also necessary when a researcher intends to replicate an earlier study. In this case the review highlights the theoretical or methodological strengths and deficiencies present in earlier, significant studies, and in so doing, supports the need for replication.

3. To help conceptualize the study. Knowing what hypotheses have been generated or tested previously, how terms have been defined, and what assumptions and limitations have been dealt with by other investigators can facilitate the task involved in the proposed study. Previous work can, in fact, be cited in a supportive manner as you establish the rationale for limiting a study in a certain way, for defining terms, for developing hypotheses to guide the study, and so on.

4. To provide clues to methodology and instrumentation. Knowing what approaches have been used before, and with what success, can save an investigator from wasting effort and expense. Depending upon the nature of a particular problem, an experi-

mental design, for example, may or may not be ethically or logistically feasible, and even if it is feasible, using this design may not lead to answering the questions of interest. Similarly, a review of the literature may uncover survey instruments, tests, and other measures that have already been validated and thus save the researcher the trouble of designing a valid and reliable instrument.

5. To offer a collective point of reference for interpreting the researcher's own findings. Prior to collecting data, the literature review is used to show how the proposed study intends to extend, revise, or refine knowledge in an area. After the data have been collected and analyzed, previous work can become a point of reference for discussing the significance that the study has to the field. One's findings can then be assessed against the previous state of knowledge to see whether the intention has been realized. By making such a comparison, the researcher gives other investigators and consumers of the research a sense of what contribution the present study has made to advancing the knowledge base of the discipline.

A literature review, then, functions as a means of conceptualizing, justifying, implementing, and interpreting a research investigation. Without it you court the possibility of duplicating earlier work or investigating an insignificant problem. Without a literature review it is also impossible to ascertain the significance of the proposed study for contributing to the knowledge base of a field.

The Search Process

The search for related literature is characterized, to a large extent, by how precisely a problem is formulated. If the investigator has a particular study in mind, the search is narrower in scope. The purposes of the search in this case are (1) to make certain no one else has done the same study, and (2) to use previous writing in support of the need for the present study. The danger in being too focused is, of course, that the study may have been done previously, or that it may be an insignificant issue, or that the investigator may not be able to find literature on the particular topic. On the other hand, having only a vague sense of a problem area may result in a search so broad as to be unmanageable. The ideal topic lies somewhere in between -- the literature both confirms that a previous study is not being duplicated (unless by intent), and also serves as a guide to actually formulating the study. Nearly all previous studies or literature reviews have suggestions for further research. Recurrent suggestions would indicate a significant research need in the field. How you delineate a manageable research topic has been discussed in a previous chapter. However, assuming that you have developed a reasonable topic and are ready to do a literature review, the search process itself can be broken into three phases: finding the literature to be reviewed, selecting the sources to be included in the review, and ending the search.

Finding the Literature

For most topics there are two kinds of literature: the theoretical or conceptual writing in the area and data-based research studies. The theoretical literature consists of writings that reflect an author's experiences or opinions. Research studies are based on the collection and analysis of data gathered from sources (people, institutions, documents) extraneous to the author. The amount of each type of literature in a problem area varies. At different points in a search, both types are helpful and important to the reviewer.

A person not well versed in a subject area would be advised to begin a search, not with a particular research study, but, rather, with an overview of the conceptual literature. An overview of the problem area can be gotten from a general text on the topic or from subject encyclopedias. Subject encyclopedias identify major trends and thinking in an area and contain bibliographies for further reading. For example, a literature review on some topic related to the education of adults could begin with encyclopedias and yearbooks that offer overviews on various topics in education:

Encyclopedia of Education
-contains short articles in various areas of education.
International Encyclopedia of Higher Education
-approximately 1,300 entries, ranging from brief articles to lengthy topical essays; arranged alphabetically through ten volumes giving a global perspective of all major aspects of international higher education.
Dictionary of Education
-gives definitions for approximately 40,000 professional terms and concepts that are used in the entire field of education.
International Dictionary of Education
-includes definitions of more than 10,000 terms used internationally in all levels of education.

Handbook of Adult Education
(1960, 1970, and 1980 Handbook Series)
-chapters on general topics such as philosophy, organization of field; some on specific topics such as women's programs, evaluating adult basic education, etc.
Training and Development Handbook:
A Guide to Human Resource Development
-edited by Robert L. Craig; contains chapters on a variety of topics related to the philosophy of training, and programmatic concerns in training and development in business and industry.
Yearbook of Adult and Continuing Education
-annual publication (1975-1981) containing articles on a wide variety of topics in adult education.
Public Continuing and Adult Education Almanac
-contains names and addresses of leading institutions and people who are involved in adult education in the United States; includes statistics about each state's involvement in adult education; published by NAPCAE.

In addition to the above references, the *Cyclopedia of Education* for historical topics, and the *International Encyclopedia of the Social Sciences* or the *Encyclopedia of the Social Sciences* can be consulted for topics of interest to educators and trainers of adults. At this stage of the search, reading is done for a general overview and understanding of the topic. Major issues, trends, points of view, people, or landmark studies should be noted.

A second step in the search involves moving on to reviews of research. Such reviews are narrower in focus than articles in subject encyclopedias and handbooks and usually provide an extensive list of studies and articles for further reading. Some general basic sources of reviews of research are:

Encyclopedia of Educational Research
-critical synthesis and interpretation of all subject areas in education; includes bibliographic references.
Review of Educational Research
-published quarterly by the American Education Research Association; contains integrative reviews and interpretations on substantive and methodological issues in education.
Reviews of Research in Education
-an annual volume published by AERA, summarizing research on specific topics in education.

Handbook of Research on Teaching
-summaries of research in several areas of education.
Research Reports
-published by both the American Council on Education and National Education Association.

In both the *Encyclopedia of Educational Research* and the *Review of Educational Research,* research dealing with adults has been reviewed periodically. Reviews on specific topics can be also found in journals such as *Training and Development Journal* and *Adult Education Quarterly* and in ERIC publications.

Up to this point the literature search will have given the reviewer a "feel" for the topic, some familiarity with basic theories, key sources, and a sense of the state of data-based research. This general reading should also have contributed to a better conceptualization of the problem down to a specific research focus. At this stage the researcher is ready to use bibliographies, indexes, and abstracts.

Bibliographies are published on nearly every topic. Finding a bibliography can be done through consulting the card catalogue or through using the *Bibliographic Index,* a volume published annually listing bibliographies in approximately 2,600 periodicals by subject area. The *Bibliographic Guide to Educational Research* includes descriptive annotations of more than 700 books, periodicals, collections of research studies, government publications, and reference works that deal with the field of education. In adult education, bibliographies exist on adult basic education, teaching methods, media and adult learning, staff development, and dissertations in adult education and training. From bibliographies you begin developing a pool of references that are particularly relevant to the research topic. At this stage you might fill out an index card on each possible source.

This pool of references expands through using indexes and abstracts. For every discipline there are indexes that list by topic (and in some cases by author) pertinent articles to be found in various journals. *Education Index,* for example, lists by topic articles from over 200 education journals. In addition, *Social Science Index* and ERIC's *Current Index to Journals in Education* and *Resources in Education* (documents other than journal articles) are essential tools in locating sources.

Once you have generated a list of sources or set of index cards, you can save many hours in the literature search by going to abstracts *before* locating the entire article or document. Abstracts can also be used for developing a bibliographic pool. Abstract resources present a full citation of the source, as well as a paragraph summary of the study or document. The most useful sources for abstracts that deal with education are the following:

Dissertation Abstracts International
-lists most doctoral dissertations written at American universities and some foreign universities. Abstracts summarize objectives, procedures, and conclusions of each study.
American Doctoral Dissertations
-complete listing of all doctoral dissertations accepted by American and Canadian universities.
Master's Theses in Education
-lists the authors and titles (no abstracts) of master's theses published by institutions throughout the United States and Canada during the year covered by each volume.
Psychological Abstracts
-nonevaluative summaries and abstracts of American and foreign books and periodicals in psychology and related diciplines.
Sociological Abstracts
-abstracts of American and foreign periodicals in sociology and political science.
ERIC
-both the *Resources in Education* (RIE) and *Current Index to Journals in Education* (CIJE) print abstracts of the documents and journals indexed. (A note on ERIC: ERIC is and acronym for Education Resources Information Center. Funded by the National Institute of Education, ERIC is a national information network that collects, organizes, and disseminates educational research information and material. The ERIC system indexes and abstracts research projects, theses, conference proceedings, project reports, speeches, bibliographies, curriculum-related materials, books, and more that 750 educational journals.)

Once you have read generally in an area of interest and have honed in on a specific research topic, a literature search can be done as outlined above, or it can be done by computer. The extensiveness of the search depends upon the library's capabilities as well as how specific your topic is. In any case, most librarians with assistance of the computer can search data bases that correspond to well-known indexes such as *Psychological Abstracts, ERIC, Sociological Abstracts*, and so on. In addition to librarian-assisted searches, arrangements can be made with search services such as Bibliographic Retrieval Services (BRS) and Dialogue to access their data bases through one's microcomputer. Both BRS and Dialogue have lower evening and weekend rates for just such usage. The most recent development in computer searches is the use of CD-ROM (Compact Disc-Read Only Memory) systems. Entire data bases such as ERIC's are placed on a compact disc. Once the discs are purchased by a library, users can search through data bases at leisure without incurring on-line costs. Whichever method one uses, the result of a computer search is a printed bibliography; that is, a list of citations (sometimes with abstracts) of articles, research reports, and a conference proceedings on the topics searched. Obviously, a computer search will save hours compared with conducting a manual search. It also allows for a comprehensiveness and flexibility not always possible in manual searching.

Selecting the Sources for Review

The thoroughness of a literature search, whether done manually or by computer, depends upon several factors: the specificity of the topic, the resources of the library where the search is being conducted, the researcher's mastery of library techniques, the time available for the search, and the ingenuity or creativeness of the researcher in uncovering relevant sources. At the end of the first stage of finding the sources, you should have accumulated a reasonable list of references that appear to be directly relevant to the problem area. Now you halt the search and begin reading some of these articles or research studies. The bibliographies at the end of an article should be checked against your own list. Seemingly pertinent references should be located and read, and the bibliography should be checked again. The process at this stage involves shifting between indexes, abstracts, actual articles and their bibliographies, and your own list of sources. You will soon notice recurrent references and major articles of either a conceptual or data-based nature. At this point you are a detective, following the trail of a research problem. During the process of moving between references and original sources, decisions must be continually made with regard to the relevance of the material and whether or not certain pieces will be included in the final literature review. A reviewer can ask the following questions to assist in making decisions for relevance:

1. Is the author of the source an authority on the topic, one who has done much of the empirical work in the area, or one who has offered seminal theory upon which subsequent research and writing has been based? If so, that author's work will be quoted by others and listed in bibliographies on the topic.

2. When was the article or book or report written? As a rule, the more recent work in an area should be included in a review.

3. What exactly was written about or tested? If a particular resource or research study is highly relevant to your present research interest, it should be included even if the "who" and "when" criteria are not met.

4. What is the quality of the source? A thoughtful analysis, a well-designed study, or an original way of viewing the topic is

probably a more significant piece of literature. In historical or documentary analysis, the quality of primary and secondary sources is a major criterion for inclusion into the data base.

As you decide which particular sources are important for inclusion in the review, how the material should be handled becomes an important consideration. If possible, a copy of the complete article, or the pertinent sections of it, should be made for reference when writing the review. If it is not possible or feasible to copy the article, notes should be taken in some systematic way. Direct quotations that state main ideas and supporting points should be extracted from conceptual/theoretical articles. At this point you cannot be certain whether the final review will include a summary of an idea or direct quotation. You can always summarize from a direct quotation, but it is impossible to resurrect a direct quotation from general notes. For data-based research articles, the abstract (if there is one) can be copied and/or notes taken on sample, methodology, and findings. Taking care in obtaining all pertinent information from a source cannot be overemphasized. Getting what seems to be too much information will save many hours searching back through the sources for a certain perfect quotation, the number in the sample, and so on.

Occasionally, there is a paucity of literature on a particular topic. This is a sign that the researcher is embarking onto a new area and that the study will form some contribution to the literature. On the other hand, the researcher cannot profit from previous work and may encounter insurmountable methodological problems or may be investigating an area of little interest to others. As stated earlier, however, there will always be some related literature. From what literature is available, it will be important to extract statements regarding the need for research or theory building in the area, the gaps or problems in what has been done, the reasons that the area has been neglected, and so on. Such statements, especially if made by authorities in related areas, can be effectively used to build support for the present research study.

The time, the energy, the resourcefulness of the researcher, and the resources of the library where the search is being conducted are among the factors that may artificially limit the search for, and the gathering of, sources. An authentic end to a literature search is one in which the investigator is satisfied that all relevant material has been uncovered and dealt with. There are two guidelines that can be used to determine when to end a search: (1) encountering lists of material already covered, and (2) a feeling of expertise in the subject area:

1. In the process of moving back and forth between indexes or abstracts and actual articles or books, the researcher becomes quite familiar with certain studies, certain names, certain publications. At some point in the process, the researcher turns to a reference list at the end of an article and discovers that *all* the listings are familiar and may, in fact, have been read. When this occurs two or three times, the reviewer can be reasonably certain that the relevant literature in an area has been uncovered. The search has, in a sense, become saturated, and no new material is likely to be found. How long it will take to reach this point and how many sources one will have to go through will depend upon prior familiarity with the topic, the amount of literature available, and the nature of the research problem or topic.

2. The second guideline is less objective. At some point in the search, a sense of expertise about the subject is acquired. This is reflected in the ability to recall and discuss major ideas, historical developments, important research topics, authors, and so on, that are relevant to the topic.

Writing the Literature Review

The process of doing a literature review is not unlike the process of doing research. In both cases, collecting the material or data constitutes half the task; writing the review or report requires an equal amount of effort. A literature review demands more than annotating a list of sources. A literature review is a narrative essay that integrates, synthesizes, and critiques the important thinking and research on a particular topic. Whether freestanding or part of a study, the review should present a systematic overview of the topic.

Several strategies can be used to transform a stack of sources on a topic into a well-written analytical essay. Two that have worked especially well for the authors can be loosely labeled the "chart" method and the "conversation" approach. In the chart method, one lists down the left side of a large sheet of paper the authors and/or titles of each source to be reviewed. This listing might be done alphabetically, chronologically, or by type of literature (e.g., conceptual versus research). Categories appropriate to the literature, such as the major theme of the article, date of the study, sample, intervention or treatment, findings, or needed research, are then listed across the top of the chart. A category titled "assessment" is the most important of all. Here the reviewer notes an opinion of the piece of literature--that is, how well the work was done and how important a contribution it is.

After each source has been entered on the chart, the reviewer stands back and asks what generalizations can be made about all of the sources. These generalizations should be written down, for it is likely that these points will form the skeletal structure of the literature review. The chart in Table 3.1 was used by one of the authors in doing a literature review. The topic of interest was the effectiveness of short-term training programs in changing people's attitudes about aging. The studies are listed chronologically in the left column. Across the top are the categories that were of interest to the reviewer. From looking at the chart, one can make the following generalizations about the literature on this topic:

1. There is no consistency in the meaning of "short-term" -- interventions range from 4 to 40 hours.
2. Significant results with the treatment groups appear to be unrelated to the length of training.
3. The majority of studies deal with changing attitudes toward death and dying; a few focus on attitudes about the elderly.
4. The sample in most of the studies is college students or personnel who work with the elderly.
5. With few exceptions, experimental designs with treatment and control groups were employed.

These observations can now be used to structure the literature review. Since the topic is the effectiveness of short-term training programs, it would be important to discuss the concept of "short-term" and how little agreement there is on its definition. A second discussion point would be the lack of relationship between length of the intervention and its resulting effectiveness. Some attention could also be given to possible explanations for the results of various studies-- the rigor of the design, the treatment itself, the nature of the sample, and so on.

While the chart in Table 3.1 is limited to data-based research studies, the same approach can be used for a literature review consisting of all conceptual/theoretical material, or one that has a mixture of opinion and data-based articles. In a review of the literature on mentoring conducted by one of the authors (Merriam, 1983) for example, a chart of all the sources revealed the following: there is no single, accepted definition of the phenomenon; there are a few studies from adult psychology, but most of the empirical studies are from business settings and relate to career advancement; the majority of literature is in the popular "how-to" vein and is almost always from the perspective of benefits to the protégé; there is a subgroup of literature consisting of

Table 3.1. Sample chart for a literature review

Short-Term Intervention Programs in Aging

Study & Date	Purpose of Study	Sample	Treatment/Control	Time	Results	Assessment
Cicchetti, Fletcher, Verner, & Coleman: 1973	To determine whether a course focusing on aging changes attitudes of first year medical students toward the elderly.	180 freshman medical students	Experimental group - Course content included aging. Control group - Course content did not include aging. Ss administered questionnaire first and last days of courses to assess attitude change toward the elderly.	18 Weekly lectures	Little change in attitudes toward the elderly as a result of course.	study doesn't add much
Nash, Connors, Gemperle: 1977	Design, implement and evaluate a short-term educational program for personnel who work with the terminally ill.	76 personnel	Interview format - yielded descriptive data.	12 hours	In general - evaluation showed that program had a positive impact on participants. Favored saturation technique (intensive workshop experience)	lack of control group

Author/Year	Purpose	Sample	Methodology	Duration	Findings	Comments
Watts: 1977	To evaluate death attitude change among students involved in a death education instructional unit within a health course.	79 college students	Experimental group (N-39) and Control group (N-40). Treatment: death education. Pre-test, treatment, and post-test format utilized for experimental group. Pre-test, nontreatment, and post-test format utilized for control group.	4 hours	Showed a favorable death-related attitude change as a result of the death education instructional unit.	rigorous, good study
Gordon, Hallaner: 1977	To examine the effects of field work and course experience with the elderly and aging on student attitudes.	110 undergraduate students	4 groups - 2 experimental and 2 control. Treatment: field work experience - "Friendly Visiting Program".	10-12 weeks	Course alone significantly altered students' attitudes toward the aged. Friendly visiting in addition had an even greater effect. Friendly visiting alone did not substantially improve students attitudes.	contact with elderly plus content best treatment
Hoelter, Epley: 1979	To assess impact of death and dying course on students and their death-related attitudes.	34 college students	Questionnaire (pre- and post-) Experimental group (N-17) enrolled in "The Sociology of Death and Dying" course; Control group (N-17) enrolled in "The Sociology of Family" course.	40 hours	No significant pre-test - post-test differences for either the experimental or control groups.	findings contradict above study
Abernathy: 1980	To determine the effect of a short-term training program on counselor attitudes toward the elderly and aging.	68 counselors from 4 urban community colleges	Experimental and control groups. Random assignment. Treatment: workshop dealing with aging and the older adult.	4 hours	No significant change was found in attitudes toward aging and the elderly as a result of the treatment.	good study - 4 hours perhaps too short

both conceptual and data-based articles dealing exclusively with women. These generalizations formed the major points of organization for the literature review.

A second strategy for transforming sources into a narrative essay is the conversation approach. Imagine that someone who has no knowledge about a topic is having a conversation with the reviewer who is becoming an expert in this subject area. The novice would obviously have to ask many questions before there would be any understanding at all. The reviewer might be asked the following:

1. Who are the major authorities on the topic, and why are they considered experts?
2. What are the major theories or points of view about the topic?
3. What is the single most important source of information on the topic?
4. When was most of the work done?
5. What were the major breakthroughs?
6. What research is currently being conducted in this subject area?
7. What research still needs to be done?
8. What is unique and worthy of note from this literature?

Written answers to these questions should provide an overview and synthesis of the material.

Both methods also help the reviewer adopt a critical stance toward the literature. Being critical does not mean being negative, but rather being able to assess the strengths and weaknesses of a body of material. In a critical approach one praises *and* finds fault. Readers of a review should gain some sense of the relative importance of particular sources as well as an overall sense of the state of the art. Brief, evaluative, critical assessments of the individual sources in the literature review are both appropriate and expected. More lengthy assessments might also be woven into summary and conclusion sections. In any case, a literature review demands more than merely presenting the content of numerous sources.

There are probably as many systems for organizing material as there are reviewers. Whatever the structure, the reviewer must make an effort to stand apart from the individual sources in order to extract generalities, major themes, and salient issues from across the entire body of literature. It is only through withdrawing from the specifics that a researcher can create an overview that integrates, synthesizes, and critiques.

Parts of the Literature Review

There is no single formula for structuring a literature review. How a review takes shape depends in part upon whether the reviewer intends to make it a state-of-the-art, freestanding review, or one that leads to a study with a particular focus. In most cases, the structure emerges from the literature being evaluated; this will be explained more fully in a discussion of the body of a literature review. However, there are usually several other parts of the review that precede and follow the body.

Like every other narrative essay, a literature review begins with an *introduction*. Here the reviewer lays out for the reader the topic to be reviewed, the nature of this topic, its scope, and its significance, The writer should assume that the reader knows nothing about the topic: therefore, the writer must be careful to introduce the subject in as clear and simple a manner as possible. Special terminology should be explained or defined. In most cases the introduction will begin very generally, explaining the nature of the subject and then gradually narrowing the focus to the specific topic to be reviewed. A review of the literature on women's reentry programs, for example, might begin with several paragraphs about the phenomenon of women returning to school. A review of the research on the dropout problem in Adult Basic Education programs should first introduce the reader to ABE in general and to the existing programs for adults who need assistance in mastering basic skills.

Once the specific topic has been identified, the author may want to discuss the *criteria* used in selecting the literature for review. Why were certain sources included and others ignored? Perhaps only literature within the last ten years was selected, or perhaps only major writers were chosen, or perhaps only certain dimensions of the topic were considered important for review. The limits of the review are set in this section. That is, the reviewer can discuss what is not to be reviewed as well as what is included. The limits depend upon how much literature is available. To review all the research studies on Piaget's theories, for example, would be unmanageable, but it would be reasonable to limit such a review to studies that applied Piaget's theories to adults. A review might also be limited to a specific type of literature such as journal articles. Stating selection criteria and reviewing limits early in the essay prevents readers from questioning why particular sources were or were not included. Where there is a dearth of relevant literature, this section of the review may include a recounting of the efforts made to find sources, the results of such efforts, and perhaps the rationale for turning to certain tangential literature.

Following the introduction and criteria for selection is the *body* of the review. This is the heart of the essay, the critical synthesis of material reviewed. The organization of this section flows logically from the nature of the literature on a particular topic. As stated earlier, developing the body of the review involves much more than merely annotating or summarizing sources. If either the chart method or the conversation approach is used, the body of the review will emerge from the generalizations extracted across all the sources. In most literature reviews, the body is organized thematically. Certain recurring themes or subtopics emerge from the literature, and these themes form the major subheadings. In the following three examples, each literature review topic is subdivided into several themes that were generated from the material itself:

Topic A.   Locus of Control: Studies with Adults
               1. Adults in higher education
Thematic   2. Disadvantaged adults
Subtopics   3. Older adults
               4. Changing the locus of control with adults

Topic B.   Middle Age
               1. When does middle age occur?
               2. What are the physical characteristics of middle age?
Thematic   3. What are the psychosocial characteristics of middle
Subtopics   age?
               4. What are the developmental tasks of middle age?
               5. Is there a midlife crisis?

Topic C.   Competency-Based Education (CBE)
               1. What does competency-based mean?
               2. How is CBE related to performance?
Thematic   3. What are the objectives of CBE?
Subtopics   4. In what settings is CBE most likely to be found?
               5. What are the political overtures of this emphasis?
               6. Does the Adult Performance Level test measure
               competence?

Under each thematic subtopic the reviewer discusses research studies or other writings appropriate to the theme. Depending upon the nature and importance of a source, some discussions may be quite detailed while other sources may be only alluded to. A particular source may contain material appropriate to several subtopics, in which case the reviewer must choose where to discuss it (perhaps several places) and how thoroughly. Within each subtopic critical comments are appropriate. For example, a review might point out the methodological weakness of a particular study, might comment on several pieces as a whole, or might enumerate reasons why a particular work is an important contribution.

The most logical organization may be chronological, particularly when reviewing historical works or public documents that are records of a particular event. As with a thematic organization, the decision to use a chronological organization should be dictated by the literature itself. Some reviews may evolve into a combined thematic and chronological organization. You might handle the early, though important, literature on the topic under a chronological heading (pre-1970, post-World War II, for example) and then move on to relevant themes characteristic of the most recent work. Conversely, the bulk of the literature might be organized thematically with the most recent work under a heading such as "recent developments."

The body of the literature review should be followed by a *concluding section*. There the writer can summarize the review, discuss overall weaknesses and strengths in the literature, point out gaps that exist in the topic's conceptual development or research efforts, or note aspects that have been well covered, even saturated.

An essential part of this concluding section is the identification of potentially fruitful avenues for future inquiry. The reviewer who has been immersed in the literature in a certain area has become an expert on that topic. It is entirely appropriate, then, to offer guidance for the future development of this body of knowledge. The concluding section is also an appropriate place to move into a discussion of the reviewer's particular research study, how it addresses the gaps or weaknesses in the field, and how it should prove to be a manageable and rewarding line of inquiry.

The parts of a review, then, include: (1) introductory material, in which the nature of the topic, the scope of the study, and the criteria or process of selecting materials for review are discussed; (2) the body of the review, which provides the critical synthesis and integration of all the important literature and is arranged by the themes that evolve naturally from the material itself; and (3) the concluding section, which summarizes, evaluates, and offers suggestions for future study.

The novice should read several published reviews to see how the points made in this discussion are applied to a content area. As an example, the reader is referred to a literature review titled "Counseling the Adult Learner: A Selective Review of the Literature" (Goldberg, 1980). This review evaluates a wide variety of sources, both theoretical and data-based, on a rather broad topic. In the introduction the author comments on the increase in participation of adults in education and the parallel demand for counseling services. The reader is told that the literature to be reviewed will cover work that links counseling needs to the larger perspective of adult developmental psychology.

The author reviewed the material under the following major themes: the need for adult counseling, meeting the adult learner's specific needs, life-span developmental perspective, new forms of counseling services, and new approaches to counseling adults. Points discussed under each of these topics were synthesized from a wide range of conceptual and data-based writing located in proceedings, books, individual papers, and journal articles. The review appears to reflect a very thorough search.

In "suggestions for further study and research," the author concludes with an overall assessment of the literature on this topic:

> Although there is general agreement in the literature supporting the thesis that distinct counseling needs for adult learners do in fact exist, a solid research base to substantiate the growing number of theories is virtually non-existent. The evidence presented in the literature thus far seems primarily limited to a blend of deductions from major theoretical works supplemented with personal experiences, opinions, intuition and insights. The research reported tends to be sparse and weak methodologically. Studies are generally based on small, non-representative, specific samples (sometimes not even adult populations), do not necessarily employ control groups and are lacking in the replication necessary to justify generalizing and implementing the findings. (Goldberg, 1980, p. 76)

The article concludes with a thorough discussion of the gaps in the literature and offers suggestions for much-needed research.

Two other examples of literature reviews can be found in the Summer, 1987, issue of *Adult Education Quarterly*. Merriam (1987) reviewed theory building efforts in adult learning. Following a discussion of the need for theory, she organized adult learning theories into three categories: theories based on adult learner characteristics; theories based on adult's life situation; and theories based on changes in consciousness. The article closes with a summary evaluation of theory-building efforts in adult learning.

In the same issue, Caffarella and O'Donnell (1987) review the research and writing on self-directed learning. This large and growing body of literature was organized into the following framework: verification studies (in the Tough tradition); nature of the method of self-directed learning (how questions); nature of the individual learner (who and what questions); nature of the philosophical position (perspectives on process); and policy questions (roles of educators, institutions, and society). They conclude their review with six suggestions for future research.

Some Helpful Reminders for Doing a Literature Review

The process of doing a literature review can be roughly divided into two parts: (1) the research process and (2) the writing of the review. The following summation will make both parts of the process easier:

1. Read generally for an overview of the problem area before defining the topic precisely.
2. Define the limits of the review. Too broad a search will overwhelm you with material; too narrow a topic might make you overlook related work or not find enough material.
3. Through indexes and abstracts, locate a reasonable number of sources and begin reading those sources. Then move back to bibliographies and abstracts. This will allow you to develop a pool of relevant sources.
4. Establish criteria for selecting materials that will be included in the review.
5. Continue the search until the sources are saturated and you feel you are an "expert" on the topic.
6. Copy the material to be reviewed, being especially careful to obtain full bibliographic data.
7. Arrange the material reviewed into categories that are suggested by the material itself.
8. Structure the review into three parts: introductory material, the body of the review, and a concluding section.

REFERENCES

Caffarella, Rosemary and Judy O'Donnell. 1987. "Self-Directed Adult Learning: A Critical Paradigm Revisited." *Adult Education Quarterly*. 37:199-211.

Goldberg, Joan. 1980. "Counseling the Adult Learner: A Selective Review of the Literature." *Adult Education*. 30: 67-81.

Merriam, Sharan. 1983. "Mentors and Protégés: A Critical Review of the Literature." *Adult Education*. 33:161-173.

Merriam, Sharan. 1987. "Adult Learning and Theory Building: A Review." *Adult Education Quarterly*. 37:187-198.

CHAPTER 4

EXPERIMENTAL
AND DESCRIPTIVE
RESEARCH

Various definitions exist to describe research designs, methods, approaches, or strategies. Some texts differentiate three major research categories -- descriptive, historical, and experimental. Others label the categories by technique, such as "survey" research; still others make finer distinctions such as "experimental" versus "quasi-experimental" designs. Each methodology presented in the next four chapters represents a systematic procedure for the collection and analysis of data. Differences in methodological purpose and procedure will be examined in the following discussion of experimental, descriptive, causal/comparative, historical, philosophical, case study, grounded theory, ethnographic, interactive, ecological and futures study designs.

Perhaps the research method most directly representative of scientific thought in the twentieth century is the experimental method. Its purpose is to determine the cause of events and to be able to predict similar events in the future. Because of their purpose and basic science origins, some experimental designs are detailed and technical. However, rather than focusing on the complex nature of various experimental designs, the emphasis here will be upon providing an overview of the purposes and procedures of experimental methods.

Experimental and Quasi-Experimental Methods

The experimental method originally was based upon a set of laws introduced by John Stuart Mill (1873) in a work titled "Methods of Experimental Inquiry." In his treatise Mill proposed a number of principles in the form of canons or rules that he contended were requirements to establishing order among controlled events. One of those laws, the method of difference, stated,

> If an instance in which the phenomenon under investigation occurs, and an instance in which it does not occur have every circumstance in common save one, that one occurring only in the former, the circumstance in which alone the two instances differ is the effect, or the cause, or an indispensable part of the cause of the phenomenon. (p. 222)

Mill is saying that if two sets of events are alike and something is either added to or taken from one event, causing a difference between those two events, the difference is attributed to what was added or withdrawn. The law of the single variable was useful in designing research for the disciplines of basic science. However, when applied to the emerging behavioral sciences, it proved less than adequate because the multivariant nature of human events made application of the law difficult. Seldom could differences in complex human events be traced to a single cause. Also, interaction of variables made isolation and observation of single variables impossible to achieve in many cases. Thus, a method of analyzing effects of more than one variable was needed in order to conduct behavioral science studies effectively.

A method that provided the capability of assessing several variables simultaneously was introduced through the science of agriculture. R. A. Fisher (1935) presented the concept of factorial design as an outgrowth of his agricultural experimentation. The method was soon adopted to serve the research needs of behavioral researchers. By standardizing conditions before the experiment, using random selection of subjects and random assignment of experimental treatment, Fisher's factorial concept permitted researchers to study effects of more than one independent variable on more than a single dependent variable.

A type of factorial design can be illustrated through an example that is similar to the earliest factorial research -- an agricultural experiment. Assuming that the study is to determine crop yield (dependent variable) in various field plots, factorial methods can be helpful in identifying the factors that contribute to yield. First, the independent variables that are expected to be related to crop yield are identified. These might include type of seed used (Brand X/Y), type of fertilizer used (Fast Grow/Slow Grow), and amount of irrigation (heavy/medium/light). Assignments of plots to these various conditions are done on a random basis. Each of the many combinations of factors is represented by at least one plot. The number of combinations is the product of the number of levels of each independent variable. In this example, seed has two variations (Brand X/Y), fertilizer has two, and irrigation has three. The different comparisons (factor combinations) are 2 x 2 x 3 or 12 combinations. At least twelve different plots are to be studied in carrying out the research.

A second example, this time from adult education, relates to participation. Our research question asks what type of learning setting produces the greatest achievement or satisfaction among participants in an evening math refresher program. Related factors might include location of the class (school/church/YMCA) and method of instruction (lecture/discussion).

Each class offered should represent a different combination of factors -- instructors using the lecture method and teaching in a school environment; instructors using the discussion method, teaching in a YMCA, etc., until all six combinations are represented. Participants are assigned randomly to a classroom setting. Assuming equal enrollment in each class, the number of participants exposed to the different conditions (independent variables) will be the same. Some measure of achievement or satisfaction is then administered at the conclusion of the course to determine effects. As Edwards (1972) stresses, factorial methodology

> means that the outcomes of the experiment provide a sounder basis for generalizing about the effectiveness of the experimental variables, since they are tested not only in isolation, but in conjunction with the effects of other variables. (p. 223)

Primary components of experimental design are a control group and an experimental group. After each group is equated through the process of random selection and assignment, the experimental group is either exposed to, or deprived of, some particular treatment (manipulation), while the control group does not receive the treatment. Changes in events associated with the experimental group are then compared with events of the control group. Because control is difficult to ensure in many natural settings of human interaction, even the best planned factorial designs do not always meet the needs of social science researchers in applied fields such as adult education and training.

Methods necessarily must be modified in order to address research problems in education. Designs that do vary from the classical model are referred to as quasi-experimental methods. If research groups are unequal in number of participants, or in dimensions one wishes to study at the beginning of an experiment, quasi-experimental designs are used to provide as much control as possible. For example, in the sample study of the best learning setting for math, preference of class location by participants makes random assignment difficult. If individual participants in the study self-select to attend a particular class, it is not possible to establish that individuals who chose to go to the church, as opposed to the YMCA, are equal regarding extraneous influences. The fact that some participants chose to attend the class at their church with friends could be an extraneous influential factor.

Designing Quasi-Experimental Research

Obtaining a sample through randomization provides the experimental researcher control necessary to study effects of the independent variable. In planning quasi-experimental research, however, randomization is not always possible. At least four other ways bring about experimental control. First, the researcher can match participants having as many like characteristics as the researcher can identify. For example, each participant in a computer training program experiment might be matched with an individual in another group according to such characteristics as equal years of computer experience, equal math training, and equal level of education. This procedure gives greater assurance that differences at the conclusion of the experiment are attributable to the experimental treatment.

Experimental control is also attained by a second method -- homogeneous selection. Participants in the computer training experiment might be selected only on the basis of age (e.g., twenty to thirty-five years old) and amount of past computer experience (e.g., over two years). A more homogeneous group of research participants controls for extraneous variables. The disadvantage of homogeneous selection is that results are not easily generalized to other situations, such as other computer programs.

A third way of achieving experimental control is by a statistical procedure called analysis of covariance. In this procedure, control is attained through a statistical analysis of differences between research groups found in the dependent variable at the beginning and end of the experiment. Also, differences in independent variables that are relevant are controlled through covariant analysis. Differences in performance of participants in the computer program at the conclusion of the experiment, for example, are statistically compared with preprogram achievement of the participants to determine actual change in performance. Also pertinent factors that may influence performance, such as past computer experience, are statistically compared with other independent variables to determine the degree of influence on participant performance.

A fourth means of gaining experimental control in addition to randomization is through the individual research participant. By subjecting the same individual to two or more experimental treatments intended to reach similar ends, the researcher has some assurance that extraneous variables have been limited. The individual, in this case, is the controlling agent. If participants in the computer training experiment, for example, were given three different experiences directed at teaching the same computer skills, an assessment at the end of each phase or experience might reveal how rapidly the individual's learning took place or/how thoroughly the skill was learned as a result of the different approaches. Though using the individual research participant as a controlling agent is efficient, an obvious disadvantage is the confounding influence of sequential training experiences. One training experience may influence participant performance in a subsequent episode, therefore the researcher cannot always be certain of the actual effects of individual experiences.

The experimental controls explained in the previous discussion are used by the researcher in designing quasi-experimental studies. Attention to control is necessary to study effects of the independent variable. This is the essence of experimental methodology. The researcher should consult authoritative sources for a more detailed explanation of quasi-experimental designs. (Kerlinger, 1986, Edwards, 1985).

Because controlled conditions are essential to experimental research, studies that employ experimental methods in adult education and training are rare. Those that are experimental usually use some form of pretest and posttest design. Research reported by Rosentreter (1979) is an example. The study examined the effectiveness of a training program for managers supervising production of work groups in a large corporation. Rosentreter studied effects of communication skills training upon the dependent variables of employee turnover, tardiness to work, appraisal of performance by managers, and number of formal grievances to the local union. Sixty-eight department managers from a large corporation, who supervised small work groups of sixteen to thirty subordinates, was the population for study. The managers were assigned randomly to experimental and control groups after being matched according to their relative employee turnover rate prior to the training. Employee turnover, employee tardiness, managerial performance ratings, and number of formal grievances were recorded for each manager prior to and following the training period. Conclusions of the study indicated that the training program significantly affected employee turnover, but did not result in significant change with regard to other dependent variables.

Two other examples of quasi-experimental research that explored adult learning processes are studies by Williams (1985) and Young (1986). Williams examined the degree to which perspective transformation, as a theory of adult learning, explained the process through which abusive behavior developed toward a spouse and how that behavior was changed through treatment. Five self-report instruments that measured factors such as self esteem, locus of control, and role preference were anticipated changes in perspective. Testing was done before and after a 12-week treatment program that included 25 self-selected male abuser participants. A follow-up of a portion of the participants twelve weeks after the treatment indicated conclusion of treatment. The process of perspective transformation was found to only partially explain abuser adaptation that led to the changes.

In the study conducted by Young (1986), cognitive restructing about world perspectives among adults who participated in a Conceptual Learning workshop was explored. Forty-two teachers, evenly divided into two groups, one of which participated in the workshop, responded to a 28-item likert instrument--Future World Perspective Values Scale. Young found a significant change in world values held by participants immediately following and six months after the workshop. Demographic variables, such as age, gender, subject taught or years of teaching experience were found not to be significantly related to cognitive restructuring.

Some terms and basic processes of the experimental method need definition.

Sample. A sample is a strategically and systematically identified group of people or events that meets the criterion of representativeness for a particular study. In order to detect causal relationships and project into the future, experimental design demands selection of research participants or events that accurately represent the total population of persons or the universe of events being studied. In research, to sample means to identify subjects or events for study in a systematic way.

Randomization. One common strategy used in selecting and assigning participants to groups for study is randomization. It "is the assignment of objects (subjects, treatments, groups) of a universe to subsets of the universe in such a way. . . that every member of the universe has an equal probability to be chosen for assignment" (Kerlinger, 1986, p. 114.). Randomization is usually carried out by using a table of random numbers. Each subject or event is assigned a number and selection to groups is done by following the list of random numbers in the table.

Variables. In identifying interrelationships between variables in a phenomenon, functional terms are used to explain relatedness -- i.e., independent, dependent, extraneous, and intervening variables. An independent variable is one that is independent from the phenomenon being studied. Conversely, a dependent variable "depends for its existence on the influence of the independent variable" (Johnston & Pennypacker, 1980, p. 27).

In the crop production study mentioned earlier, the amount of irrigation and type of fertilizer both are independent of any property of the crop being grown and are, therefore, referred to as independent variables. In contrast, crop growth is dependent upon cultivation and moisture; therefore, crop growth is functionally described as the dependent variable.

Extraneous variables are variables that may influence the dependent variable but are not or cannot be identified by the researcher. For example, undetected detrimental chemical elements in the soil could constitute an extraneous variable in crop production. An intervening variable is one that is observed to have an influence during the experiment, but cannot be controlled, i. e., an outbreak of leaf blight.

Treatment and Control. Part of experimental design is observing or introducing different independent variables in the research procedure to see their effects upon the dependent variable. The process of introducing different variables is referred to as manipulation, or treatment. To ensure that any influence of independent variables on the dependent variable is accurately assessed, rigid controls are used in the research design of an experimental study. Control of experimental conditions reduces the possibility of influence from extraneous variables. In the factorial design study previously discussed, method and location of the refresher course were independent factors that were observed to see their influence upon achievement and satisfaction in math. In this case, the control to minimize effects of possible extraneous variables, such as teacher personality or type of participants attending the program, was a 2 x 3 design which combined each independent variable with all other variables. By including two different combinations of site and instruction, extraneous factors of teacher personality and type of participant are at least partially equated.

Observation. The word observation is frequently used in experimental methodology. Although the term does include "viewing" behavior or events, it is generally thought of as any form of assessment, in addition to visual observation. For example, an assessment of events represented by performance on pretests and posttests is a form of observation. It simply is documentation of events associated with the phenomenon being studied.

Internal and External Threats to Validity. Basic to conducting experimental research are steps to ensure the validity of research results. The degree to which a study is valid is important in that it indicates to the research consumer how accurately cause was established and future events can be predicted. The degree to which a study may be judged valid is determined in two ways -- internally and externally. Steps to ensure both types of validity are carefully considered in planning experimental research studies.

Validity is of concern to any researcher in carrying out research, but threats to validity are of particular concern in the design of an experimental study because the researcher hopes to make predictions from the research results.

Internal threats to validity may be interpreted as those factors which affect the degree to which the research procedure measures what it purports to measure.

1. History of events in the experiment
2. Maturation of subjects through time
3. Effects of testing upon subjects

4. Errors of measurement or observation
5. Biased selection of subjects
6. Statistical regression.

External threats pertain to the extent results of a study are generalizable to other situations.

1. Extent of randomization in subject selection
2. Effects of pretesting on subjects
3. Effects of the experimental setting (Hawthorne/placebo effects)
4. Effects of multiple treatments in the experiment

The effects of life experience (history) or physical and emotional development (maturation) of research participants during the course of a study, for example, are internal threats that may affect the validity of results generated. Participants change through experience and develop over time and, therefore, may naturally respond differently at the end of a study from how they responded at the outset of the experiment. Also, the way research subjects are selected is sometimes biased: one type or group of persons may have a better chance of being selected, for example, or may learn through the experimental process, beyond what is intended by the treatment. Additionally, simple errors in observation and measurement by the researcher, along with statistical regression -- the tendency for participant scores to move closer to the mean upon retesting -- all may contribute to invalid research results.

Generalizability of findings is influenced by the degree a study is controlled through the research design. Lack of representativeness within the sample group is an example of a potential external threat. Changes brought about because of the aura of experimental conditions or the secondary influences of experimental treatment also are external threats that affect the researcher's ability to generalize research beyond the present study.

Hypothesis. A hypothesis is a tentative explanation of phenomena that may be empirically tested and gives direction to the research (Ary, 1985). Each hypothesis developed to guide the experimental study is usually related to an important variable or set of relationships that make up the phenomenon under study. Research hypotheses are converted to quantitative, negative statements, or null hypotheses, for use in statistical testing. The null hypothesis states that no significant difference exists between the experimental and control groups pertaining to the specific variables mentioned in the hypothesis. Inferential statistics are used as tools to test hypotheses, as well as to estimate parameters -- the type of distribution of the population being used in the study. The inferential test is to prove the null hypothesis incorrect and permit the researcher to reject the null hypothesis. Rejection of the null and acceptance of the original or alternative hypothesis indicates that a difference does indeed exist. Acceptance or rejection of the null hypothesis is done using standard levels of probability. The level of probability indicates the extent to which observed differences could have resulted by chance.

An obvious advantage of experimental research methods includes the predictive nature of results. Theoretically, the method makes it possible to accurately predict events in similar settings without actually observing those events. Another advantage is the careful delineation of research phenomena that takes place through the experimental process; meticulous care is taken to sort out and examine factors that may influence outcomes of the study.

A disadvantage is the difficulty of implementing the method in the study of human events. True experimental conditions are difficult to arrange in natural settings. Consequently, researchers are forced to use quasi-experimental methods in the educational enterprise, and the use of quasi-experimental methods reduces the predictive power that the researcher has available. Another disadvantage of the experimental method is the narrow scope of investigation induced by the empirical/deductive mode of inquiry. Use of intuitive sources of knowledge, for example, are minimized, and reality is reduced to minuscule, stop-action snapshots. The power of experimental design lies in precision; its major limitation is narrowness of scope as related to the on-going milieu of human events.

In summary, the assumption upon which experimental methodology rests is that use of tightly controlled conditions and application of statistical probability lead to determination of causal relationships. Adherence to the experimental method allows the researcher to generalize results of one study to other similar situations.

As stressed in the discussion of advantages and disadvantages, not all research problems can or should be pursued using experimental methods. Actually, with some research problems, the researcher merely wants to describe relationships surrounding a phenomenon. Descriptive research methodology -- that which describes rather than predicts -- is discussed in the following section.

Descriptive and Causal/Comparative Methods

One of the most commonly used methodologies in the study of adult education and training is the descriptive method. Its purpose is to describe systematically the facts and characteristics of a given population or area of interest. Description may include (1) collection of facts that describe existing phenomena, (2) identification of problems or justification of current conditions and practice, (3) project or product evaluation, or (4) comparison of experience between groups with similar problems to assist in future planning and decision making.

A form of descriptive research that has many of the design characteristics of the experimental method is causal/comparative (or ex post facto) research. Here the investigator attempts to explain phenomena that already have taken place. Such studies do not predict events in the future; rather, they seek results indicating the relationships that may point to cause.

Research done on the effect of using seat belts in automobiles is an example of causal/comparative research that influenced development of safety equipment. Reports of research indicated individuals who used seat belts experienced fewer injuries and fatalities. This research led to legislation dictating that all new cars purchased after January 1, 1968, must have lap and shoulder belts installed (*U.S. News & World Report*, 1968). The Swedish Volvo report that followed indicated drastic reduction of skull and facial injuries among accident victims who used shoulder/lap belts.

Another example of causal/comparative research is the study reported in *Americans in Transition: Life Changes as Reasons for Adult Learning* (Aslanian & Brickell, 1980). A representative sample of approximately 2,000 adults in the United State over twenty-five years of age was surveyed using face-to-face and telephone interviews. Research questions included "Why do adults choose certain learning activities?" "Do certain demographic characteristics correlate with adult learners?" and "Why are more adults choosing to take part in learning activities?" The researchers found that of those engaged in learning, over 80 percent described some change in their lives as the reason for learning. More than half of the transitions were career related; a smaller but substantial fraction were family or leisure transitions. The findings therefore suggest that transitions in adult life lead to learning. Results also confirmed findings of earlier participation studies -- adult learners tend to be younger, more highly educated, and from higher income levels.

A precaution researchers should take in using the causal/ comparative method is not to assume independent variables either do or do not cause outcomes reflected in the dependent variable. Arriving at conclusions of cause based on relational data in causal/comparative research is referred to as "post hoc fallacy." In the *Americans in Transition* study, for example, the researchers did not say that transitions cause learning, only that transitions and learning are related, which suggests cause.

An example of coming to unsupported conclusions using the causal/ comparative method is found in the following example. A researcher is interested in attrition of adults in evening classes at a particular community college. In pursuing the study the researcher gathers various descriptive data related to participants in the evening program and discovers that females between the ages of eighteen and twenty-five who attend the community college are more persistent in attending classes than are females in the twenty-six to forty age range. A conclusion that the researcher might incorrectly draw is that being younger causes participants to be more persistent in attending classes. In fact, we may find the cause to be the responsibilities of child care, stronger commitment to career, or numerous other factors, if variables were manipulated under experimental conditions. Data gathered after the event has taken place can only indicate relationship and give clues to probable cause.

The central focus of descriptive research is to examine facts about people, their opinions and attitudes (Kerlinger, 1986). Its purpose is not to give value to sets of relationships between events, but simply to draw attention to the degree two events or phenomena are related. Because social science researchers find arranging subjects into experiments for manipulation or treatment to be artificial, descriptive research is a common choice of method. In descriptive research, the researcher does not manipulate variables or control the environment in which the study takes place.

The researcher who engages in descriptive research finds that the way data are sampled to be of great importance. Generally, three different procedures are used to gather descriptive research data when large populations are being studied -- cross-sectional, longitudinal, and cross-sequential sampling. These three designs have two main distinguishing characteristics: (1) the time at which data are collected, and (2) the type, or nature of the sample (Wiersma 1986). A discussion of descriptive data sampling follows.

Descriptive Data Sampling

In a cross-sectional design, data are sampled at a single point in time, whereas a longitudinal design gathers data from the same sample on several occasions. The combination of these two -- cross-sectional and longitudinal -- is referred to as cross-sequential. Each design has a special use that may be valuable to the researcher, depending upon the purpose of a study. The following examples of sampling designs are taken from adult development and learning research, an area of study that has impact upon both education and training. The examples are selected to illustrate how the three designs are distinct and to discuss strengths and limitations of each one.

In cross-sectional developmental study, the performances of people from different age groups are measured at the same point in time. For example, a group of twenty-year-olds, forty-year-olds, and sixty-year-olds are tested, and their mean scores compared. A major reason for using this methodology would be to simply survey difference in people of various age groups.

The major problem in cross-sectional research is the construing of *age differences* in performance or attitudes as *age-related* changes. With cross-sectional studies, one can say that people of a given age or stage are characterized a certain way. One cannot say that people will change in a certain way as they grow older.

In longitudinal research, the performance of a group of subjects is compared with their own performance at another period in time. A group of twenty-year-olds, for example, may be observed at age twenty, again at age twenty-five, thirty, thirty-five, and so on. This design allows for age-related conclusions to be drawn. However, because only one cohort is being studied, generalizations can safely be made only to people born at the time that group was born. Other limitations with this design are: the long-term commitment of money, time and personnel needed for such a study; survivor bias, that is, those who survive for successive rounds of study are most likely healthier and more intelligent than those who do not survive; the practice effects of successive testing; and changing interest of the researcher in topics for study.

Besides the basic problems of internal and external validity common to all research, studies in adult development and aging are particularly sensitive to the following methodological problems:

1. Selective Sampling. Cross-sectional studies have the problem of achieving representative samples for each age group tested. In addition, those who volunteer tend to be above average in intelligence and of a higher socioeconomic status than those who do not.

2. Survivor Bias. A given population at birth changes its composition as the members age. The survival rate of cohort members is

correlated with intelligence, socioeconomic factors, and psychopathology. Successively older groups in a cross-sectional study and survivors in longitudinal studies represent samples unrepresentative of their birth cohorts.

3. Selective Dropout. A longitudinal sample measured later may not be comparable to the earlier sample because the dropout from the sample may not follow the random pattern that would be equivalent to attrition of the larger population. Consequently, results will be biased.

4. Testing Effects and Instruments. A longitudinal design assumes that repeated measurements with the same sample have no effect on the dependent variable. Practice effects and increased sophistication at test taking do, however, become sources of error. Measurement or test instruments themselves pose an additional problem. The difficulty of finding or designing instruments that measure the same attribute, such as intelligence in young adults and older adults, is no small task. Age differences in performance on an instrument may indicate that different attributes are being measured rather than age-related changes of the same attribute.

5. Generation Effects. Generation effects hamper the internal validity of cross-sectional designs and the external validity of longitudinal designs. In cross-sectional designs, samples vary by age and by generation cohort, and measurement differences thus reflect age and cultural changes. In longitudinal designs, the same cohort is measured, and thus differences are not confounded by generation differences. On the other hand, changes are specific to that generation only.

To control for testing and generation effects, several sequential design strategies -- the third type of design -- have evolved in the study of development and aging. Sequential or "mixed" designs are characterized by the simultaneous application of cross-sectional and longitudinal factors. Age changes are assessed at the same time for several groups over a period of time. For example, a group of twenty-, forty-, sixty-year-olds are measured, and then either the same subjects or different subjects from the same cohort are tested again in ten years, adding a new group of twenty-year-olds. The original twenty-year-olds are now thirty, the forty-year-olds are now fifty, and the sixty-year-olds are now seventy. With this method, age changes occuring within generations can be contrasted with age differences between generations at a given point in time. Also, environmental impact is constant for all age groups, thus allowing the differences that emerge to be attributed to maturation. Once the researcher settles upon the appropriate data sampling design, techniques for gathering data are the next consideration.

Descriptive Techniques

The most common technique used for gathering data in descriptive research is the survey. Subjects are asked to respond to a written or orally administered schedule of questions. Written forms of surveys are questionnaires; orally administered surveys are interviews. Typically surveys are carefully planned to elicit whatever information is needed.

An advantage of using questionnaires to conduct research is the opportunity for careful construction and validation of questions in advance of conducting the study. Also, written instruments are usually easier to administer. In some cases, the researcher's presence is unnecessary, thus reducing time required and expense. Many surveys are administered through the mail, which permits access to a potentially larger group of subjects.

An advantage of the interview technique is its effectiveness in surveying special populations and gaining in-depth information. Interviewing is particularly useful in gathering data from "hard-to-reach" populations, such as persons who are handicapped, illiterate, or culturally different. Also, when it is not possible to anticipate all that the researcher may need to know in preparing the schedule of questions before meeting the research subjects, an unstructured interview may yield more reliable data than a written questionnaire. A personal, face-to-face interview is recommended to develop rapport and gain the widest range of data. The telephone interview, however, may be used in gathering data from subjects that are otherwise hard to contact.

When research procedures require gathering data about the performance and interaction of people, another descriptive research method --structured observation -- is sometimes used. This method is also used for collecting data from documents, in which case it is commonly referred to as content analysis or document analysis. If the object of the study is to explore, unstructured observation is often employed. Tests that reflect attributes such as aptitude, achievement, or personality are the third type of technique used in descriptive research. Each of these techniques is more thoroughly discussed in Chapter 7 of this book.

Contributions of Descriptive Research

Numerous research methods are effectively used to study the education and training of adults. However, descriptive research has made a significant contribution in the early development of these fields. The first major adult education survey was completed in England in 1851 (Hudson, 1969). Since that time several extensive surveys to study adult participation have been conducted (e.g., Johnstone and Rivera, 1965; Tough, 1979, 1982; Boshier & Collins, 1985; Dimmock, 1985). Interest in why adults participate in education appears to be a perennial source of descriptive survey research.

Dickinson and Rusnell (1971) indicated that 86 percent of research reported in *Adult Education* during the twenty-year period (1950-1970) used the survey technique as a basis of the study. Also, a review of graduate student scholarship revealed wide use of the survey technique (Grabowski, 1980). In looking to future trends for the field, Dickinson and Blunt (1980) forecast that because of persistent needs of an evolving discipline of social practice (adult education), the survey will continue to be the major means used in conducting research.

Descriptive research is the most common form of research used in adult education. Because of immediate need to define and describe the fields of practice, this methodology will continue to be important in advancing knowledge. The researcher should be aware, however, that descriptive research also has certain strengths and limitations.

Strengths and Limitations of Descriptive Research

One obvious advantage or strength of the descriptive method is its ease of use. It produces data that are accurate and representative. It describes "what is." The rigor of research design in descriptive research is not typically as demanding as in experimental studies.

A second advantage is that it allows the researcher to study relationships or events as they happen in human life situations. None of the contrived or manipulative techniques that are common in experimental methods are used.

A third advantage is the exploratory nature of the descriptive methods. Not only can variables be studied that indicate probable cause, but additional variables may be discovered that shed new light upon the phenomenon.

One prominent disadvantage or limitation is the lack of predictive power. The researcher discovers and describes "what is," but is unable to generalize or predict "what will be."

An aspect of research methodology that seems to be both a positive and a negative influence in conducting research is the application of statistics. Statistical explanation and analysis can give the researcher the advantage of greater power of expression in the case of descriptive research, and increased power of prediction when experimental methods are used. However, substitution of statistical terms for narrative discourse in the analysis and reporting of research often perplexes, frustrates, and discourages researchers and research consumers.

In experimental and descriptive research, as well as in many other methods of research, statistics are commonly used for comparison of data, analysis of data, and interpretation of research findings. It is important to be aware of the ways in which statistics assist or hinder the researcher.

Numerous statistical techniques are available. A full treatment of type and methods of conducting various statistical precedures is found in sources devoted to the topic of statistical design (Kerlinger, 1986; Edwards, 1985).

Use of terms such as statistic, control, treatment, and sample in a discussion of research methods raises some ethical questions. For example, What is the moral or ethical responsibility of the researcher to participants in a study? or What are the boundaries of intervention in the lives of research subjects in the name of science? Persons conducting experimental and descriptive research are particularly sensitive to the concerns these questions represent. Although definitive answers are difficult to provide, a discussion of factors that are related to the researcher's ethical responsibility is important to understand planning and conducting research.

Ethical Treatment of Participants

The ethical treatment of research participants has become a growing concern in social science research. At the heart of the issue is society's right to know and an investigator's right to inquire versus a person's right to safety and privacy (Brockett, 1987). Because human behavior is involved, the issues are extraordinarily complex. Guidelines suggesting what is ethically and morally acceptable in gathering information from human subjects have been established by most professional associations, funding agencies, and universities. These guidelines do not answer the many questions involved in doing research on human behavior, but they do reflect a common-sense approach to ensuring the privacy of participants, ensuring protection from harm, and obtaining informed consent. More specifically, most guidelines recommend that:

1. Respondents should be told the purpose of the research and how the data they are being asked to provide will be used.

2. Respondents should be informed of the nature of the research before data are collected and should be allowed to withdraw at any given point.

3. There should be no unpleasant or damaging effects on the individual, the setting, or others close to the participant either during or subsequent to the research.

4. The investigator must respect the privacy of the respondents and, whenever possible, ensure anonymity or confidentiality.

5. There should be no unprofessional behavior required of the participants.

6. The participant should be given an opportunity to learn from the research. (Fox, 1969, p.p. 384-486) This can be achieved by debriefing participants and/or by sharing the results of the research with the participants.

Each of the six areas mentioned is to some extent problematic when the guideline is put into practice. For example, informing participants of the purpose of the study may in some cases obscure the purpose of the study. If managers were told that they were being studied to determine the extent to which the sex of an employee determined promotability, their behavior may well be different from the way it would be if they were unaware of the purpose of the study. Even the implementation of the third guideline -- that there be no unpleasant effects or damage to participants -- can be problematic. It is not always possible to determine ahead of time whether there will be unpleasant effects or the extent of those effects. If an experimental study were designed to test a new method of teaching adults to read, for example, it certainly would be difficult to say whether or not those receiving the treatment would be set back or would advance in their reading progress. If the method were tremendously successful, one might also wonder how ethical it is to deprive the control group of the benefits of the method. Diener and Crandall (1978) suggest that the best

criterion deciding what information should be given to individuals before a study is what a 'reasonal or prudent person' would want to know. This legal term captures the essence of a common-sense approach to the problem. . . . Subjects have an *uncondi-*

tional right to know of any potential danger or of any rights to be lost during the study. (p. 43)

Approaching the problem of the ethical treatment of research participants from a common-sense position suggests at the very least that reasonable measures be taken to ensure the safety of participants, that subjects be treated by the researcher as if the researcher were a subject, that the respondents give their consent to participate, and that all information be kept confidential.

Although it is not within the scope of this text to elaborate, the subject of ethics in research involves areas in addition to the treatment of research participants The researcher's responsibility to report findings honestly and accurately needs to be considered. Also, ethical standards to be adhered to in the writing of research reports and articles with colleagues are important. Finally, there is the larger issue of ethics and social values and their relationship to research in a particular time. Researchers interested in these issues are referred to more extensive coverages of the topic such as those found in (Beauchamp et al. 1982).

In summary, experimental and descriptive research methods are two of the most commonly used methods in the social science fields. Each provides a unique approach to inquiry. Experimental research attempts to establish cause by isolating the independent variable(s) that influence change observed in the dependent variable. Descriptive research, on the other hand, describes the variables, describes the phenomenon of which the variables are part, and may indicate degrees of relationship existing between them. Results of causal/comparative descriptive research may even point to potential cause.

Experimental research provides the power of prediction through carefully designed studies utilizing treatment, control, and statistical probability. The multivariant nature of the educational enterprise and the natural, human settings in which research related to education and training of adults is conducted, however, make experimental research of limited use. Ethical considerations regarding rights and propriety of research participatants also limit the researcher's application of experimental methods.

Descriptive research utilizes various forms of survey, observation, and testing techniques in gathering data. Cross-sectional, longitudinal, or cross-sequential sampling are some of the ways the researcher gathers descriptive data. The strength of the descriptive research method is in the exploratory capability it provides -- a feature that has resulted in significant contributions to developing fields, such as the education and training of adults.

REFERENCES

Ary, D., Jacobs, L. C., and Ragevich, A. (1985). *Introduction to Research in Education*. (3rd ed.). New York: Holt, Rinehart and Winston.

Aslanian, Carol B. and Henry M. Brickell. (1980). *Americans in Transition: Life Changes as Reasons for Adult Learning*. New York: College Entrance Examination Board.

Beauchamp, T. L., et al. (eds.) (1982) *Ethical Issues in Social Science Research*. New York: Holt, Rinehart and Winston.

Boshier, R. and Collins, J.B. (1985). "The Houle Typology After Twenty-Two Years: A Large-Scale Empirical Test," *Adult Education Quarterly*. 35:113-130.

Brockett, Ralph G. (1987). *Ethical Issues in Adult Education*, San Francisco: Jossey-Bass Publishers.

Dickinson, Gary and Dale Rusnell. (1971). "A Content Analysis of Adult Education." *Adult Education*. 21: 177-185.

Dickinson, Gary and Adrian Blunt. (1980). "Survey Research" in *Changing Approaches to Studying of Adult Education*, (eds.). Huey B. Long, Roger Hiemstra and Associates, San Francisco: Jossey-Bass.

Diener, E. and Crandall, R. (1978). *Ethics in Social and Behavioral Research*. Chicago: The University of Chicago Press.

Dimmock, K.H. (1985). "Models of Adult Participation in Informal Science Education," Unpublished Doctoral Dissertation, Northern Illinois University.

Drew, Clifford J. (1985). *Introduction to Designing and Conducting Research*. St. Louis: The C. V. Mosby Company.

Edwards, A. L. (1985). *Experimental Design in Psychological Research*. (5th ed.). New York: Holt, Rinehart and Winston.

Edwards, A. L. (1972). *Experimental Design in Psychological Research*. (5th ed.). New York: Holt, Rinehart and Winston.

Fisher, Ronald A. (1935). *The Design of Experiments*. Edinburgh: Oliver and Boyd.

Fox, David J. (1969). *The Research Process in Education*. New York: Holt, Rinehart and Winston.

Grabowski, Stanley M. (1980). "Trends in Graduate Research" in *Changing Approaches to Studying of Adult Education*, (eds.) Huey B. Long, Roger Hiemstra and Associates, San Francisco: Jossey-Bass.

Hudson, J. (1969). *The History of Adult Education*, London: Woburn Press.

Johnston, J. M. and Pennypacker, H.S. (1980). *Strategies and Tactics of Human Behavioral Sciences*. Hillsdale, New Jersey: Lawrence Erlbaum Associates.

Johnstone, J. W. C. and R. J. Rivera. (1965). *Volunteers for Learning: A Study of Educational Pursuits of American Adults*. Chicago: Aldine Company Publishing.

Kerlinger, F. N. (1986). *Foundations of Behavioral Research*. New York: Holt, Rinehart and Winston. (3rd ed.).

Mill, James S. (1873). *A System of Logic*. New York: Harper and Row.

Rosentreter, Gary. (1979). "Evaluating Training by Four Economic Indices." *Adult Education*. 24:234-241.

Tough, Allen. (1979). *The Adults' Learning Projects*. Toronto: Ontario Institute for Studies in Education.

Tough, Allen. (1982). *Intentional Changes*. Chicago: Follett Publishers.

U.S. News & World Report, January 29, 1968.

Wiersma, W. (1986). *Research Methods in Education*. (4th ed.). Boston: UC
Williams, G. B. (1985). "Perspective Transformation As An Adult Learning Theory to Explain and Facilitate Change in Male Spouse Abusers," Unpublished Doctoral Dissertation, Northern Illinois University.
Young, J. D. (1986). "An Examination of Cognitive Restructuring In An Adult Continuing Education Workshop," Unpublished Doctoral Dissertation, Northern Illinois University.

CHAPTER 5

HISTORICAL
AND PHILOSOPHICAL
INQUIRY

Research can be thought of as systematic inquiry. Some approaches have already been discussed in Chapter 4. The particular system or method followed depends upon the nature of the problem and the type of question being asked. Historical and philosophical inquiry each has its own "system" for answering questions about the past or about underlying assumptions and beliefs. The purposes of this chapter are to discuss how history and philosophy can be used in the understanding of a field of social practice, and secondly, to discuss how to systematically engage in historical or philosophical study.

Historical Inquiry

Like other areas of research, historical inquiry is motivated by curiosity: it begins with wondering about some event, institution, idea, or person. In applied fields like allied health, vocational education, or human resource development, there are many historical questions to be asked. One might be curious about the inception, purpose, or evolution of a particular institution or practice or ideal. For example, how has the current emphasis on career counseling come about in the field of counseling? What has been the black person's experience in vocational education? Why is the federal government willing to finance adult basic education but not liberal education programs?

A meaningful research topic not only arises out of curiosity, but also relates in some way to a larger problem or broader question. In focusing upon a particular segment of a problem, the researcher hopes to contribute to understanding the larger problem area. It is not enough, for example, to chronicle the history of an institution such as an adult *role*

evening school or a community health clinic. One must also ask questions about the role of that particular institution in society, and the sociohistorical context in which it evolved. This anchors the specific question in a larger context, the understanding of which may lead to a better appreciation of present practice. Carlson (1981) writes that historical and philosopical research are in fact the *most* effective methodologies for understanding practice. They "provide the sort of perspective that lets us determine where we have come from, what we are doing and why, where we appear to be going, and how we might influence events in a humane direction" (p. 3). Whether articulated or not, all the planning and decision making that practitioners do in their work (and in their personal lives as well) are based on former experiences, knowledge, and values. The more knowledge one has, the more informed one's decisions in practice can be.

Thus, significant historical questions in applied fields are those that relate to the practice of that field. Using the Chautauqua movement of the nineteenth century as an example, Rose (1982, p. 15) distinguishes between the "traditional historian" and an adult educator involved in historical research. The traditional historian would be "primarily interested in questions which were derived from the period" such as Chautauqua's relationship to reform and social gospel movements, or its intellectual origins. While not ignoring these questions, adult educators would focus on issues of "participation and actual impact" such as

> Where did participants come from; how did they hear about Chautauqua; did they buy homes on the lake or were they visitors; how long did the average person stay; what was the educational background of participants; is there a connection between the growth of a summer community such as this and large resorts which were also being developed during the same period; what were the differences? Finally, what does participation tell us about how adults viewed learning during this time? (p. 15)

Many historical research problems in applied fields deal with events, institutions, or persons. Historical research may also deal with ideas, concepts, or theories that have had an effect upon practice. Stubblefield (1988) for example, discusses the ways in which the first generation of American adult education thinkers began to theorize about the field. He traces the development of notions of the diffusion of knowledge and culture, liberal education, and social education. Other concepts that might be the subject of a historical investigation are human resource development, patient education, distance learning, and community development.

Perhaps because they are young, fields such as adult education, human resource development, gerontology, social work, and such have sought to establish their own body of knowledge through more "scientific" methodologies. Historical research has tended to be descriptive of institutions and programs. While chronicling has its place, historical inquiry is of greater service to a field when it is used to examine

1. The origin of assumptions held to be "true" in the field
2. A field's failures as well as its "great feats" (Rockhill, 1976, p. 196)
3. The impact a practice has had on people's lives (Rose, 1982, p. 19)
4. The total context of an event, not just the event itself (Rose, 1982, p. 18)

Thus, engaging historical research with an applied field involves more than detailing the chronological history of some aspect of that field. It is looking at the context of the event, examining assumptions related to the topic, and being cognizant of its impact on the lives of participants. This approach holds the potential for adding to the knowledge and understanding of present practice. It may even offer some guidelines for future practice, although prediction per se is not a goal of historical research. Instead, historical studies offer "clues to *possible* rather than *probable* behavior," allows one to "*anticipate* rather than to *predict,* to take *precautions* rather than to *control*" (Gottschalk, 1963, p. 269).

Doing Historical Research—Doing historical research necessitates having a historical topic. As noted earlier, problems arise out of a curiosity about the past of an event, institution, concept, or person. Studies have already been conducted of such diverse topics related to the education and training of adults as university extension, settlement houses, and adult basic education. Occasionally one begins with a question about present practice and finds that it leads to a historical problem. For example, a question about the effectiveness of using programmed instruction materials with adults might lead to wondering how long programmed instruction has been used, how it was originally developed, how it found its way into present practice, why it was adopted as an instructional technique, and what the impact of its use has been on adults.

Having a general topic and posing some questions about the topic is sufficient to begin a historical study. Working through material on the topic will eventually lead to a thesis or proposition to be argued. At the outset, however, a researcher "should judiciously refrain from stating hypotheses, locking into a social science theory, or articulating the study in the form of a problem. . . .Historical research is not the discipline with which to 'solve problems' but a means of exploring the mystery that is man" (Carlson, 1980, p. 44).

After becoming acquainted with the general topic, the task becomes one of focusing upon a particular seqment of the problem area. As with other types of research, knowing what is a manageable topic in historical research is a trial-and-error process. If the topic is too broad or too narrow, it can be reduced or expanded by manipulating the extent of geographical area covered, the number of persons involved, the span of time covered, or the scope of human activity included (Gottschalk, 1963). For example, the history of adult illiteracy in the United States may be too broad a topic for an individual to handle. Using Gottschalk's suggestions, the topic could be narrowed by (1) studying the history of illiteracy in one section of the country or in one state; (2) limiting the investigation to a segment of the population such as women, immigrants, Jewish Americans; (3) focusing on a prominent person who fought illiteracy; or (4) limiting the study to a particular time frame such as adult illiteracy during colonial times.

In delineating a manageable topic or focusing a study, one is probably already "doing" historical research. Furthermore, there is no standardized format that all historians subscribe to. L. P. Curtis (1970) discovered this when he attempted to pull together an anthology revealing "just how historians went about choosing their subjects, doing their research, shaping their interpretations and writing up the results" (p. xi). Several prominent historians who were invited to contribute declined with comments like "I am a bad person to write about methods--I have none," or "If all the contributors complied really honestly with your request, the history profession would be shattered fore and aft. What we now merely suspect would be proved without question--that nobody proceeds as the research manuals say we should" (Curtis, 1970, p. xv).

However elusive the techniques of historical research might be, all who do historical research are concerned with obtaining the best information available on the topic. The handling of historical material is very systematic and involves distinguishing between primary and secondary sources.

Primary sources are the basic materials used in historical studies. Under the leadership of the Syracuse University Kellogg Project, efforts are now underway by North American adult educators, historians, and archivists to identify and preserve primary source material and collections of historical interest to adult education. Oral or written primary sources are those where the author was a direct observer, or eyewitness, of the event. Barzun and Graff (1963) differentiate between "intentional" and "unpremeditated" transmitters of facts. Intentional primary sources are (1) written records including chronicles, annuals, memoirs, inscriptions, (2) oral recordings, and (3) works of art such as portraits, paintings, and films. Unpremeditatied sources are relics such as human remains, public documents, language and customs, tools, or other artifacts (pp. 132-134).

Secondary sources report the observations of those who did not witness the actual event. These secondary or secondhand sources can be useful in familiarizing the researcher with the topic and in suggesting new areas for further study. While the best primary sources are those recorded closest in time and place to the phenomenon, the farther removed a secondary source is from the phenomenon, the better, for such sources draw from the accumulated wisdom of earlier scholars.

It is not always possible to separate sources into primary and secondary categories. An eyewitness account may also include the observations or opinions of others, and, interestingly, a particular source may be classified primary or secondary depending upon the research problem. For example, a director's report of how a program has interpreted adult vocational education legislation would be a primary source if the study were investigating how federal legislation is translated into practice. The same report would be a secondary source in a study of the history of adult vocational legislation.

Locating primary sources is followed by the researcher's assessing the value or worth of the sources. In general, the best sources will meet the following criteria:

1. Proximity. The account closest in time to the event is preferable to others.
2. Competence of the author. The better record is one written by a person trained to observe the matter at hand. An instructor is not expected to be an expert on the institution's public policy, for example, yet a police officer is expected to record events accurately.
3. Purpose. The document that has as its purpose an impartial recording of events is likely to be more accurate than a spontaneous impression. Public records such as sports events, election returns, census data, and so on attempt to be accurate. At the same time, documents such as personal correspondence that are intended to be read by a few people are likely to be more revealing than those written with a large audience in mind.

In determining the genuineness of a document, the researcher attempts to establish authorship, time and place of writing, and whether it is an original copy. Internal criticism ascertains the trustworthiness of the information *within* the document. A researcher looks internally for the biases and motive of the author, as well as for incongruities in the account which may indicate exaggeration, misinterpretation, distortion, or outright fabrication. While full discussion of the principles of criticism is beyond the scope of this chapter, a person who undertakes a historical study should become acquainted with the procedures and problems inherent in assessing the value of the sources used.

Being careful about the material used for a historical study and being systematic in the handling of those sources help ensure that what is said about a phenomenon is as close an approximation of the truth as possible. But because the past can never be replicated, and we can never have complete faith in the facts found in primary sources,

> truth absolute is not at hand; the original with which to match the copy does not exist. . . .the historian finds truth by the unremitting exercise of his and his peers' judgement upon the material. Judgment is a comparative act that takes in the evidence and the report. . .and eliminates the untenable. The resulting truths are built, not reached. . . . (Barzun, 1974, p.p. 147-8)

In the end, Felt (1976, p. 6) writes, "all of us have to settle for the highest probabilities we can get, based on whatever observations, documents, and confirmations of deductive and inductive reasoning we can muster." As Barzun and Graff (1957) point out, we can trust history to the extent that we have documents that are critically tested, that our judgments are governed by probability, and that the notion of replicating the past as it actually was is a "delusion" (p. 144).

In recent years historical research has experimented with new methods in an attempt, one historian feels, to become more "scientific" (Barraclough, 1978), more certain, more precise. The use of measurement and quantification has "affected practically every branch of historical research during the last one or two decades" (Barraclough, 1978, p. 84). Any phenomenon that can be counted or measured (such as voting behavior, settlement patterns, and so on) may be the subject of a quantitative history employing sophisticated statistical techniques and computer analysis. Among the applications of quantitative analysis to history are:

1. Collective biography -- delineating biographical characteristics of a particular group of individuals such as Swedish immigrants, Civil War congressmen, prohibition-era police officers.

2. Content analysis -- establishing the frequency of certain ideas, attitudes, or words within a particular body of material. For example, the employment opportunities for women during the 1950s might be ascertained by doing a content analysis of period newspapers.
3. Historical demography -- studying the composition of the population, such as birthrate or age of marrying. This can be determined by aggregating public records. These and other quantitative history methods are discussed at length in Beringer's *Historical Analysis: Contemporary Approaches to Clio's Craft* (1978).

In addition to quantitative history, psychosocial history has become an accepted historical method. Broadly defined, this approach uses modern psychological and sociological theories and concepts to interpret personalities, events, groups, or movements of the past. Examples of this approach are Erikson's psychobiography of Luther (1958), and Donald's interpretation of abolitionist behavior in terms of status and reference group theory (1956).

Both approaches to historical research have their supporters and their critics. While it is not within the scope of this chapter to enter the debate over these methods it can be pointed out that each is an attempt to deal more precisely with the problems of an increasingly complex world through historical analysis. Barzun, a critic of these approaches, nevertheless recognizes the reason for their popularity:

> The joint popularity of psycho- and quanto-history is not an accident or a contradiction; for although nothing is more impalpable than the Id and more dense than town-hall records, they stand respectively for the individual and society, and the past of one or the other or both may well contain the influential secret about present and future. The two branches of the new history give an equal hold to the strong desire mentioned in an earlier connection: to solve pressing problems. (Barzun, 1974, p. 78)

Like history itself, the methods of historical inquiry are changing, but each new method represents an attempt to find the best way to uncover the truths of the past. Researchers in applied fields--especially those dealing with the training and education of adults--more often than not have been trained in other disciplines and so may be quite familiar with other theories and methods of doing research. Creative applications of these methods to historical questions may lead to a better illumination of the past.

Interpretation—Doing historical research is more than collecting information by various means from primary data sources. "History," Halle (1982, p. 2) writes, "is not simply a heap of details, any more than the cathedral of Chartres is a pile of stones. Just as the individual stones are not what count in Chartres, so the details are not what count in history." The collection of facts must be arranged into some order and given some interpretation. It is this task of interpreting the data, of bringing insight and coherence to a set of facts, that requires skill and imagination on the part of the researcher. "The greatest historians," Commager writes, "have been the interpreters. . .that is they tried to extract some meaning out of the inchoate raw materials of history, or to impose some philosophy upon it" (1965, p. 6).

Explaining how a person actually interprets a set of facts is as difficult as explaining how to have insight or how to make a discovery. Interpretation is dependent upon the individual researcher. The facts can be organized and interpreted in many ways. Such multiplicity of histories "mirrors the character of mankind, which is no more at one in its view of the present or recently endured past than it is about any other subject, including the past past" (Barzun, 1973, p. 101).

While the process for arriving at interpretation cannot be delineated, some of the characteristics of the interpretive step can be pointed out. As noted above, the narrative is more than a listing of facts. It also involves ideas. An idea is "an image or a suggestion that goes beyond the bare facts. . . .The statement of a fact gives the impression of ending with itself, whereas an idea leads us on" (Barzun and Graff, 1957, p. 117). Ideas link facts together and infuse the narrative with meaning.

A historical account is a personal interpretation of the best, most relevant evidence available to the researcher. The researcher exercises judgment at two points in this process -- first, in deciding what is "relevant" evidence, and then in choosing how to present the evidence in narrative form. Carlson (1980) captures the subjective dimension of historical research in the following passage:

> Historians present a reasoned argument regarding the past, based on evidence and their own values. . . .Historians interpret the past by sifting through the available relevant evidence and by mixing this information with their own values and philosophy. Through this sometimes agonizing process, they create or discover patterns in the thinking, action, motivation, and relationships that occurred in the past. Disciplined only by reality and their own common sense, historians tease out, dream up, and spin out their interpretation of why the events they are describing have occurred. (p. 42)

Just as the brilliance of a historical interpretation is dependent upon the imagination and intellect of the researcher, the perspective of the interpretation is shaped by the investigator's biases and values. One limitation of the historian that is particularly difficult to overcome is what Commager calls " 'present-mindedness' -- our instinctive habit of looking at the past through our own eyes, judging it by our own standards, recreating it in our own words or reading back into the language of the past our own meanings, assuming that whatever happened, happened in some 'past' and forgetting that every past was once a present" (1965, p. 46). While researchers cannot divest themselves of the present, an effort can be made to understand events from the point of view of those participating in them. For example Lemisch (1968) recounts how merchant seamen in early America had been portrayed by historians as irresponsible, boisterous, and manipulated, because little attempt was made to understand their behavior from the perspective of the seamen themselves. Lemisch (1968) argues that historical research from the point of view of the "inarticulate" may well dispel some erroneous assumptions and preconceptions about the history of a field. In a parallel example from adult education, Seller (1978) uncovered a whole new facet of immigrant education by examining records of educational opportunities--opportunities offered by the immigrants themselves.

Summary—Historical research in applied fields can bring some clarity to the practice of that field. Training in history or historical methods, although desirable, is not necessary to engage in a historical study. The researcher does need to be curious about the past of an institution, event, person, or practice; about its relationship to the times in which it occurred; and curious about the people involved. Then the researcher can acquire the knowledge needed to examine sources for their authenticity and value in answering the questions posed by the study. Finally, the information must be skillfully organized into a narrative that both explains and interprets the past. In so doing, the present becomes enlightened.

Philosophical Inquiry

The many methods of doing research presented in this text have in common the systematic handling of data and the interpreting of that data for others. Philosophical research or, as it is more commonly referred to, philosophical inquiry is no exception. Like historical inquiry, philosophical inquiry begins with a question or problem, proceeds to the selection and examination of data according to certain rules, and ends with an insightful interpretation of the question. Philosophical inquiry has been grouped with historical inquiry in this chapter because both forms of inquiry are concerned with the foundations of a discipline or field of practice. Historical inquiry goes back to the past events and people--the early building blocks of a field--in order to illuminate present practice. Phiosophical inquiry examines the underlying opinions, beliefs, values, and assumptions to bring clarity to a field of practice. What distinguishes philosophical research from historical inquiry is the nature of the questions raised and the methods philosophers employ in addressing those questions.

To some extent all human beings wonder about their lives, the things they experience, and where they fit into the world as a whole. Wanting to know, to understand, to satisfy curiosity are urges characteristic of us all:

> Even the least educated or the most simple-minded, are of necessity engaged in a ceaseless effort to find meaning behind apparent meaninglessness, to discover unity beneath surface diversity, and (above all) to impose some degree of order on the seeming chaos of our personal experience. Much of this effort may be unconscious or unarticulated, but we cannot escape making it. (Mead, 1962, pp. 23-34)

In contrast to most other people, philosophers are those who "do" philosophy consciously and systematically. How one "systematically" approaches answering philosophical questions is at the heart of philosophical inquiry as a research methodology.

Like other forms of inquiry, philosophy attempts to uncover truth and to add to our knowledge. The subject matter of philosophical inquiry is the ultimate nature of things. Of course no one person could manage an investigation of "all things." Rather, we wonder about a selected segment of the world and our existence in it. To bring some order to such an undertaking, problems of a philosophical nature traditionally have been divided into categories. There are *epistemological questions* dealing with the origins and nature of knowledge and how we know something is true, *metaphysical questions* dealing with what is ultimately real, *axiological questions* about value--the nature of good, the beautiful and so on--and *questions of logic* which focus on rules of correct reasoning.

These basic classifications are useful in thinking about problems in applied fields. A simple statement such as: "All adults should have access to learning opportunities," for example, can be analyzed philosophically from several perspectives. What constitutes the classification of a person as "adult"? Why "should" adults have access to learning opportunities? Who are "all" adults? What does "access" mean? What are "learning opportunities"? How can such an ideal become a reality? Answering any of these questions would bring some clarity to the practice of adult education. Philosophers strive for clarity, for perspective, for a sense of order and wholeness. Thus, philosophical questions or problems in an applied field arise out of curiosity or uncertainty about the assumptions underlying practice. In education, a philosophical problem often centers on the aims of the endeavor, education's relationship to society, the teaching-learning process, and curriculum.

Methods of Philosophical Inquiry—Philosophical inquiry is as systematic and rigorous as any other form of inquiry. Its method depends upon the philosophical school with which the investigator is aligned. "The endorsement of a method," Johnstone notes, "amounts to the same thing as acceptance of a view of the nature of philosophy" (1965, p. 19). If, for example, one believes that the ultimate nature of things lies in human consciousness, one would investigate consciousness according to certain procedures, and those procedures would be different from those of the person who believes answers to philosophical questions can be found in language or in rational thinking or in experience.

While methods of philosophical inquiry are usually considered within the framework of a particular school of philosophy, at least "three fundamental methods" of inquiry have been delineated by grouping several schools of thought together (McKeon, 1965). Each of the three methods reflects a different conceptualization of the nature and purpose of philosophy itself.

1. Dialectic. This method aims to reconcile disputes and unify experience. It seeks a whole within which seemingly disparate assertions can coexist. McKeon points to Plato, Hegel, and Marx as major philosophers employing this method. The various forms of dialectic have a common purpose: "to transcend or remove contradictions as they are eliminated in the processes of nature, in the sequence of history, or in the insights of art, the stages of scientific thought, or the interplay of group inquiry in conversation" (McKeon, 1965, p. 94).
2. Logistic. This method does not concern itself with resolving contradictions but instead seeks to "trace knowledge back to the elements of which it is composed and the processes by which they

are related" (McKeon, 1965, p. 94). For example, certain philosophers have proposed that axioms and postulates are the simple elements of mathematics, rules of logical syntax are the basic elements of language, and simple ideas are the basis of formal knowledge.

3. Problematic. This method is "aimed at solving particular problems one at a time and without reference to an all-inclusive whole or to a simplist part. A solution is regarded as acceptable just so long as it 'works' " (Johnstone, 1965, p. 22). William James and John Dewey made extensive use of this method.

Dialectic, logistic, and problematic methods are general approaches to doing philosophical research. Being more specific about the steps involved in a philosophical investigation or the "rules" one might employ to ensure that an inquiry is systematic necessitates becoming familiar with a particular philosophical system. The process of inquiry as exemplified in its application to phenomenology and linguistic analysis will be discussed later. For now, however, two additional observations about philosophical inquiry in general are worth noting.

First, the "data" one gathers and examines in a philosophical investigation can be anything the researcher feels will reveal the truth. In the past philosophers have used faith, reason, material objects, observation, intuition, and language as the data in their search. Once the source of data has been selected, philosophical inquiry becomes a disciplined mental activity. Most philosophers would agree that the only equipment necessary for this activity is language. Language is the medium through which philosophers reflect upon their data and by which they record their observations.

Second, there is no standard format for reporting the findings of philosophical research, other than that they be "presented *systematically,* in the form of an orderly, consistent development of the thinker's views" (Matczak, 1975, p. 27). Matczak discusses several different formats that have been used by philosophers from various schools of thought:

1. Dialectic or conversational approach -- used by Socrates, Plato, Hume, Hegel, Engels, and Marx.
2. Commentaries -- works that comment on original philosophic work such as modern interpretations of St. Thomas Aquinas.
3. Literary forms -- Expressing one's views in dramas and novels, used by modern existentialists such as Camus and Sartre.
4. Confessions or journals -- especially common among philosophers concerned with questions of faith such as Kierkegaard and St. Augustine.

5. Mathematical form -- expressing one's views with mathematical precision using numbers and equations, such as in the writings of Spinoza and Wittgenstein.

To summarize, philosophical research cannot point to a single source of data, a preferred format for disseminating findings, or a standardized method for investigating a problem. These aspects of the research process are defined by particular schools of thought. Thus, in order to give the reader a better sense of what it means to *do* philosophical research, it is necessary to become better acquainted with particular approaches. Following is a brief discussion of two contemporary schools of philosophy and their methods of inquiry. Linguistic analysis and phenomenology have been selected for discussion because of their prominent position in modern Western philosophy. More importantly, each has a well-defined method for doing research that is easily applied to a field of practice.

Linguistic Analysis—Linguistic analysis, also called conceptual analysis or analytic philosophy, uses human language as its data base. Unlike traditional philosophy, linguistic analysis is not concerned with developing a system of thought that encompasses human nature, knowledge, the universe, and so on. Rather, philosophical analysis is interested

> fundamentally in the clarification of basic notions and modes of argument rather than in synthesizing available beliefs into some total outlook, in thoroughly appraising root ideas rather than in painting suggestive but vague portraits of the universe. (Scheffler, 1960, p. 7)

Just as all people, to some extent, attempt to make sense out of their lives, everyone at one time or another has felt the need to clarify a concept or the meaning of a statement or the definition of a word. For linguistic analysts, language is the key to understanding "the many puzzles and paradoxes of traditional philosophy" (Elias and Merriam, 1980, p. 180). While there are several variations in emphasis within the school itself, all linguistic analysts believe "that by studying the ways in which words are used we can shed a great deal of light on philosophical problems and in many instances avoid becoming the victims of 'pseudoproblems' " (Kurtz, 1966, p. 36).

Two general types of analyses are undertaken by proponents of this school. One type strives for precision in explaining what language means for those who use it. Korner (1969, p. 26) labels this "exhibition

-analysis" because its aim is "to exhibit the meanings of expressions used by a group of speakers and thinkers." The second type -- "replacement-analysis" -- goes beyond making meanings and rules of language explicit. The aim of replacement-analysis

> is to replace a concept or set of concepts, which is in some ways defective, by another concept or set of concepts, which is free from these defects, but nevertheless preserves those features which are useful and desirable. (Korner, 1969, p. 29)

Actual steps involved in analyzing language usage employ standard tools of logic such as pointing out fallacies, establishing criteria for truth and falsehood, and defining terms. In addition, linguistic analysts have developed conventions or procedures of their own. Specifically, the type of question being asked is determined, cases that exemplify the concept are sought, and a definition that best reflects the concept's usage is given.

Analysts first determine what type of question is being raised. There are questions of fact -- How many millions of dollars are spent on training adults each year? questions of value -- Who should participate in training programs? and questions of concept -- Is training the same as education? Philosophical analysis concerns itself with questions of concept. Once these have been answered, questions of fact and value become easier to answer. If, for example, we can distinguish training from education, then the extent of training becomes easier to assess. Likewise, if we know exactly what training is, we might more readily determine who should participate.

In analyzing concepts, researchers turn to model cases, contrary cases, and borderline cases. Model cases are those instances "in which the concept is used in such a way that everyone would agree that this a good use of the concept" (Elias and Merriam, 1980, p. 184). Everyone would agree, for example, that General Motors, Bell Telephone, and the Army "train" their employees. Contrary cases are those instances where the term cannot be used. We do not think of a church as "training" its adult members. Borderline cases are situations in which a concept is stretched or applied beyond its common usage. We might say that faculty members at a particular college are being trained to use computers, but it has an odd ring to it. One would be more likely to say that faculty are *learning* to use computers.

Concepts can also be ambiguous -- that is, have several meanings -- or they can be vague -- that is, have varying degrees of a quality. For example, "program" has several meanings and is therefore classified as ambiguous, whereas "age" is a vague concept because it refers to a quality that exists in degrees. By exposing ambiguity and vagueness in language, linguistic analysts bring clarity to thinking and to everyday activity.

Conceptual clarity is the presumed end product of language analysis. As noted above, some thinkers prefer to "exhibit" the essential meaning or definition or criteria of a concept. Others may find it necessary to go a step further and "replace" a defective concept with a better one. Definitions of concepts can be stipulative, descriptive, or programmatic. A stipulative definition specifies the ways in which a term or concept is to be used. Descriptive definitions explain the common usage of a term. Programmatic definitions "overtly or implicitly" reveal "what should be done rather than what is done" (Elias and Merriam, 1980, p. 186).

In discussing questions, models, and definitions, we have attempted to introduce the reader to some of the techniques linguistic analysts employ in doing research. The techniques of this particular school of philosophy can be applied to any area of human endeavor. Several writers have, in fact, extensively analyzed the field of adult education from this perspective. Two British analysts, Lawson (1975) and Paterson (1979), have done pioneering work in analyzing such fundamental concepts in adult education as adult training, the teaching-learning process, and adult education. One American philosopher, Monette (1979), has published articles analyzing the concept of need in adult education and training. His philosophical analysis of the literature of need reveals that the field has had an overly technical preoccupation with meeting needs to the exclusion of political and ethical considerations.

There are many concepts yet to be analyzed -- "lifelong learning," "accountability," "community education," and "adult development" are but a few examples. The value of this type of research is tested by the extent to which it can bring clarity to conceptual confusion and the extent to which such clarity affects the practice of a field.

Phenomenology—Phenomenologists also deal with language and, on occasion, engage in an analysis of concepts or linguistic expressions as part of their inquiry. Stanage (1987, p. 53) points out that linguistic phenomenology "is a way of articulating as precisely as possible the distinctions within what adults say in direct investigation and descriptions of phenomena which we feel, experience, and conscious (know-with)." Rather than an end in itself, however, linguistic analysis for a phenomenologist is "merely preparatory to the study of the referents, i.e., of the phenomena meant by the expressions. Phenomenological analysis, then, is analysis of the phenomena themselves, not of the

84 / A Guide to Research for Educators and Trainers of Adults

expressions that refer to them" (Spiegelberg, 1965, p. 669). Language is thus an insufficient basis for studying phenomena: too many dimensions of life and experience cannot be captured by language.

Phenomenologists are also dissatisfied with modern science's efforts to categorize, simplify, and reduce phenomena to abstract laws for theories. Rather, phenomenology is expansive as it seeks to deepen our level of consciousness and broaden our range of experiences. Phenomenology requires us to go directly " 'to the things themselves'. . . to turn toward phenomena which had been blocked from sight by the theoretical patterns in front of them" (Spiegelberg, 1965, p. 658). Phenomenologists are interested in showing how complex meanings are built out of simple units of direct experience. This form of inquiry is an attempt to deal with inner experiences unprobed in everyday life. Such an arena, phenomenologists feel, has been abandoned by science as too subjective. Common in phenomenology are descriptive studies concerned with the themes of perception, intention, time-consciousness, and the origin of experiences and the relationship among experiences.

That phenomenological research lends itself to applied fields of study is evidenced by several investigations. In one study, adult learning was explored from the perspective of the inner experiences of adults and their reflections upon experiences with learning (Bates, 1979). In another study, the theoretical basis for the practice of competency-based education was investigated phenomenologically (Collins, 1980). In a third example, "throwing like a girl" and other "feminine" body movements were analyzed. (Young, 1980). Finally, Stanage's book on *Adult Education and Phenomenological Research* (1987) deals with "the four fundamental questions, Who am I? What Can I Know?, What Ought I To Do?, What May I Hope?, as vital questions in the lives of adults" (p. 3). These questions are addressed in his book by considering definitions of adult education, by reflecting upon the meaning of being an adult, by clarifying what phenomenology is and what scientific methods are, and how all of this relates to problems of curriculum and methods in adult education practice.

The "data" of a phenomenological investigation are phenomena, or more precisely, the conscious experience of phenomena. "Phenomena" includes both the acts -- such as thinking, believing, perceiving -- and the things to which these acts are related -- such as ideas or material objects. Experience is thus "intentional," that is, directed upon some object. One does not, for example, merely experience fear or love, but rather one experiences fear or love *of* something, such as fear of heights or love of beauty. Beliefs about the reality of objects are held in abeyance; no preconceived theories or persuppositions are allowed to determine the analysis of the experience itself. The basic method for this type of research is "seeing" or "intuiting" or "reflecting" upon one's experiences. Its objective is "to trace the elements and structure of the phenomena obtained by intuiting" (Spiegelberg, 1965, p. 669).

Essential to the method of phenomenology are the pure description of inner experiences and something Edmund Husserl, founder of phenomenology, calls "phenomenological reduction." This involves the suspension of one's natural attitude or beliefs toward the world and everyday activities (Korner, 1969). The reality of our world "is not denied but temporarily 'put into brackets' " (Collins, 1981, p. 5). In suspending our beliefs, consciousness *itself* becomes heightened, and can then be examined rather than examining the object of consciousness. While the description of inner experience and the suspension of our attitude toward that experience are essential characteristics of phenomenology, the process of phenomenological inquiry involves several specific steps. Spiegelberg describes how phenomenology arrives at "systematic and intersubjective knowledge":

> it does so by (a) describing first what is subjectively experienced ('intuited') insofar as it is experienced, whether real or not (the 'pure phenomenon') in its typical structure and relations ('essences' and 'essential relations'), and by (b) paying special attention to its modes of appearance and the ways in which it constitutes itself in consciousness. (1975, p. 112)

If, for example, we were to try to phenomenologically analyze our own learning, we would first describe what is "subjectively experienced," such as the setting, the feelings, and reactions to the content involved. In attending to its "modes of appearing," we might see that learning involves a sensory experience, a mental activity, and/or an emotional dimension. Finally, the ways in which learning "constitutes itself in consciousness" involve tracing the sequence of steps through which learning establishes itself or takes shape in our consciousness. Perhaps there is first an interest in the nature of the thing being learned, then there might be the gathering of information about the thing to be learned, then an organization of the information in the mind, and so on.

Spiegelberg (1965, pp. 659-700) presents seven steps in the phenomenological method, which include the above activities. While all phenomenologists would not agree with all seven or the order in which they are listed, the steps do offer us some glimpse into the rigor of a phenomenological inquiry.

Step 1. Investigating Particular Phenomena. This step includes "the intuitive grasp of the phenomena, their analytic examination, and their description" (p. 659).

Step 2. Investigating General Essences. Here we intuit the general essence of the phenomena being investigated. We can look at particular examples before or simultaneously with intuiting the general essences (several instances of learning can lead to a sense of its general essence, for example).

Step 3. Apprehending Essential Relationships Among Essences. Here we assess whether the components of the internal relations within an essence are essential and in what way there are relationships between several essences.

Step 4. Watching Modes of Appearing. This is the "systematic exploration of the phenomena not only in the sense of *what* appears, whether particulars or general essences, but also of the way in which things appear" (p.684).

Step 5. Exploring the Constitution of Phenomena in Consciousness. At this stage we analyze how a phenomenon has come into our consciousness.

Step 6. Suspending Belief in Existence of the Phenomena. This is the same as "bracketing" the phenomena, of suspending judgment as to its existence or qualities.

Step 7. Interpreting the Meaning of Phenomena. Once the experience has been brought into consciousness and analyzed, an attempt is made to grasp the meaning of the experience.

In summarizing phenomenological inquiry, Spiegelberg highlights some of its characteristic features that set it apart from other forms of philosophical inquiry. In the words of Spiegelberg:

One might describe the underlying unity of the phenomenological procedures as the unusually obstinate attempt to look at the phenomena and to remain faithful to them before even thinking about them.
. . .What distinguishes phenomenology from other methods is not so much any particular step it develops or adds to them but the spirit of philosophical reverence as the first and foremost notion of the philosophical enterprise. (1965, pp. 700-701)

Conclusion

This chapter has discussed the nature and techniques of two research methodologies--historical and philosophical inquiry. Both are foundational methods in the sense that each is concerned with fundamental questions of human existence. History turns to the past for an explanation of how things have come to be as they are. Philosophy applies the mind to itself or to some other phenomenon in grappling with the nature of human existence. Both forms of inquiry are foundational in a second sense: they provide a means for exploring the foundations of a discipline or field of study. Historical inquiry asks what happened and what meaning the past has for the present. Philosophical inquiry asks what assumptions, values, or ideas constitute the framework by which human behavior can be understood. In applied fields of study, historical and philosophical research can have very practical ramifications. Knowing how something was done in the past, why it was done the way it was, can clarify present practice and shape future practice. Likewise, understanding the assumptions and values upon which everyday activity rests can permeate even the most mundane daily activities with a sense of purpose and vision.

REFERENCES

Adams, James T. 1944. *Frontiers of American Culture: A Study of Adult Education in a Democracy.* New York: Charles Scribner's Sons.

Barraclough, Geoffrey. 1978. *Main Trends in History.* New York: Holmes and Meier Publishers, Inc.

Barzun, Jacques. 1974. *Clio and the Doctors.* Chicago: The University of Chicago Press.

Barzun, Jacques and Henry F. Graff. 1957. *The Modern Researcher.* New York: Harcourt, Brace and World, Inc.

Bates, Heather. 1979. "A Phenomenological Approach to the Study of Experience." *Adult Education Research Conference Proceedings.* Ann Arbor, Michigan.

Beringer, Richard E. 1978. *Historical Analysis: Contemporary Approaches to Clio's Craft.* New York: John Wiley and Sons.

Carlson, Robert. 1980. "Humanistic Historical Research" in *Changing Approaches to Studying of Adult Education,* (eds.) Huey B. Long, Roger Hiemstra and Associates. San Francisco: Jossey-Bass.

Carlson, Robert A. November, 1981. "Philosophical and Historical Research: The Importance of a Humanistic Orientation in Adult Education." Paper delivered in Finland. Available from Carlson, University of Saskatchewan, Saskatoon, Saskatchewan, Canada.

Collins, Michael. February, 1981. "Phenomenological Perspectives in Adult Continuing Education: Implications for Research and Practice." Paper presented at Lifelong Learning Conference, College Park, Maryland.

Collins, Michael. 1980. "Competency in Adult Education: Applying a Theory of Relevance." Unpublished Doctoral Dissertation, Northern Illinois University.

Curtis, L. P., Jr. 1970 *The Historian's Workshop: Original Essays by Sixteen Historians.* New York: Alfred A. Knopf.

Daniels, Robert V. 1966. *Studying History.* Englewood Cliffs, New Jersey: Prentice-Hall, Inc.

Donald, David. 1956. *Lincoln Reconsidered: Essays on the Civil War Era.* New York: Alfred A. Knopf.

Elias, John and Sharan Merriam. 1980. *Philosophical Foundations of Adult Education.* Malabar, Florida: Krieger Publishing Company.

Erikson, Erik. 1958. *Young Man Luther: A Study in Psychoanalysis and History.* New York: W. W. Norton and Co.

Felt, Thomas E. 1976. *Researching, Writing, and Publishing Local History.* Nashville: American Association for State and Local History.

Gottschalk, Louis. 1963. *Understanding History.* New York: Alfred A. Knopf.

Grattan, C. Hartley. 1955. *In Quest of Knowledge: A Historical Perspective on Adult Education.* New York: Association Press.

Halle, Louis J. 1982. "The Historian's Vocation." *Manas.* 35:1-2,7.

Helmstadter, B. C. 1970. *Research Concepts in Human Behavior.* New York: Appleton-Century-Crofts, Inc.

Johnstone, Henry W., Jr. 1965. (ed.). *What Is Philosophy?* New York: The Macmillan Company.

Knowles, Malcolm. 1962. *The Adult Education Movement in the United States.* New York: Holt, Rinehart and Winston.

Korner. Stephen. 1969. *What Is Philosophy?* London: Allen Lane.

Kurtz, Paul. 1966. (ed.). *American Philosophy in the Twentieth Century.* New York: The Macmillan Company.

Lawson, K. G. 1975. *Philosophical Concepts and Values in Adult Education.* Nottingham, England: Barnes and Humby, Ltd.

Lemisch, Jesse. 1969. "Listening to the 'Inarticulate'." *Journal of Social History.* 3:1-29.

Matczak, Sebastian. 1975. *Philosophy: Its Nature, Methods and Basic Sources.* New York: Learned Publications, Inc.

McKeon, Richard. 1965. "Philosophy and Method," *What is Philosophy?* (ed.) Henry W. Johnstone, Jr. New York: The Macmillan Company.

Mead, Hunter. 1962. *Types and Problems of Philosophy.* (3rd ed.), New York: Holt, Rinehart and Winston.

Monette, M. 1979. "Need Assessment: A Critique of Philosophical Assumptions." *Adult Education.* 29:83-95.

Paterson, R. W. K. 1977. *Values, Education and the Adult.* Boston: Routledge, Kegan, Paul.

Rockhill, Kathleen. 1976. "The Past as Prologue: Toward an Expanded View of Adult Education." *Adult Education.* 26:196-208.

Rose, Amy D. March 31, 1982. "The History of Adult Education: Questions of Context and Utility." Paper presented at the Mini-Conference on Historical Research in Adult Education, Adult Education Research Conference, Lincoln, Nebraska.

Scheffler, Israel. 1960. *The Language of Education.* Springfield, Illinois: Charles Thomas.

Seller, Maxine. 1978. "Success and Failure in Adult Education: The Immigrant Experience." *Adult Education.* 2:83-99.

Snyder, Phil L. 1958. (ed.). *Detachment and the Writing of History: Essays and Letters of Carl L. Becker.* Ithaca: Cornell University Press.

Spiegelberg, Herbert A. 1965. *The Phenomenological Movement.* The Hague: Martinus Nijhoff. Vol. 2.

Speigelberg, Herbert A. 1975. *Doing Phenomenology.* The Hague: Martinus Nijhoff.

Stanage, Sherman. 1987. *Adult Education and Phenomenological Research.* Malabar, FLA: Robert E. Krieger Publishing Company.

Stubblefield, Harold. 1988. *Toward a History of Adult Education in America.* New York: Routledge, Chapman and Hall.

Walsh, Warren B. 1962. *Perspectives and Patterns: Discourses on History.* New York: Syracuse University Press.

Young, Iris Manon. 1980. "Throwing Like a Girl: A Phenomenology of Feminine Body Comportment, Motility and Spatiality." *Human Studies.* 3:137-156.

CHAPTER 6

ETHNOGRAPHY, CASE STUDY, GROUNDED THEORY

Within the last several years there has been a growing interest in using ethnographic techniques, case study, and grounded theory approaches to illuminate the practice of training and educating adults. Ethnography is the methodology used by anthropologists to study peoples and their cultures. Case study is probably the most familiar of the three methodologies, having long been used in medicine, law, social work, and psychology. Basically, the case study is an intensive description and analysis of a phenomenon or social unit such as an individual, group, institution, or community. Grounded theory is a methodology that was developed and refined by sociologists Glaser and Strauss (1967) and has as its major purpose the building of theory. Each of these methodologies can be grouped together as forms of qualitative research.

Common Characteristics

Ethnography, qualitative case study, and grounded theory all depend upon the researcher being the primary conduit for data collection and analysis. While surveys, tests, or inventories might be used in support, the investigator assumes the major burden for collecting and processing data. Guba and Lincoln (1981) delineated the following characteristics to differentiate human instruments from other collection instruments:

> Responsiveness. "He is responsive because he must first 'sense' the dimensions of a context, then seek to make those dimensions explicit" (p. 130).
> Adaptability. The researcher as instrument in exploring a context can adapt a data collection mode to suit the circumstances; the human as instrument can also collect several types of data simultaneously.

Holistic Emphasis. The totality of a context can be considered rather than a particular segment.

Knowledge Base Expansion. An investigator can extend "awareness of a situation beyond mere propositional knowledge to the realm of the felt, to the silent sympathies, to the unconscious wishes, and to the daily unexamined usages" and in so doing "will lend depth and richness to our understanding of social and organizational settings" (p. 136).

Immediate Processing of Data. The human being as instrument can simultaneously collect and process data leading, if necessary, to refining data collection procedures. Unlike other instruments, the investigator can use his or her powers to guide the inquiry.

Opportunities for Clarification and Summarization. The human instrument can clarify questions and responses immediately; summarization of material is a credibility check in that the interviewee can endorse or critique the researcher's interpretation of material.

Opportunity to Explore Atypical or Idiosyncratic Responses. "Within the boundaries of standardized inquiry the atypical or idiosyncratic response would be lost, masked, or treated as a statistical deviation. . . . The ability to encounter such responses and to utilize them for increased understanding is possible, in fact only with human. . . instruments" (p. 138).

A second characteristic that the three methodologies have in common is that each usually involves field work. The researcher physically goes to the site, the group of people, the institution, "the field" to collect data. This is, of course, always the case in anthropology where the intent is to learn about people of different cultures. And in most instances, investigations that build theory (grounded theory) or describe and interpret a social process or unit (case study) necessitate field work. Field work involves becoming intimately familiar, through observation and interviews with the phenomenon under study, whether it be a case investigation of a single individual or a grounded theory study of a complex social interaction. Occasionally, qualitative case studies and grounded theory studies have been conducted using written documents alone, but these are the exceptions.

The third factor common to ethnography, qualitative case study, and grounded theory research is that each methodology leads to an increased understanding of the phenomenon by clarifying concepts, generating hypotheses, or constructing explanatory frameworks. These methodologies are, in fact, particularly appropriate to use where there is little knowledge about the problem. If there is a lack of theory, or if existing theory does not adequately explain the phenomenon, hypothesis cannot be used to structure an investigation. Rather, the researcher goes into the field and studies as much of the problem as possible with the intent of interpreting, explaining, hypothesizing, or theorizing about the phenomenon. Selltiz et al. (1976) call this type of research "insight-stimulating." In addition to formulating a problem for more precise investigation or developing hypotheses, "insight-stimulating" research may have other functions of:

> increasing investigators' familiarity with the phenomenon they wish to investigate in a subsequent, more highly structured study, or with the setting in which they plan to carry out such a study; clarifying concepts; establishing priorities for further research; gathering information about practical possibilities for carrying out research; gathering information about practical possibilities for carrying out research in real-life settings; providing a census of problems regarded as urgent by people working in a given field of social relations. (p. 91)

Briefly, ethnography, case study, and grounded theory are three research methodologies that have in common (1) the development of, rather than the testing of, hypotheses and theory; (2) fieldwork (in most instances) as the usual means of collecting data; and (3) reliance upon the investigator as the primary instrument for data collection and analysis. Each approach is distinguishable from the other two, however. Following is a more detailed discussion of each methodology's purposes, procedures, and techniques.

Ethnography

Ethnography is the research methodology developed by anthropologists to study human society and culture. Recently the term *ethnography* has been used interchangeably with *field study, case study, naturalistic inquiry, qualitative research,* and *participant observation.* Anthropologists and others familiar with ethnography, however, do not find these terms interchangeable. The term *ethnography* has two distinct meanings. Ethnography is (1) a set of methods or techniques used to collect data, and (2) the written record that is the *product* of using ethnographic techniques.

Ethnographic techniques are the methods researchers use to uncover the social order and meaning a setting or situation has for the people actually participating in it. The five procedures commonly used in this type of investigation are participant observation, in-depth interviewing, life history, documentary analysis, and investigator diaries (records of the researcher's experiences and impressions). Employing any one of these procedures involves going into the field, "immersing oneself in a collective way of life for the purpose of gaining firsthand knowledge about some facet of it" (Shaffier et al., 1980, p. 6). Fieldwork involves entering the chosen setting, establishing rapport with the residents of that setting, maintaining some type of relationship with the subjects, and, finally, leaving the setting. The archetypical anthropologist that comes to mind here is one who travels to exotic places, lives with the people for a period of time, and returns home to write an account of their cultural norms and social practices. Not all ethnographic researchers travel to foreign places, however. Much fieldwork has been conducted with particular social groups within the ethnographer's own society. In the United States, ethnographic studies have been published on many segments of society including ghetto dwellers, coal miners, and suburban housewives.

Participant observation is the cornerstone technique of ethnography, and a researcher might assume any of several variations of this technique. Junker (1960, pp. 35-38) describes four variations:

1. Complete participant. The researcher becomes a member of the group being studied, concealing the fact that he or she is observing as well as participating.
2. Participant as observer. The observer's activities are not concealed but are clearly "subordinated to activities as participant" (p. 36).
3. Observer as participant. The role of observer is publicly known, and participation becomes a secondary activity.
4. Complete observer. The observer is invisible to the activity (as in the case of a one-way mirror or hidden camera) or tries to become unnoticed (camera crews that live with their subjects, classroom observers).

The role assumed depends upon the type of information being sought and the idiosyncracies of the group being investigated. The researcher's role can also shift during the process of the investigation. In an interesting account of her firsthand experiences in a home for the aged, Judith Posner (1980) relates how she moved from being a participant observer as a volunteer worker, to complete participant as a programmer, to the stance of observer participant.

Participant observation is a time-consuming and demanding technique. One must establish rapport and trust with a group and become familiar enough to gain insights into the meaning of their lives. At the same time, one must be an observer, remaining as objective as possible while collecting information. This schizophrenic condition is exacerbated by medical problems, ethical issues, and the psychological stress inherent in employing a relatively unstructured research procedure in unfamiliar settings (Saffir et al.; 1980, p. 18). Indeed, several writers have commented upon the lack of description of fieldwork techniques and the lack of guidelines for conducting fieldwork (Saffir et al.; 1980; Berreman, 1968; Pelto, 1970). Pelto (1970) recommends that

> any extensive discussion of the art of fieldwork should include (among other things) sections on selection of informants, on gifts and payments, on when to take notes, on tactics with photographic equipment, on interactions with outsiders, on the giving of parties, on when to break taboos, and on many other subjects related to the central issue of 'impression management.' (p. 225)

Another ethnographic technique used in fieldwork -- interviewing -- has been described and refined in recent years. Prospective researchers can take courses in interviewing techniques, or they can read about the technique in the many books and articles on the topic. An interview is a "conversation with a purpose" (Dexter, 1970, p. 136). In ethnographic research, interviewing usually follows, or is integrated with, participant observation. Observation will often reveal which persons are important to interview as well as the type of information the researcher wants to extract in the interview. Interviewing is an indispensable tool in certain situations. "The ability to tap into the experience of others in their own natural language, while utilizing their value and belief frameworks, is virtually impossible without face-to-face and verbal interaction with them" (Guba and Lincoln, 1981, p. 155).

There are several types of interviews that can be employed in an investigation: team and panel interviewing, covert or overt interviewing, oral history interviewing, structured and unstructured interviewing (Guba and Lincoln, 1981). In most ethnographic studies, interviews are open ended or loosely structured so that the respondents' views of the topic can be obtained. By using an open-ended format, investigators hope to avoid predetermining subjects' responses and, hence, their "views" of reality. Interviewing as a data collection technique is discussed more fully in Chapter 8.

Occasionally interviewing key informants (people who have a great amount of knowledge and can conceptualize their group's norms and beliefs) leads to the collection of life histories. Life histories are intensive autobiographical studies of selected members of the sociocultural group under study. "The richness and personalized nature of life histories afford a vividness and integration of cultural information that are of great value for understanding particular life ways" (Pelto, 1970, p. 99).

In addition to using participant observations, interviews, and life histories, an ethnographer may want to evaluate all available documents on the phenomenon being studied. As a resource, documents and records often (1) are easily accessible, low-cost, or free; (2) "constitute a legally unassailable base from which to defend oneself against allegations"; (3) represent the context of the research problem; (4) may be more objective sources of information than an interview; and (5) provide a base for further inquiry (Guba and Lincoln, 1981, pp. 232-234).

Fieldworkers are also encouraged to keep a diary (in addition to fieldnotes) of each day's happenings and record personal feelings, ideas, impressions, or insights with regard to those events. This diary becomes a source of data and allows researchers to trace their own development and biases throughout the course of the investigation.

From the foregoing description of ethnographic techniques, the role of investigator as instrument emerges as a paramount consideration. Several writers have elaborated on the personal qualities essential in a researcher who intends doing ethnographic research. Most suggest that the researcher needs to be empathetic, bright, flexible, energetic, imaginative, and adventuresome. Guba and Lincoln (1981), commenting on the many lists of desirable attributes, note that a person who possessed all of the suggested qualities

> not only could be a good inquirer but undoubtedly would make a good president, a fine doctor, another Margaret Mead, or could lead the United Nations to a peaceful resolution of world conflict. . . . They are above all human beings who attend carefully to the social and behavioral signals of others and who find others intrinsically interesting. Many of these skills can be taught: others can be continuously cultivated and refined. (pp. 144-145)

The centrality of the investigator in ethnographic research has remained untouched even with the introduction of quantitative research methods. Statistical tools have become important aids in gathering demographic information, in assessing the magnitude and regularity of certain cultural behaviors and values, and in evaluating the strength of relationships among cultural phenomenon. But, as Mitchell (1967) points out,

> The fieldwork data, quantitative or qualitative, which social anthropologists use to base their conclusions on are all derived ultimately from observation. From this point of view there is no essential difference in the two types of data. Quantification has no magical property to confer accuracy on the data: if the basic

observations are inaccurate or incomplete, statistics derived from them will assuredly also reflect those weaknesses. What quantification achieves is a condensation of facts so that the regularities and patterns in them are more easily discernible. (pp. 25-26)

The techniques of ethnography -- participant observation and interviewing in particular -- have been adopted by people in applied fields of study where research problems or questions have warranted an exploratory, rather than hypothesis-testing, approach. However, anthropologists take issue with educators and others who use ethnographic techniques and then think they are doing ethnography. For ethnography is more than techniques; it is also an account of the data, an account that interprets the data within a sociocultural framework. Ethnography has as its intent the interpretation of a situation that incorporates the participants' symbolic meanings and ongoing patterns of social interaction. Concern with the cultural context is what distinguishes ethnography from grounded theory -- which builds theory -- and case study -- which describes and interprets a situation or social unit from the perspective of the researcher. Wolcott (1980) makes this distinction between technique and account:

> Specific ethnographic techniques are freely available to any researcher who wants to approach a problem or setting descriptively. It is the essential anthropological concern for cultural context that distinguishes ethnographic method from fieldwork techniques and makes genuine ethnography distinct from other 'on-site-observer' approaches. And when cultural interpretation is the goal, the ethnographer must be thinking like an anthropologist, not just looking like one. (p. 59)

Many of the same techniques of ethnography are used in case studies and grounded theory studies. Case study and grounded theory approaches do not have as a major focus sociocultural interpretation and so are even more useful to educators and trainers of adults who wish to conduct exploratory research within their field of practice.

Case Study

The case study is an intensive description and analysis of a phenomenon or social unit such as an individual, group, institution, or community. In contrast to surveying a few variables across a large number of units, a case study tends to be concerned with investigating many, if not all, variables in a single unit. By concentrating upon a single phenomenon or entity ("the case"), this approach seeks to uncover the interplay of significant factors that is characteristic of the phenomenon. The case study seeks holistic description and interpretation. "The content of a case study is determined chiefly by its purpose, which typically is to reveal the properties of the class to which the instance being studied belongs" (Guba and Lincoln, 1981, p. 371). If conducted over a period of time, the case study may be longitudinal; thus, changes over time become one of the variables of interest. Other case studies are concerned with describing a phenomenon as it exists at a particular time.

Unlike ethnography, which has been associated with only one discipline in particular, the case study method can be appropriately used in many fields. There are legal case studies, medical case studies, psychological case studies, and social case studies; there are even anthropological case studies of primitive cultures. Perhaps because of its widespread use, case study is sometimes confused with the terms *case work, case method, and case history*. Case study, as defined above, refers to an intensive study of a particular social unit, whereas *case work* denotes "the developmental, adjustment, remedial, or corrective procedures that appropriately follow diagnosis of the causes of maladjustment" (Good and Scates, 1954, p. 729). *Case method* is an instructional technique whereby the major ingredients of a case study are presented to students for illustrative or problem-solving purposes. *Case history* -- the tracing of a person, group, or institution's past -- is sometimes part of a case study.

The case study is a basic design that can accommodate a variety of disciplinary perspectives (Merriam, 1988). In particular, case studies in education often draw upon concepts, theory, and research techniques from anthropology, history, sociology, and psychology. Thus a sociocultural analysis of a single social unit or phenomenon would produce an ethnographic case study, whereas a description of an institution, program or practice as it has evolved over time would be a historical case study.

One of the characteristics of the case study approach is its adaptability to different research problems in many fields of study. Merriam (1988, pp. 11-13) has delineated four essential properties of a qualitative case study. Case studies are:

1. Particularistic. Case studies focus on a particular situation, event, program, or phenomenon;
2. Descriptive. The end product of a case study is a rich thick description of the phenomenon under study;

3. Heuristic. Case studies illuminate the reader's understanding of the phenomenon under study. They can bring about the discovery of new meaning, extend the reader's experience, or confirm what is known;

4. Inductive. Qualitative case studies for the most part rely upon inductive reasoning for the formulation of concepts, generalizations, or tentative hypotheses.

The process of conducting a case study consists of several steps, the first of which is the selection of the "case" to be analyzed. The selection is done purposefully, not randomly; that is, a particular person, site, program, process, community, or any other social unit is selected because it exhibits characteristics of interest to the researcher. The next step is to collect raw data. A wide range of data-collection techniques can be used by the case study researcher; observation, interviewing, and document analysis are probably the most common, although surveys and other instruments are sometimes used, depending upon the unit under investigation.

As information from various sources is being collected, the researcher may begin aggregating, organizing, and classifying the data into manageable units. Data can be organized chronologically, categorically, or placed within a typology. Aggregation is a process of abstracting generalities from particulars, of looking for patterns characteristic of most of the pieces of the data. Several recent publications give detailed instructions for organizing of most of the pieces of the data. Several publications give detailed instructions for organizing and analyzing data (Merriam, 1988; Miles and Huberman, 1984; Patton, 1980; Strauss, 1987). Following is the sequence of procedures described by Guba and Lincoln: First, any item of information from interviews, observations, or documents should be abstracted onto index cards and cross-referenced to the source. The cards are then sorted into piles, the first card beginning the first pile; "the second card is then assessed to determine whether it is similar or different from the first. If it is similar, it is placed into the same pile, but if it is different, a new pile is formed" (p. 314). Each pile is then given a name that best reflects the content of the cards in that pile. This name becomes a category or concept central to the study. As new data are collected, these categories become refined and reinforced. New data may also necessitate the formation of a new pile, and thus a new category.

The data organization procedure described by Guba and Lincoln is essentially inductive and results in the uncovering of new categories and concepts. Maimon et al. (1981) make the suggestion that grouped observations might also be labeled according to theoretical concepts already present in the social sciences, for example, "in child development -- sibling rivalry, attention-getting behavior, motor skills, language development; in sociology -- alienation, conformity, deviance; in psychology -- identity diffusion, depression; in political science -- single-issue campaigning, fear mongering" (p. 225).

Writing the case study narrative constitutes the final step in the process. The narrative is a highly readable, descriptive picture of a phenomenon or social entity, "making accessible to the reader all the information necessary to understand." It should "take the reader into the case situation, a person's life, a group's life, or a program's life" (Patton, 1980, p. 314).

As with other research strategies, the case study has obvious strengths counterbalanced by limitations. The strengths of the case study approach are that it offers large amounts of rich, detailed information about a unity or phenomenon; it is useful as supporting information for planning major investigations in that it often reveals important variables or hypotheses that help structure further research; it allows researchers the flexibility to understand and even to answer questions about educational processes and problems. Some of the limitations of the case study are the following:

- Case studies can be expensive and time consuming.
- Training in observation and interviewing techniques and/or documentary analysis is necessary.
- Case study narratives tend to be lengthy documents, which policy makers and others have little time to read; also, writing the narrative to meet the needs of potential, though perhaps unknown, readers is a difficult task.
- Findings from case studies cannot be generalized in the same manner as findings from random samples; generalizability is related to what each user is trying to learn from the study.

In applied fields such as the education and training of adults, counseling, and vocational education, the case study has been used to describe and/or evaluate the efficacy of a new program or new approach to ongoing problems. For example, Kline (1981) conducted a case study of a return-to-industry program for vocational instructors at a junior college. At the time of her study, such a program was considered an innovative approach to keeping postsecondary faculty technically updated and well informed. The purpose of her study was to document the process of collaboration between an educational institution and business and industry, and to assess the impact of the program upon the instructors as well as participating agencies. The researcher went to the program site, observed and interviewed participants and staff associated with the program (including business and industry personnel), and examined documents and records related to the in-service program. Using fieldnotes to build categories and group data, she developed a model of the collaborative process and presented categories descriptive of the impact of the program for both instructors and participating businesses and industries.

In an example of a case study approach used to assess a new approach to an old problem -- the best way to teach adults to read -- Driessen and Pfyer (1975) investigated the importance of setting in adult basic education. Here, 208 adult basic education students were instructed in their homes rather than in a classroom setting. Data were collected through interviews with students, teachers, aides, project administrators, through observation of lessons in the home, and through analysis of diaries kept by the investigators. The result was a case study narrative that described and interpreted the interplay of an informal setting (the home) with a formal occasion (instruction).

Finally, readers are referred to a case study by Zeph (1989) of a career enhancement award program for community-based adult educators. Data were collected through interviews with participants, through observations of three group seminars, and through reviewing documents related to the program including the participants' applications for the award. Zeph found that involvement in the program resulted in significant personal development, which she labeled "The Expanded Self," and significant career development, labeled "The Reflective Practitioner."

In summary, the case study is a particularly useful methodology for exploring an area of a field of practice not well researched or conceptualized. In-depth describing and understanding of a phenomenon is needed before generalizations can be made and tested. Case study, which has as its purpose the description and interpretation of a unit of interest, can result in abstractions and conceptualizations of the phenomenon that will guide subsequent studies.

Grounded Theory

Grounded theory is a distinctive research methodology popularized in the late 1960's with the publication of Glaser and Strauss's book, *The Discovery of Grounded Theory* (1967). As with ethnography and case study, the investigator in a grounded theory study is the primary instrument of data collection and analysis, and the mode of investigation is characterized by inductive fieldwork rather than deductive hypothesis testing. The end result of a grounded theory study is the building of theory -- theory that emerges from, or is "grounded" in, the data.

Grounded theory research emphasizes discovery: description and verification are secondary concerns.

As a qualitative, exploratory methodology, grounded theory is particularly suited to investigating problems for which little theory has been developed. The explanation of an area of human interaction or a social process emerges from a grounded theory study as either substantive or formal theory. Substantive theory deals with phenomena limited to particular real-world situations such as nursing home care, the academic life of community college adult students, or the budgeting of community resources. Formal theory is more abstract and general (Weber's theory of bureaucracy, for example) and usually requires analysis of data from more than one substantive area.

In one scholar's opinion, generating substantive theory "is, or should be, a concern of researchers in applied professional fields such as adult education" (Darkenwald, 1980, p. 67). Darkenwald goes on to list several substantive areas well suited to grounded theory building: "literacy education in developing countries, program development in university extension, rural community development, and continuing professional education" (p. 69). The major purpose of doing grounded theory research in an applied field "is to improve professional practice through gaining a better understanding of it" (Darkenwald, 1980, p. 69).

Just how professional practice is enhanced is discussed at length by Glaser (1978) in a follow-up publication to the original book on grounded theory. Glaser recognizes that practitioners are knowledgeable, efficient, even expert in their particular fields of practice. "What the man in the know does not want is to be told what he already knows. What he wants to be told is how to handle what he knows with some increment in control and understanding of his area of action" (Glaser, 1978, p. 13). A practitioner's knowledge is usually experiential and nontheoretical. The researcher can offer ideas, categories, and a theory that integrates the diverse elements of practice. Grounded theory -- if it has truly been generated from the situation and is "grounded" in the data -- will give the practitioner a conceptual tool with which to guide practice. As Glaser (1978) points out:

> With substantive theory the man in the know can start transcending his finite grasp of things. His knowledge which was heretofore not transferable, when used to generate theory, becomes transferable to other areas well known to him. His knowledge which was just known but not organized, is now ideationally organized. This allows him perceptible breakthroughs. (p. 13)

Grounded theory, whether substantive or formal, consists of categories, properties, and hypotheses. Categories, and the properties that define or illuminate the categories, are conceptual elements of the theory. Categories and properties need to be both analytic -- "sufficiently generalized to designate the characteristics of concrete entities, not the entities themselves" -- and sensitizing -- "yield a 'meaningful' picture, abetted by apt illustrations that enable one to grasp the reference in terms of one's own experience" (Glaser and Strauss, 1967, p. 38). Hypotheses are relationships among categories and properties. Unlike hypotheses in experimental studies, grounded theory hypotheses are tentative and suggestive rather than tested. In a study of a college faculty's participation in in-service workshops, for example, the researcher identified "workshop credibility" as one of several categories explaining faculty participation (Rosenfeldt, 1981). A property that helped to define workshop credibility was called "identification with sponsoring agent." The author hypothesized that "workshop participation will depend on the extent to which faculty members identify with the workshop sponsors. Namely, the greater the identification of the potential participants with the sponsoring agent, the greater the likelihood that professors will participate in a given workshop" (Rosenfeldt, 1981, p. 189). In another grounded theory investigation, a study of middle-aged men uncovered "career malaise" as a category reflective of the career situation of most of the men in the study. "Boredom," "inertia," and "feeling trapped" defined the category. It was hypothesized that the more acute one's "career malaise," the more burdensome the sense of responsibility to one's children and one's parents (Merriam, 1980).

Two studies that investigated concepts related to continuing professional education were ones by Wagner (1988) and Ritt (1989). Wagner used grounded theory methodology to identify factors that influenced professional nurses who were recognized by their colleagues to be "lifelong learners." Her study resulted in two major propositions -- (1) lifelong learning for the professional nurse is a value developed early in life through family support as part of the socialization process that is strengthened through professional education; and, (2) the result of lifelong learning is an expanded personal and professional understanding of self that is the source of empowerment.

In a contrasting grounded theory study, Ritt (1989) examined the evolution of a rather recent phenomenon in the nursing profession -- the role of the nurse consultant. Through indepth interviews with nurse consultant practitioners, Ritt discovered how an individual becomes a nurse consultant and interventions that appropriately prepared the nurse to function in that role. The study resulted in a theoretical framework that described the development of the role of the nurse consultant.

In most grounded theory studies, data come from interviews and participant observations. Glaser and Strauss (1967) note that a wide variety of documentary materials, fiction, and previous research are also potential sources of valuable data. Procedures for collecting and handling data can best be understood through familiarity with the techniques of grounded theory research. Theoretical sampling, comparison groups, constant comparative analysis, and saturation are grounded theory techniques that determine what data to collect, how to handle the data, and when to stop gathering data.

Data collection is guided by *theoretical sampling* in which "the analyst jointly collects, codes, and analyzes his data and decides what data to collect next and where to find them, in order to develop his theory as it emerges" (Glaser and Strauss, 1967, p. 45). An initial sample is chosen by its logical relevance to the research problem. The reader uses insights gleaned from early analysis to determine where to go next for more data. In a grounded theory study of adult education growth in New Jersey community colleges (MacNeil, 1981), for example, data were originally gathered from divisions of continuing education and community service. Early fieldwork revealed that studying adult student participation could not be limited to a single administrative unit. Subsequently, data were collected from interviews with a wide range of personnel involved in adult education programming.

The discovery of grounded theory is facilitated through the use of *comparison groups*. Comparing several groups reveals quickly the similarities and differences that give rise to theoretical categories. The strength of these emerging categories is tested by collecting data from diverse groups. In Glaser and Strauss's study of the process of dying (1965), premature babies who died were first studied, and the emergent concepts then tested with terminal cancer patients. Glaser and Strauss (1965b) describe the use of comparison groups as follows:

> Significant categories and hypotheses are first identified in the emerging analysis, during the preliminary fieldwork in one or a few groups and while scrutinizing substantive theories and data from other studies. Comparison groups are then located and chosen in accordance with the purposes of providing new data on categories or combinations of them, suggesting new hypotheses, and verifying initial hypotheses in diverse contexts.... These groups can be studied one at a time or a number can be studied simultaneously. They can also be studied in quick succession in order to check out major hypotheses before too much theory is built around them. (pp. 292-293)

The basic procedure in grounded theory research is the *constant comparative analysis* of data, which consists of four stages (Glaser and

Strauss, 1967; Strauss, 1987). In the first stage one compares incidents, generates tentative categories and/or properties to cover the incidents, and codes each incident into as many tentative categories as are appropriate. The researcher also records in memo form any insights that occurred during the comparison of incidents.

In the second stage the comparison of units changes from "incident with incident" to "incident with properties of the category" (Glaser and Strauss, 1967, p. 108). The researcher attempts to integrate categories and their properties.

The third stage is characterized by the delimitation of the theory. Here, similar categories are reduced to a smaller number of highly conceptual categories; hypotheses are generated; data are further checked for their "fit" into the overall framework. The simultaneous collection and analysis of data ends when the categories become saturated. *Saturation* means that "no additional data are being found" whereby the researcher "can develop properties of a category" (Glaser and Strauss, 1967, p. 61). Further incidents of that category need not be coded since so doing "only adds bulk to the coded data and nothing to the theory" (p. 111).

The fourth stage -- the actual writing of the theory from coded data and memos -- occurs when "the researcher is convinced that his analytic framework forms a systematic substantive theory, that it is a reasonably accurate statement of the matters studied, and that it is couched in a form that others going into the same field could use" (Glaser and Strauss, 1967, p. 113).

In order to assess the credibility of theory generated through constant comparative analysis of comparison groups, it is essential that readers be told how data were collected, how coding was done, and how the categories, properties, and hypotheses emerged from the data. The value of the theory itself can be determined by the following criteria suggested by Glaser and Strauss (1967):

1. Fitness. A theory must fit the substantive area to which it will be applied; a theory that is closely related to the reality of the substantive area of investigation is one that has been carefully inducted from the data.
2. Understanding. Laypersons working in the substantive area should be able to understand and use the theory.
3. Generality. Categories of the generated theory "should not be so abstract as to lose their sensitizing aspect, but yet must be abstract enough to make. . .theory a general guide to multiconditional, everchanging daily situations" (p. 242).
4. Control. A theory must provide understanding of enough con-

cepts and their interrelations "to enable the person who uses it to have enough control in everyday situations to make its application worthwhile" (p. 245).

Grounded theory as a research methodology is not without its critics. Some consider the approach to be undisciplined and impressionistic. The constant comparative method, if used properly, however, allows for a very systematic and even rigorous handling of data. Admittedly, the success of a grounded theory investigation depends to some extent upon the sensitivity and analytical powers of the investigator. Discovery, or the process of arriving at an insight that may later form a category or property in the theory, is not a process that can be mapped out for other researchers to follow. Only the tools that may facilitate discovery can be given to the researcher. The investigator remains central to this type of research.

Finally, the charge has been made that other investigators would have evolved different theories from the same data. While this may be true, it does not mean that the theory that has been developed is invalid or inconsistent with the data. Rather, the validity of the theory is judged by its overall explanatory power, by how well assertions are supported, by how well integrated the elements are, and by whether there is an internal, logical consistency to all dimensions of the theory. These same canons are applied to *any* theory.

Most would agree that applied professional fields such as those related to the education and training of adults do not yet have theoretical bases sufficient to structure all of future research. These fields can be advanced by the addition of theoretical frameworks derived from practice. These frameworks, in turn, can be tested by professionals who are concerned with expanding the knowledge base of their field.

REFERENCES

Berreman, Gerald D. 1968. "Ethnography: Method and Product" in James A. Clifton (ed). *Introduction to Cultural Anthropology*. Boston: Houghton Mifflin Company.

Darkenwald, Gordon G. 1980. "Field Research and Grounded Theory" in *Changing Approaches to Studying of Adult Education*, (eds). Huey B. Long, Roger Hiemstra and Associates. San Francisco: Jossye-Bass.

Dexter, Lewis A. 1970. *Elite and Specialized Interviewing*. Evanston, Illinois: Northwestern University Press.

Driessen, Jon J. and Julen Pyfer. 1975. "An Unconventional Setting for a Conventional Occasion: A Case Study of an Experimental Adult Education Program." *Sociology of Education*. 48:111-123.

Glaser, Barney G. 1978. *Theoretical Sensitivity*. Mill Valley, California: The Sociology Press.

Glaser, Barney G. and Anselm L. Strauss. 1967. *The Discovery of Grounded Theory*. Chicago: Aldine Publishing Company.

Glaser, Barney C. and Anselm L. Strauss. 1965a. *Awareness of Dying*. Chicago: Aldine Publishing Company

Glaser, Barney G. and Anselm L. Strauss. 1965b. "The Discover of Substantive Theory: A Basic Strategy Underlying Qualitative Research." *The American Behavioral Scientist*. 8:5-12.

Good, Carter V. and Douglas E. Scates. 1954. *Methods of Research*. San Francisco:

Guba, Egon G. and Yvonne S. Lincoln. 1981. *Effective Evaluation*. San Francisco: Jossey-Bass.

Helmstadter, G. C. 1970. *Research Concepts in Human Behavior*. New York: Appleton-Century-Crofts, Inc.

Junker, Buford H. 1960. *Field Work*. Chicago: The University of Chicago Press.

Kline Barbara H. 1981. "A Case Study of a Return-to-Industry Program and Inservice Approach for Vocational Instructors at a Two-Year Post-Secondary Institution." Unpublished Doctoral Dissertation, Virginia Polytechnic Institute and State University.

MacNeil, Pauline. 1981. "The Dynamics of Adult Education Growth in Community Colleges." Unpublished Doctoral Dissertation, Rutgers University.

Merriam, Sharan. 1980. *Coping With Male Mid-Life: A Systematic Analysis Using Literature as a Data Source*. Washington D.C.: University Press.

Merriam, Sharan. (1988). *Case Study Research in Education; A Qualitative Approach*. San Francisco: Jossey-Bass Publishers.

Mezirow, Jack, Gordon Darkenwald, and Alan Knox. 1975. *Last Gamble on Education*. Washington, D.C.: Adult Education Association of the USA.

Miles, Matthew, B. and A. Michael Huberman. (1984). *Qualitative Data Analysis: A Sourcebook of New Methods*. Newbury Park, CA: Sage.

Mitchell, J. Clyde. 1967. "On Quantification in Social Anthropology," in *The Craft of Social Anthropology* (ed.) A. L. Epstein. New York: Tavistock Publications.

Patton, Michael Q. 1980. *Qualitative Evaluation Methods*. Beverly Hills: Sage Publications.

Pelto, Pertti J. 1970. *Anthropological Research*. New York: Harper and Row.

Posner, Judith. 1980. "Urban Anthropology: Fieldwork in Semifamiliar Settings," in *Fieldwork Experience* (eds.) William B. Shaffier, Robert A. Stebbins, Allan Turowetz, New York: St. Martin's Press.

Ritt, E. (1989). "The Evolving Role of the Nurse Consultant," Unpublished Doctoral Dissertation, Northern Illinois University.

Rosenfeldt, Ana B. 1981. "Faculty Commitment to the Improvement of Teaching Via Workshop Participation." Unpublished Doctoral Dissertation, Virginia Polytechnic Institute and State University.

Selltiz, Claire, Lawrence S. Wrightsman and Stuart W. Cook. 1976. *Research Methods in Social Relations*. 3rd Edition. New York: Holt, Rinehart and Winston.

Shaffir, William B., Robert A. Stebbins, and Allan Turowetz. 1980. *Fieldwork Experience*. New York: St. Martin's Press.

Strauss, Anselm. (1987). *Qualitative Analysis for Social Scientists*. Cambridge, England: Cambridge University Press.

Wagner, P. A. (1988). "Select Factors Influencing Lifelong Learning of Professional Nurses," Unpublished Doctoral Dissertation, Northern Illinois University.

Wolcott, Harry F. 1980. "How to Look Like an Anthropologist Without Really Being One." *Practicing Anthropology*, 3:1

Zeph, Catherine. (1989). *A Case Study of Participants Experiences in a Career Enhancement Award Program*. Unpublished Doctoral Dissertation, Department of Adult Education, The University of Georgia.

CHAPTER 7

INTERACTIVE, CRITICAL, AND FUTURES RESEARCH

Researchers in applied fields of study, such as those involved with the education and training of adults, are constantly searching for more appropriate means to acquire knowledge. This search often leads to entirely new conceptualizations, not only of the role research is to play in the pursuit of knowledge, but also in the purpose for knowledge itself. The three research methodologies discussed in this chapter -- interactive, critical, and futures research -- represent conceptualizations of knowledge and techniques for acquiring knowledge that depart from the more conventional methods discussed in previous chapters.

These unconventional paradigms differ primarily in their definition of what is considered valid knowledge (Reason & Rowan, 1981). In the traditional research paradigm, validity rests with the methods used in seeking knowledge and the extent to which those methods achieve internal and external control. For the newer paradigms discussed in this chapter, valid knowledge is defined in terms of those "doing" the knowing. As Reason and Rowan (1981, p. 241) point out, validity in this context "must concern itself both with the knower and what is to be known; valid knowledge is a matter of relationship."

The authors have chosen to discuss interactive, critical, and futures research from among several possibilities because of the potential contribution each may make to the study of education, social and developmental psychology, community development, and human resource development.

Interactive Research

Several characteristics distinguish interactive research from other forms of social science research:

1. The researcher serves as a facilitator for problem solving and, in some cases, as a catalyst between the research findings and those individuals most likely to benefit or take action from the findings.
2. Results of research are intended for immediate application by those engaged in the research or by those for whom the research was initiated.
3. The design of interactive research is formulated while the research is in progress, rather than being totally predetermined at the outset of the study.

Three types of interactive research -- action, participatory and critical -- are discussed.

Action Research—Interactive research can be used to solve specific, practical, social or individual problems that may be found in a community, a social agency, a school, a classroom, or even within an individual researcher. This is action research. According to Isaac and Michael (1981, p. 42), action research is designed "to develop new skills or new approaches and to solve problems with direct application to the classroom or other applied setting." In a broader definition Bogdan and Biklen (1982) describe action research as "the systematic collection of information that is designed to bring about social change" (p. 215).

Action research methods may be traced to a study by Kurt Lewin (1942) that reported on change in people's food habits. Lewin studied the effects of lecture and discussion on the food habits of adult women from various income levels. The problem focused on getting women to use less popular, but more accessible and nutritious foods during World War II. Half the women in each income group were given a thirty-minute lecture by a nutritionist, followed by a fifteen-minute question-and-answer session. The other half participated in a discussion, with the nutritionist acting as a resource person. Lewin found that ten times more women who participated in the discussion groups tried the recommended food, as compared with women who experienced the lecture and question session. According to Marrow (in Sanford, 1981), Lewin's greatest contribution to research may have been "the idea of studying things through changing them and seeing the effect"(Sanford, p. 174). The theme or principle around which Lewin patterned action research was that in order to gain insight into a process, the researcher must create a change and then observe the effects and new dynamics of the change.

Action research departs from more conventional methods in the following ways:

1. Its purpose is to obtain knowledge that can be applied directly to a particular situation, (e.g., class, school, social agency, community).
2. The research problem emerges from events that are disturbing the researcher, such as efficiency of a teaching method or a local pollution problem in the community.
3. The problem is stated generally -- hypotheses are seldom used.
4. Secondary sources of literature, rather than primary sources, are used extensively; the researcher simply wants an idea about the phenomenon being studied.
5. The participants are not systematically sampled or selected; they are part of a natural "flow" of human activity.
6. Procedures for conducting research are only planned generally at the beginning of a study and are altered as needed throughout the course of investigation.

Little attention is given to control and experimental conditions in conducting the study (Borg, 1987). Bogdan and Biklen (1982) point out that action researchers sometimes collect data to change practices of social injustice, such as discrimination or creation of a harmful environment (pp. 218-19). Action research is used to effect social change by: (1) collecting information that identifies people and institutions that have a negative affect upon lives of other people: (2) helping people to become more aware of problems, to understand themselves, and to develop more commitment to addressing problems; and (3) serving as a catalyst to get people involved, organized, and active concerning particular issues within the community.

An example of action research at a practical, local level would be a study conducted by a teacher that focuses upon effective methods for teaching English as a second language. In this instance, the teacher becomes the researcher. During the progress of a class, the teacher recognizes that participants are having difficulty with the curriculum material. In search of a more effective method, the teacher tries a different set of materials with some individuals in the class. Over a period of time, the teacher observes carefully the progress of participants using the new material. By using each set of materials for approximately the same amount of time and by giving the same proportion of instructional attention to each group, the teacher attempts to follow procedures that will give her confidence in the study results. After a period of time, an assessment of participant achievement and satisfaction is conducted by the teacher. Since no attempt is made to strategically select a sample from the class for the study, no application of results to other second language classes is made. Through this action research activity, the teacher arrives at results that will assist in choosing second language curriculum material for the entire class later in the term.

A more assertive stance with regard to the meaning of action research is espoused by researchers at Deakin University in Australia (Kemmis and McTaggart, 1987). The Deakin version of action research focuses primarily upon the mileau of formal educational systems. Briefly, it is a form of collective self-reflective inquiry undertaken by participants in social situations for the purpose of improving the rationality and justice of their own social and educational practices and to better understand these practices and situations. Participants can be parents, teachers, principals or students -- anyone with a concern. It is action research only "when it is collaborative activity that is achieved through criticaly examined actions of individual group members," Kemmis and Mc-Taggart (1987, p.5) point out.

The method is further explained through the interrelationships of three domains of individual and cultural action -- language, activity and social relationships. Reform requires both individual and cultural action. Therefore, educational reform requires examination and modification of institutional forms of language, activity and social relationships that constitute education.

An example of this form of action research was carried out throughout a series of projects that addressed Aboriginal education and teacher education in Australia. The projects conducted by Deakin University personnel were intended to guide the preparation of Aboriginal teachers. Beginning with a self-examination by the faculty, followed by a review of problems that existed within the curriculum, placing emphasis upon non-aboriginal and aboriginal participant involvement, the projects led to a teaching education concept of "both ways" education, eventually offered by Aboriginal teachers. This concept development promoted and encouraged communities to remain bi-cultural -- to retain and strengthen two alternative modes of life -- the new way of living along with the traditional.

In each case, the action process is one of analysis, getting facts, identifying the problem, planning and taking action on the problem, then repeating the cycle as new concepts and information result from the process.

The benefits of this method are that it is relevant to an actual situation in the field of practice, it focuses on a systematic process for problem solving and project development, and it is responsive to experimentation and innovation (Isaac & Michael, 1981). As with the case of the Deakin teacher training projects in Australia, the method may lead to social change on a large scale. However, action research also has limitations. Because it lacks external and internal controls, generalizability of results are limited to the specific circumstances and conditions in which the research was done.

Participatory Research—Another purpose of interactive research, taking a broader perspective of the term "problem," is the political empowerment of people through group participation in the search for and acquisition of knowledge. Interactive research that has empowerment and human equality as its aim is referred to as "participatory research."

Participatory research methodology is supported by a social philosophy of human equality (Hall, 1979). As with action research, one of the strengths of this method is its immediate application. Although participatory research methods are closely associated with processes of community development, one distinction between them is the role played by the researcher and research subjects. In participatory research, the one conducting research activities plays an active part and is not just an objective observer of data. The researcher is a catalyst in achieving research results to solve social problems. Research subjects take on a role of colleagues in collecting and analyzing data. Through the participatory process, the researcher is integrated into the community and, with community members, seeks solutions to social problems.

Participatory methodology is a reaction against highly empirical, deductive methods commonly found in the social sciences. Its proponents argue that it is less oppressive than these more traditional methods. Hall (1979) makes three major distinctions between social science methods and participatory approaches to research (p. 43). Social science research methods imply value, whereas participatory methods attempt to be free of values. Second, techniques used in social science research have a "hidden process" to manipulate subjects of research, whereas, those engaged in participatory research control the research. Third, most social science research is conducted and reported for other researchers; therefore, the monopoly of knowledge is with intellectuals. Research results should be usable, Hall suggests, by those individuals in the world recognized as subjects of inequality.

Participatory research is a tool for individuals working in groups to address problems of social inequality and to curb exploitation of those persons with less economic and political power (Participatory Research Network, 1982). Participatory research permits individuals to study and better understand the influences that social institutions have upon them. Better understanding leads to more economic and political control of their lives by consolidation of information and effort within the group. Participatory research focuses upon the subtle and overt psychological and social dimensions of oppression -- messages transmitted through public media, religious institutions, government, and educational institutions, for example. The method challenges the way knowledge is produced and disseminated through traditional channels of social institutions and attempts to bring knowledge back to people.

Participatory research involves three interrelated processes:

1. Collective investigation of problems and issues with the active participation of the constituency (community) in the entire process
2. Collective analysis, in which the constituency develops a better understanding not only of the problems at hand but also of the underlying structural causes (socioeconomic, political, cultural) of the problem
3. Collective action by the constituency aimed at long-term as well as short-term solutions to these problems (p.2)

Beginning with a "problem posing" session, participants work together to identify and solve a problem of mutual concern, such as inadequate housing, unemployment, or poor health conditions. The process leads the group to better understand the problem and to question its underlying causes. Paulo Freire made a significant contribution to the concepts and methods of participatory research by introducing the terms "conscientization" and "thematic investigation" in his work in South America (Freire, 1974). The concept involved in conscientization is explained as "learning to perceive social, political, and economic contradictions and to take action against the oppressive elements of reality" (p. 3). The method that grows from conscientization -- thematic investigation -- involves participants in the analysis of words and experiences common to their reality, and identification of inconsistencies that lead to increased understanding of their reality. Participatory research has been conducted primarily in Third World countries in South America, Central America, and Africa.

Table 7.1 shows Hall's (1981, p. 55) comparison of participatory research characteristics and those of more traditional methodologies.

According to Kassam and Mustafa (1982), features that distinguish participatory research from the so-called "objective" social sciences are (1) a subjective commitment on the part of the researcher to the people under study; (2) close involvement of the researcher with the researched community; (3) a problem-centered approach that utilizes data gathering, from which action may be taken; (4) an educational process for both the researchers and people for whom the research is

Table 7.1. Comparison of research approaches

Issues/Actions	Participatory Research	Most Common Survey Approaches
Problem identification	Community or group experiencing the problem	Most often researcher or other outside person
Focus of Choice of methods for gathering data	Community	Researcher
Methods of data gathering	Wide variety, including group meetings, use of videotape, seminars, workshops, surveys, use of drama and photographs Developmental and reformable Focus on collective response	Some variety, but most often based on some form of survey Fairly static Focus on individual response
Analysis and interpretation of data	Emphasis on collective analysis and interpretation by those involved in the problem	Individual analysis by researcher, *sometimes* with limited "feedback" from clients
Use of results	Directed, planned for, and applied by the community	Serendipitous, not usually an integral part of the process

conducted; and (5) respect for the capability and potential of people to produce knowledge and analyze it (pp. 70-71).

Antecedents of participatory research, as explained by Hall (1981), can be traced to the early field work of Engels and his association with working classes of Manchester, England, as well as to the use of the "unstructured interview" with French factory workers by Karl Marx. Parts of the work of Dewey, George Herbert Mead, and the Tavistock Institute in London have provided guidelines for this type of social investigation, which departs from empirical postivism -- the research approach that dominated the scene in the 1950s and 1960s, according to Hall (p. 8).

Participatory research received its major thrust from the International Council of Adult Education in the mid-1970s, within which the Participatory Research Project grew under the direction of Budd Hall. The general objective of the project is to "investigate methods of research in adult education and related social transformation programmes which focus on the involvement of the poorest groups or classes in the analysis of their own needs" (Status Report on the Participatory Research Project International Meeting, 1977, p. 1). Hall (1981) stresses that the purpose of participatory research is to democratize research -- to let more participate in carrying out the research and more benefit from results of research. Evidence that democratization of research is beginning to take place, according to Hall, includes (1) the shift of research being conducted in metropolitan countries to countries in the Third World, (2) shift of responsibility for conducting research from "outside" persons to people within the country, (3) increased involvement of untrained persons in professional research roles, (4) increased interest in making research accessible to local decision makers, and (5) the increased involvement of the poor and exploited in the research process.

Some examples of participatory research in nonformal adult education around the world include evaluation of a cooperative weaving project in Botswana, evaluation of literacy programs in Tanzania, development in Canada of a curriculum for teaching English in the workplace, and development of women's clubs in Aadias, India (Hall, 1981).

The Rockford, Illinois Interactive Media Project reported by Niemi and Stephens (1979) is an example of participatory research at a local community level in the midwestern United States. The project focused on the encouragement of adults in a low-income community to participate in public decision making through use of videotape recordings. The project incorporated use of interactive media (videotape recordings) as a tool for solving community problems. Based upon work by Henaut (1971) and Theodore (1975), the project taught community members about the use of videotape recordings as a means of problem posing. Through this medium, issues were examined and community member viewpoints on the issues were disseminated to decision-making agencies within the community. The strength of interactive media as a research tool, Niemi and Stephens point out, is "that it brings the vital elements of dialogue and consensus-formation -- and thus a more vigorous problem-solving capacity -- to community groups" (p. 5).

Objectives of the project included: (1) training community residents to use video media equipment and to edit what they recorded; (2) analyzing and preparing collaboratively conceived objectives and strategies of several participating agencies and organizations; (3) documenting community activities related to the objectives, using the newly acquired techniques of community participants; and (4) disseminating the information back to the participating agencies and organizations. The emphasis in this type of participatory project is upon the process used to increase adult participation in community action.

Another example of participatory research conducted within the community setting is the study done by Wright (1988) that compared two nontraditional adult education programs -- participatory research and technical assistance programs -- used with residents of two Chicago public housing developments. Although Wright could not conclude that one program was superior to the other, the study did provide evidence of the compatibility of participatory research methodology when low-income family concerns are being addressed. The study also detected major obstacles, such as how to help people to move toward empowerment when residents within the groups have had limited experience with being in power.

An example of participatory research conducted in a larger setting is the Citizen's Research Project in Appalachia (Gaventa and Horton, 1981). In this project an Appalachian Alliance was formed to study land ownership. The problem identified was that land ownership patterns were resulting in conditions detrimental to residence along the Appalachian range -- destruction of land due to strip mining, lack of land for housing, low tax bases and poor services, flooding, loss of agricultural land, and irregular deeding and leasing of land.

Approximately 100 citizens from some eighty counties in Alabama, Kentucky, North Carolina, Tennessee, Virginia, and West Virginia were brought together to study who actually owned the land on the Appalachian range. Reported findings of the study confirmed (1) all the land and minerals in Appalachia are owned by relatively few people, (2) Appalachian land and mineral resources are absentee-owned, (3) large corporations dominate the ownership picture in much of Appalachia (40 percent of land and 70 percent of mineral rights), and (4) mineral rights are greatly under-assessed for property tax purposes (p. 34). In keeping with the participatory concept, findings of the study were disseminated through pamphlets, local papers, community meetings, workshops, and regional meetings. Three months after research results were reported, activities that indicated action being taken by local groups included efforts to organize a tax reform coalition in Kentucky, tax challenges in Tennessee, and a multicounty coalition organized around gas and oil taxes and drilling practices in West Virginia.

Philosophic differences that exist between participatory research -- emphasizing the acquisition and use of knowledge by people for their empowerment -- and conventional social science research -- stressing the importance of selective inquiry and funding of knowledge -- make judging the merits of the former difficult. Strengths and weaknesses of either paradigm are premised on a particular philosophic viewpoint of the purpose for research.

Criticism regarding participatory research is advanced by some individuals who represent the conventional paradigms of social science research. For example, Griffith and Cristarella (1979) suggest that "the term participatory research is a misnomer, applied idiosyncratically to activities not conducted primarily to advance knowledge, but rather to promote community development" (p. 18). Participatory research does not, in their opinion, contribute to a body of knowledge, which conventional social science researchers see as the single most important function of the research process.

The strengths and weaknesses of participatory research are much the same as those for action research. The results can be applied directly to practice, but these results can rarely be generalized to other situations. On the other hand, greater involvement by participants in the research may ensure better application of research results. As more forms of applied social science research methodology appear, it will be interesting to observe the relative status of action and participatory research.

Critical Research

One form of interactive research -- critical research -- has developed from a more definite Marxist reform philosophy. The basis of critical research method is the theory of "knowledge -- constitutive interests" proposed by Habermas (1974). The method, often referred to as Verstehen, leads to knowledge of practical interest -- knowledge that translates into interpretive understanding that can inform and guide practice.

Kemmis (1988) who readily interchanges critical with action research, explains that critical education research exists in practice within the margins of the culture and technology of educational policy and practice. The tension created by a demand for self-awareness, on one hand, and threats of institutionalization on the other, form the dialectic on which critical research is based. Critical research, as described through the words of Marx (1967 p. 212), is critical in the sense that, . . . "we do not anticipate the world dogmatically, but rather wish to find the new world through criticism of the old; for all times is not our task, what we have to accomplish at this time is all the more clear; relentless criticism for all existing conditions, relentless in the sense that the criticism is not afraid of its findings and just as little afraid of conflict with the powers that be."

A critical researcher assumes an oppositional stance in four distinct ways -- epistemologically, cognitively, culturally and politically. Epistemologically critical research practitioners reject empirism and idealism, also positivism and interpretivism. This translates into rejection of most foundations upon which much social and educational research is based. Cognitive opposition -- the second way of being critical -- is in the form of acknowledgement and struggling against interpretations of the world as they are decoded and structured through language, culture and traditions. This type of cognitive opposition is demonstrated by how the researcher treats familiar ways of understanding human activity and social relationships as problematic. This method questions such phenomena as human rationality, values associated with productive activity, and justice of social relationships.

The third mode of opposition in critical research practice -- cultural opposition -- is closely linked to cognitive opposition. It brings to focus the possibilities of how culture can sustain irrationality, unfulfilling lifestyles and social injustice, revealing the degree to which certain ways of life within a culture are strategically organized to preserve the interests of some members of society at the expense of others.

Cognitive and cultural criticism together form the fourth way, or sense of opposition -- political opposition. Critical research creates conditions within which individuals can work cooperatively as knowing human beings, as both products and producers of history who help "to find the new world through criticism of the old" and act together in bringing a new world into being. (Carr & Kemmis, 1986). This pattern of critical research practice becomes more than opposition, Kemmis emphasizes, it is a form of resistance, by awakening people to the critical sense of what is possible and organizing them into action.

To further describe critical research methodology and compare it with other conventional forms of research practice, Carr and Kemmis (1986) provide a classification of alternative styles of educational research. (See Table 7.2).

Five formal requirements characterize a critical social or educational science, according to the authors. These requirements are articulated in the philosophy of the "Frankfort School," a school associated with development of the critical thought movement. Carr & Kemmis (1986) emphasize that any adequate approach to educational research and theory must:

1) reject positivist notions of rationality, objectivity and truth; 2) accept the need to employ the interpretive categories of teachers and

Table 7.2 Alternative Styles of Educational Research

	FORM OF RESEARCH		
	POSITIVIST (Empirical-analytic)	INTERPRETIVE (Historical-hermeneutic)	CRITICAL
Presumed nature of education as an object of research	Education as a 'phenomenon'; schooling as a deliver-system (technology)	Education as a developmental process; schooling as lived experience	Education as a social project; schooling as an institution for social and cultural reproduction and transformation.
Research methods	Natural-scientific; experimental; 'quantitative'	Historical interpretive; 'qualitative'; ethno-methodological; illuminative	Critical social science; emancipatory action research
Form of research knowledge	Objective; nomological; causal explanation	Subjective; idiographic; interpretive understanding	Dialectical; reflexive understanding aimed at critical praxis
Examples of substantive theoretical forms	Functionalist psychology; structure-functional sociology, anthropology	Structuralism in psychology, sociology, anthropology	Ideology-critique; critical curriculum theorising by collaborating teachers
Human interest	Technical	Practical	Emancipatory
Practical purpose and form of reasoning	Improvement of the 'technology' of schooling; instrumental (means, ends) reasoning	Enlightenment of practitioners; practical-deliberative (informs judgement)	Rational transformation of education; critical reasoning (i. e., practical reasoning with emancipatory intent)
Theory of human nature	Deterministic	Humanistic	Historical-materialist
Educational philosophy	Neo-classical, vocational	Liberal-progressive	Socially-critical, democratic
Educational values	'Moulding' metaphor. Individuals prepared for a given form of social life	'Growth' metaphor. Self-actualisation of individuals within meritocratic form of social life	'Empowerment' metaphor. Individuals collectively producing and transforming existing forms of social life through action in history
View of educational reform	Research, development and dissemination; bureaucracy, corporate management	Enlightened action; liberal-individualist, reconstructionist	Contestational, communitarian; reproduction and transformation through collective action

Carr, W. and Kemmis, S. (1986) *Becoming Critical: Education, Knowledge and Action Research*, London, Falmer (and Geelong, Victoria, Deakin University Press).

other participants in educational processes -- it must be based upon the self-understandings of practitioners; 3) provide ways of distinguishing idealogically warped interpretations from interpretations that are not, and provide explanations of how to overcome those distorted self-understandings; 4) address identification and exposition of those aspects of the social order that interfere with pursuit of rational goals and provide theoretical explanations to practitioners that raise awareness to how these interferences may be eliminated or conquered. Finally, an adequate approach to educational theory and research should be practical, in the sense that the practice of criticism, according to Carr and Kemmis, should always be directed toward transformation of ways that participants see themselves and their situations, so that obstacles that stand in the way of attaining their objectives can be identified and overcome.

Futures Research

Several terms describe the study of the future -- futurism, futurology, futuribles, and futuristics to name a few (McHale, 1978). The term "futures research," however, appears to best describe the actual purpose for this type of research -- the study of possible futures. A concept that Cornish (1977) uses in describing futures research is "applied history." Futures researchers emphasize the importance of the past in that it can illuminate the future. Futures study attempts to use many forms of knowledge we now have to understand future possibilities.

Futurologists commonly use two principles in their study: the Principle of Continuity and the Principle of Analogy (Cornish, p. 103). The Principle of Continuity suggests that observing what exists now that will continue in the future is the way to study the future. This principle assumes that the future is to be very much like the present. The Principle of Continuity allows us to predict that what we observe today will not change, or will change in the same way it has changed in the past. By accepting the Principle of Continuity, for example, we can count on the rivers to flow tomorrow, the air to be present next year, and the sun to shine in the year 2000. An example of applying the Continuity concept in the field of adult education might be that the gradual, but inevitable increase in the median age of adults and a larger workforce within the U.S. means more training will be required for adults in the future.

The Principle of Analogy involves observing recurring patterns or cycles of events as means of studying the future. For example, a study of the decreasing temperatures in the late fall may be used to predict snow, or the southward flight of geese may be a predictor of winter weather.

McHale (1978) points out three current approaches to futures research in which these principles are applied:

1. Descriptive approach (the "imagined future") -- including conjectures, speculations, and imagined situations as in many classical utopian futures (*20,000 Leagues Under the Sea* by Jules Verne and *War of the Worlds* by H. C. Wells).
2. Exploratory Approach (the "logical future") -- forecasting based on methodical and relatively linear extrapolation of past and present developments into the future (RAND Corporation Report, 1964).
3. Prescriptive Approach (the "willed future") -- normatively oriented projections of the future in which explicit value insertions and choices are made about how a specific future may be viewed or attained, e.g., *The Year 2000* by Kahn & Wiener (1968) and Plan Europe 2000 group's publication *The Future is Tomorrow* (1973).

McHale also suggests that these categories overlap a great deal in actual practice. Research activities may be grouped according to type and range of activity. Some activities focus on forecasting causal relationships, while others concentrate upon long-range planning. Futures research tends to be oriented toward a time frame of "the next two to three decades and beyond" (McHale, p. 10).

Contributions such as those of Sir Thomas More *(Utopia)* and Francis Bacon *(New Atlantis)* in the sixteenth century opened the era of modern futurism. A number of methods for studying the future have developed since the beginning of this modern era. The methods discussed here -- intuititive and creative thinking, trend extrapolation, Delphi technique, scenario, and simulation modeling and gaming -- are commonly used in applied fields of social science.

Intuitive and Creative Thinking—To the researcher of futures who applies intuitive and creative thinking, the future is viewed as an ill-structured problem (Mendell, 1978). Human creativity and intuition are applied to generate ideas about unseen and unimaginable forms of reality that may exist in the future. Thinking about the future consists not only of creating new patterns, but of getting rid of old patterns. This latter process is what Mendell (1978) refers to as "the practice of intuition" (p. 149). Development of intuition includes freeing the mind from thinking conventionally by recognizing incomplete answers, overgeneralization or polarization, and habitual solutions to problems. Other facets of the practice of intuition are empathizing -- "wearing other people's heads"; analogizing -- looking for patterns; playing mind games; devising leading questions about institutions; and browsing for additional information. Futures research that uses intuitive and creative methods of thinking attempts to develop future worlds from the ingenuity of the human mind.

Trend Extrapolation—A second method is trend extrapolation. As defined by Hill (1978), a trend is "a tendency for the values in a time series to increase or decrease with some steady regularity" (p. 249). Based on the Principle of Continuity, this form of futures research also uses graphic displays of significant statistical information, such as the average number of deaths per year over a number of years, or employee attrition on a monthly basis over several months. Other statistical procedures include use of correlation analysis, which quantitatively describes the relationship of events over time. Trends can be identified by regression analysis, observing the degree to which events adhere or depart from statistically predicted patterns of events.

Other phenomenona that may be analyzed using this technique that have relevance for adult education and training are population trends, work patterns, migration patterns, and housing patterns.

Trend extrapolation can also be conducted through a review of literature. Ilsely (1982), for example, used phenomenological analysis to study images of the future through noted adult education literature. In the study Ilsely examined the potential for images of the future as a conceptual base for analyzing issues in the field of adult education.

In contrast Hoare (1982) did a comprehensive review of adult education and related literature for the decade of the 70's to determine issues that might impact the future of adult education. Various techniques were used in the trend study, such as conference proceedings, surveys, action-inquiry forums, and informed opinion of experts. Future issues that were identified from Hoare's research were related to various forms of education -- work and leisure education, education for aging, health education, continuing professional education, social and civic responsibility, personal adaptation, functional competency and adult teacher education.

Delphi Technique—In a report by the RAND Corporation, "Report on Long-Range Forecasting Study" (Helmer and Gordon, 1964), a third method of studying the future was introduced -- the Delphi technique. The aim of the RAND study was to determine "the direction of long-range trends, with special emphasis on science and technology, and their probable effects on our society and our world" (Linstone, 1978, p. 273). Since its introduction, the method has gained acceptance in areas other than the business world for forecasting the future. The process involves a series of questionnaires, each one being more structured and requiring more focus by the respondent than the preceding one. The Delphi process includes the following steps:

1. Formation of a team to undertake and monitor a Delphi study on a given subject
2. Selection of one or more panels to participate in the exercise -- normally experts in the subject or area
3. Development of the first round Delphi questionnaire
4. Testing of the questionnaire for proper wording (e.g., ambiguities, vagueness)
5. Transmission of the first questionnaire to the panelists
6. **Analysis of the first round responses**
7. Preparation of the second round questionnaires (and possible testing)
8. Transmission of the second round questionnaire to the panelists
9. Analysis of second round responses (Steps 7 to 9 repeated until desired or necessary data are gathered)
10. Preparation of a report by the analysis team to present conclusions of the exercise (Linstone, pp. 274-75)

The original process used in the Delphi technique incorporated three important elements: (1) structuring of information flow, (2) feedback to the participants, and (3) anonymity for the participants.

As Linstone (1978) points out, the Delphi method can be used in discovering priorities of personal values and social aims, examining the pros and cons of an issue, evaluating budget allocations, assessing the importance of a historical event, and even sorting out perceived and real human motivations.

Two particularly useful situations in which the Delphi method may be applied are (1) when the problem does not lend itself to precise analytical techniques, but can benefit from subjective judgments on a collective basis, and (2) when the individuals who need to interact cannot be brought together in a face-to-face exchange because of time or cost constraints (Linstone, p. 275). Also, the technique minimizes the influence of strong personalities. An obvious weakness of the Delphi technique is the amount of time required to conduct a thorough study.

Scenarios—Most dictionary definitions of "scenario" apply when it is used as a method of studying the future -- the scenario is "dramatic, fictional and sketchy" (Wilson, 1978). These descriptions are all essential, according to Wilson, in futures research, because the purpose is to raise consciousness. A more specific definition of scenario used for futures studies is "an exploration of an alternative future" (p. 225).

Scenarios can be described as being hypothetical -- a suggested alternative; sketchy -- only an outline that seeks to map the branching points of the future; and multifaceted or holistic -- an attempt to paint a broad picture of future possibilities.

One of the earliest futures scenarios was Plato's description of the ideal state in *The Republic*. From this source Sir Thomas More developed his treatise, *Utopia*. A recent, well-known scenario is *The Limits of Growth* (Meadow et al., 1972) which deals with population explosion and ecological change. *The Future of Adult Education; An Inductively Derived Scenario* (Boshier, 1979) is an example of a scenario which used the Delphi method to gather information from a group of conference participants in projecting the future of a field of study.

Strengths of the scenario as a means of studying the future include helping individuals and organizations to plan environments by sorting out priorities and options. The method can also free planners from the conventional environment and allow them to see the future holistically, rather than in pieces. A limitation of the method is that scenarios, no matter how creative, are developed from and perceived through the data of the present.

Simulation Modeling and Gaming—A fifth method for futures study is the use of simulation models and games. A simulation model is a set of variables and equations that represent, or substitute for, reality and relationships within that reality. It mathematically imitates a system. A model can be static -- representing a system at one point in time -- or the model can be dynamic -- attempting to trace the operation of a system over time (McLean, 1978). In most instances, the complexity of mathematical models requires use of the computer. The purpose of simulation models is to "reproduce the historical behavior of a system and project that behavior into the future for the purpose of forecasting" (p. 331). It is the urgent need to understand complex economic, technical, and social systems -- the growth of industry or changing patterns of urban structure -- that prompts futures researchers to build simulation models.

Simulation gaming differs from simulation modeling in that games are developed to assist people in conveying views and explaining alternative situations. Simulation gaming is not a device for projecting, but for explaining and helping us prepare for the future.

There are four basic functions of simulation games:

1. To transmit information
2. To extract information
3. To establish discussion between players
4. To motivate players and prepare them for future experience (McLean, p. 345)

Some examples of simulation games are the HEX Game developed to study the human settlement planning in Third World nations for UNESCO, the Metro-Apex Game used by the United States government as an air pollution control training method, and SNUS (Simulated Nutrition System) Game developed to implement nutrition planning in Third World nations. Ultimately the individual employing simulation gaming as a method of studying the future is trying to acquaint research participants with the future. The game creates an environment for self-instruction that permits a number of perspectives and opinions in investigating the future. The researcher also attempts to provoke participants in the game to think expansively -- to enlarge their perceptions and to reach logical conclusions only after exploring a problem or situation from multiple angles.

Summary

Each of the methodologies discussed in this chapter departs in some way from the conventional modes of social science research. They represent less conventional approaches to inquiry that either have contributed concepts and procedures to the education and training of adults or have shown potential for making such contributions in the future.

Nonconventional and conventional methods differ in how validity of research is viewed. In unconventional methods, not only is validity judged by external and internal measures carried out by design, but the researcher is instrumental in the process of "knowing." Interactive research (action and participatory) contributes the element of immediate application of research results and participant participation in the research process. Critical research methodology, on the other hand, contributes to the concept "knowledge of practical interest" -- knowledge that helps participants in the research more fully understand themselves and their circumstances. Critical methodology leads to knowledge that can inform and guide practice.

REFERENCES

Bogdan, Robert C. and Sari K. Biklen. (1982). *Qualitative Research for Education: An Introduction to Theory and Methods*. Boston: Allyn and Bacon.

Borg, Walter. (1987). *Applying Educational Research*. New York: Longman.

Boshier, Roger. (1979). "The Future of Adult Education: An Inductively Derived Scenario." *Adult Education Research Conference Proceedings*. Ann Arbor, Michigan.

Carr, W. and S. Kemmis. (1986). *Becoming Critical: Education, Knowledge and Action Research*. London: Falmer (and Geelong, Victoria, Deakin University Press).

Cornish, Edward. (1977). *The Study of the Future*. Washington, D.C.: World Future Society.

Freire, Paulo. (1974). *Education for Critical Consciousness*. New York: Seabury Press.
Gaventa, John, and Billy D. Horton. (1981). "A Citizens' Research Project in Appalachia, USA." *Convergence*. 14:30-42.
Griffith, William S. and Mary C. Cristarella. (1979). "Participatory Research: Should It Be a New Methodology for Adult Educators?" in *Viewpoints on Adult Education Research*, (ed.) John Niemi. Columbus, Ohio: ERIC Clearinghouse on Adult, Career and Vocational Education. pp. 43-70.
Habermas, J. (1974). *Theory and Practice*, (trans.) John Veirtel, London: Heinemann.
Hall, Budd L. (1979). "Participatory Research: Breaking the Academic Monopoly," in *Viewpoints on Adult Education Research*, (ed.) John Niemi.
Hall, Budd L. (1981). "Participatory Research, Popular Knowledge and Power: A Personal Reflection," *Convergence*. 14:6-19.
Helmer-Hirschberg, Olaf and T. J. Gordon. (1964). "Report on Long-Range Forecasting Study," Santa Monica, California: RAND Corporation.
Henaut, Dorothy. (1971). "The Media: Powerful Catalyst for Community Change," in *Mass Media and Adult Education*, (ed.), John Niemi. Englewood Cliffs, New Jersey: Educational Technology Publications.
Hill, Kim Quaile. (1978). "Trend Extrapolation," in *Handbook of Futures Research'* (ed.) Jib Fowles. Westport, Connecticut: Greenwood Press.
Hoare, C. H. (1982). "Future Issues in Adult Education: A Review of the Literature of the Seventies," *Adult Education*, 33:55-59.
Ilsely, P. J. (1982). "The Relevance of Future in Adult Education A Phenomenological Analysis of Images of the Future." Unpublished Doctoral Dissertation, Northern Illinois University.
Isaac, Stephen and William B. Michael. (1981). *Handbook in Research and Evaluation*. 2nd Ed. San Diego: EDITS Publishers.
Kassam, Yusaf and Kemal Mustafa. (1982). *Participatory Research: An Emerging Alternative Methodology in Social Science Research*. Khanpur, New Delhi: Society for Participatory Research in Asia, Series No. 2.
Kemmis, S. and R. McTaggart. (1987). *The Action Research Planner*. Geelong, Victoria: Deakin University Press.
Kemmis, S. and L. Fitzclarence. (1986). *Curriculum Theorizing: Beyond Reproduction Theory*. Geelong, Victoria: Deakin University Press.
Kemmis, S. (1988). *Critical Educational Research*. A paper prepared for a meeting of the Critical Theory PreConference of the North American Adult Education Association Research Conference, University of Calgary, May.
Lewin, Kurt. (1947). "Group Decision and Social Change," in *Reading in Social Psychology*, (eds.) T. M. Newcomb and E. L. Hartley. New York: Holt, Rinehart and Winston.
Linstone, Harold A. (1978). "The Delphi Technique," in *Handbook of Futures Research*, (ed.) Jib Fowles, Westport, Connecticut: Greenwood Press.
Marx, K. (1967). *Writings of the Young Marx on Philosphy and Society*, ed. trans. L. D. Easton and K. H. Guddat. New York: Anchor Books.
McHale, John. (1978). "The Emergence of Futures Research," in *Handbook of Futures Research*, (ed.) Jib Fowles. Westport, Connecticut: Greenwood Press.
McLean, J. Michael. (1978). "Simulation Modeling," in *Handbook of Futures Research*, (ed.) Jib Fowles. Westport, Connecticut: Greenwood Press.
Mendell, J. S. (1978). "The Practice of Intuition," in *Handbook of Futures Research*, (ed.) Jib Fowles. Westport, Connecticut: Greenwood Press.
Niemi, John A. and Stephanie Stephens. (August 1979). "The Rockford Interactive Media Project," Title 1-A HEA, Evaluation Report.
Participatory Research: An Introduction. (1982). Khanpur, New Delhi: Society for Participatory Research in Asia.

Reason, Peter and John Rowan. (1981). "Issues of Validity in New Paradigm Research," in *Human Inquiry: A Sourcebook of New Paradigm Research* (eds.) Peter Reason and John Rowan. Chichester: John Wiley and Sons, pp. 239-250.

Sanford, Nevitt. (1981). "A Model for Action Research," in *Human Inquiry: A Sourcebook of New Paradigm Research*, (eds.) Peter Reason and John Rowan. Chichester: John Wiley and Sons, pp. 173-182.

Status Report on the Participatory Research Project International Meeting, 1977.

Theodore, Tedwilliam. (1975). *Social and Political Intervention: Video Field Experience.* Chicago: Communications for Change.

Wilson, Ian H. (1978). "Scenarios," in *Handbook for Futures Research*, (ed.) Jib Fowles. Westport, Connecticut: Greenwood Press.

Wright, Lewis E. (1988). "Participatory Research: A Study of Empowerment in Public Housing Through Resident Management," Unpublished Doctoral Dissertation, Northern Illinois University.

CHAPTER 8

DATA COLLECTION PROCEDURES AND TECHNIQUES

The collection of data, though interesting and inspiring at times to the researcher, can also be tedious and boring. Consequently, the "reward" of doing research is seldom considered to be data collection; it is more often what results from the collection. The routine and sometimes monotonous steps necessary to conduct research effectively may lead the novice researcher or casual consumer of research to lose interest. The experienced researcher, however, accepts the tedium, knowing that repetition and thoroughness in the process are necessary to produce supportable results. The process of conducting research is simply the deliberate choice and use of means that best answer research questions. Techniques and procedures for conducting research are to the researcher as the chisel and hammer are to the stone sculptor: their careful and consistent use brings new images of reality.

The technique or procedure chosen for collecting data is derived from the particular research method. Depending upon the emphasis of the study (e.g., rational/empirical, intuitive, historical, or philosophical), appropriate procedures and techniques emerge during the planning of the research. If the study is planned to test hypotheses deductively, for example, rational and empirical techniques such as questioning and observing may be used. Or, if the inquiry is of a historical nature, internal and external criticism of research documents through content analysis may be most appropriate.

For purposes of discussion in this chapter, the term *procedure* refers to the steps or activities that describe the general way data is gathered. For example, the use of questions for research participant response before and after an experience is a general procedure for gathering data. A *technique*, on the other hand, refers to the specific device or means of recording the data, such as an interview, a test, or a projective inventory.

The Nature of Research Data

The researcher gathers data -- facts, impressions, beliefs, and feelings -- that are related to the phenomenon being studied in order to systematically reach conclusions. Research *data* is an elusive term which, to the beginning researcher, may seem analogous to an answer to the research question. With experience, one realizes that data gathering is but one phase of inquiry. In fact, research answers come from the comparison of data; the data are relatively meaningless without such a comparison, and they cannot provide answers to research questions all by themselves.

Data gathered as a sample of the phenomenon under study are chosen to represent accurately those behaviors and events that are part of the phenomenon. The task of the researcher is to cull from the many bits of data those that are representative, and to shape accurate and meaningful conclusions. In many research studies, the researcher is limited by the amount of data that can be gathered. This limitation results from inaccessability of data, or the sheer volume, which make collecting *all* pertinent data unrealistic. Therefore, one judgment that the researcher must make in designing and conducting the study concerns validity -- how accurately do the data represent the phenomenon? The researcher must also recognize that a sample of research data is only an approximation of the phenomenon being studied and, in a sense, can never be completely accurate. Even data collected systematically provide only a partial glimpse of the total picture.

Accurate approximations of the larger picture being researched require some type of measurement procedure, which Selltiz et al. (1976, p. 161) describe as "*a technique for collecting data, plus a set of rules for using these data.*" The purpose of any measurement procedure is to produce trustworthy evidence relevant to the research question being asked. For example, if we wanted to know the attitudes of black adults in the ghetto of a metropolitan city about a training program offered in their neighborhood, we might use a type of attitude scale that yields a score. Using this score, we could place individual responses on a continuum from unfavorable to favorable for comparison. This technique provides a way of gathering the data and also a guide for use: one individual can be compared with another by the position of each on the scale. But another way to gather the same kind of data is by using an unstructured interview. General questions about attitudes toward the training program could be asked of the same adults as before. However, a coding system -- that is, set of rules for using the data -- is necessary to approximate the participants' degree of favorable or unfavorable attitude.

The choice of which of these two techniques to use should be based upon the research problem, characteristics of the black adults, and conditions within the research environment. The following planning questions might be asked: Is the attitude scale valid for use with this sample population? How easily is it administered? Are norms based upon the population available for comparison? All of these questions must be considered in deciding whether or not to use the scale. If the participants are sensitive to filling out forms, or if the researcher is not certain about all the data needed, the unstructured interview may be more productive.

Data coded and represented by numerical scores are typically referred to as *quantitative* or *statistical* data. Data not transferable to statistics are called *qualitative* data. In the previous example, the scores produced from the attitude scale are quantitative data, while the unstructured interview produced qualitative data. Both types of data are useful in the process of systematic inquiry related to adult education and training.

The researcher has three major ways of collecting data: by asking questions through a survey, by observing, or by testing. Each procedure also includes choices of various research techniques. The choice of technique used for collecting data depends upon the type of research method already selected and conditions surrounding the research phenomenon. Primary techniques for gathering data are discussed in the following section.

Surveying

Of all data-gathering techniques available to the researcher, the survey -- either written or oral -- is used most extensively. The term *survey* represents a broad category of techniques that use questioning as a strategy to elicit information. Written forms of survey are referred to as questionnaires; surveys conducted orally are interviews. Although they serve similar purposes in gaining information, each provides unique advantages to the researcher.

Construction and Use of Questionnaire—Questionnaires vary in design according to the purpose suggested by the research problem. Two general types of questionnaires are the open questionnaire and closed (or forced-choice) questionnaire. An open questionnaire has items that allow greater freedom of response, whereas with a closed questionnaire, the person is forced to choose one of the alternatives provided.

Responses from closed questionnaires are more easily analyzed because data essentially have been categorized prior to beginning the data gathering. Items on a closed questionnaire represent factors surrounding the research phenomenon that are the focus of the investigation. The researcher, anticipating alternatives, simply has the research participant choose from information, attitudes, etc., provided within the instrument. Thus, analysis and statistical manipulation are made easier for the researcher after the data are gathered.

The following are examples of items used in a closed questionnaire:

Example 1. The HRD training program offered at Benx Industries serves members of the Metrocity community by:
   a. providing more jobs
   b. making members more aware of positions in industry
   c. teaching specific transferable job skills
   d. upgrading the educational level of the community

Example 2. The methods used in the program at Paulson Community College to prepare students for the General Education Development (GED) Test are:
   a. effectively meeting the needs of all participants
   b. meeting the needs of most participants
   c. meeting the needs of a few participants
   d. ineffectively meeting the needs of participants

The open-ended questionnaire, being less structured, requires time for coding and developing categories after the responses to the instrument are made. Since the researcher does not preconceive appropriate answers, variation in response means more work in the analysis and identification of categories. For example, those responding to the questionnaire might be asked:

Example 3. What is your opinion of the effectiveness of the HRD program at Benx Industries?

Example 4. What is your opinion about the effectiveness of the Paulson Community College program for General Education Development (GED) Test preparation?

Another advantage of the closed form is that it allows the researcher to guide participants along pertinent lines of thought associated with the phenomenon. The open-ended questionnaire, on the other hand, has the advantage of eliciting a wider latitude of possible responses from participants, and, consequently, information may result that is unanticipated by the researcher. The open-ended questionnaire is also less threatening and frustrating to certain special populations of participants -- e.g., undereducated, culturally different, or marginally literate.

Generally it is preferable to design questionnaires in a closed form, if the research problem permits. However, an open questionnaire may be useful if the researcher cannot determine appropriate items for a closed questionnaire. Responses from an open questionnaire can assist the researcher in developing a more focused, closed-form questionnaire later on. Construction of both becomes easier with experience and practice. Kerlinger (1986) suggests the following preparation guidelines:

1. Is the question related to the research problem and objectives?
2. Is the type of question appropriate?
3. Is the item clear and unambiguous?
4. Is the question a leading question?
5. Does the question demand knowledge and information that the respondent does not have?
6. Does the question demand personal or delicate material the respondent may resist?
7. Is the question loaded with social desirability? (pp. 444-445)

In addition to the basic criteria for developing questions -- that of focus, clarity, and supplying appropriate alternatives -- it is important to be aware of the general socioeconomic and cultural backgrounds of participants.

Borg (1987) uses the following questions to evaluate the closed questionnaire:

1. Was the questionnaire pretested?
2. Did the questionnaire include any leading questions?
3. Were any psychologically threatening questions included in the questionnaire?
4. Were the subjects who received the questionnaire likely to have the information requested?
5. What percentage of subjects responded to the questionnaire?
6. What steps were taken to contact nonrespondents, and how many ultimately responded? (pp. 109-110)

All the questions raised here reflect upon the validity of the questionnaire and ultimately upon the data collected through its use. Pretesting an instrument helps work out problems that may arise after the data have been collected. Also, previewing the questionnaire for leading and threatening items will guard against bias and weak reliability of results.

Researchers who distribute questionnaires through the mail face another problem. Mass mailing sometimes results in limited return.

Low return rate, in turn, affects the degree to which the researcher is assured of a representative sample. A return of 60 percent or higher is acceptable, but 75 percent or over is desirable. A well-constructed and pretested questionnaire will assist in getting an adequate number of responses from participants.

Because the questionnaire is self-administered, a well-constructed questionnaire always includes precise and detailed instructions (Mannheim, 1981). Physical appearance and size will contribute to legibility and clarity. The way items are sequenced is another factor for the researcher to consider. Questionnaire items usually are sequenced in the following way: items appearing first focus on identifying the respondent; the next items, upon demographic information; and finally, the focus is upon substantive questions. Figure 8.1 (Hauser, 1980) is an example of portions of a well-planned questionnaire.

Each item should pertain to a corresponding factor in the research phenomenon being studied. Avoid trivial or unrelated questions, no matter how interesting they may be. Problems identified by Wiersma (1986) that lessen the validity of the questionnaire are:

1. There is excessive nonresponse.
2. Items are poorly constructed or organized.
3. Respondents are not truthful in their responses.
4. Questions deal only with trivial information.
5. Data from different questions are difficult to synthesize.
   (p. 186)

Use of the Interview—The interview adds a dimension to the gathering of survey data that is not provided by the questionnaire -- namely, the interview ensures a face-to-face encounter with the research participant. Like questionnaires, interviews have two major types of formats: structured and unstructured. The researcher who uses a structured interview format, rather than a questionnaire, has the advantage of becoming an extension of the schedule of questions. Clarification, restatement, and explanation are all available for use in eliciting responses from participants. On the other hand, the researcher essentially *becomes* the research instrument when using an unstructured interview. The unstructured interview only guides the researcher through areas for investigation. The validity of results, however, rests more with the interviewing skill of the researcher than with the interview format. It is the responsibility of the interviewer to elicit pertinent information in the investigation.

PROFESSIONAL DEVELOPMENT INVENTORY

The following inventory is designed to provide information about the needs of trainers for continuing professional development. Such information is useful in designing professional programs.

Please answer the following, and *return this survey* in the enclosed envelope. *Thank you* for your professional cooperation.

1. Age: ___ 21-32 ___ 33-44 ___ 45-56 ___ 57 & over

2. *Sex*: ___ Male ___ Female

3. Number of *years* in the training profession:

___ 0-4 ___ 5-10 ___ 11-24 ___ 25 or more

4. Please indicate your *highest* level of education:

___ High school   ___ B.A. or B.S. degree plus grad hours
___ Associate degree   ___ Master's or equivalent
___ College, no degree   ___ Master's plus grad hours
___ B.A. or B.S. degree   ___ Doctorate

5. Indicate the *major* area of study in which your degree(s) were earned:

Associate: _____
B.A./B.S.: _____
Master's: _____
Doctorate: _____

6. How many *hours per week* would you estimate you spend on professional development (reading journals, attending classes, seminars, workshops, study groups, etc.)?

___ 0 ___ 1-5 ___ 6-10 ___ 10 or more

7. Check *EACH CATEGORY* within which you have received professional development assistance in the past *TWO* years.

___ College or university   ___ In-house program (internal staff)
___ Community   ___ In-house program
     college   (external consultant)
___ Professional organization ___ Other: _____

8. Please indicate what percentage of your *time* is spent in each of these roles, for example 20%, 30%, and 50%.
___ Learning Specialist   ___ Administrator   ___ Consultant

Figure 8.1. Sample questionnaire

PROFESSIONAL DEVELOPMENT NEEDS ASSESSMENT

You may feel the need for new or additional professional development. Your needs are probably higher in some areas than in others. Below, please indicate your level of need for additional professional development in each of the competencies listed. CIRCLE the number that best corresponds to your need.

Level of Need

	High need					No need
1. Developing material resources- scripts, artwork, other instructional materials.	5	4	3	2	1	0
2. Determining appropriate training approaches- evaluate alternatives, commercial and in-house.	5	4	3	2	1	0
3. Needs analysis and diagnosis- construct and administer instruments, analyze and interpret data.	5	4	3	2	1	0
4. Group and organization development- apply techniques of team building, role playing, simulations, etc.	5	4	3	2	1	0
5. Job-related training- analyze job requirements, performance problems, programs for.	5	4	3	2	1	0
6. Conduct classroom training- lecture, lead discussion, operate equipment, evaluate, etc.	5	4	3	2	1	0
7. Individual development planning and counseling- career, development needs, plans, programs.	5	4	3	2	1	0
8. Manage internal resources- obtain, train, supervise, and evaluate instructor personnel.	5	4	3	2	1	0
9. Professional self-development- attend seminars, conferences and keep abreast of training practices, concepts, and theories.	5	4	3	2	1	0
10. Training research- design and implement studies, interpret data in reports, influence future trends.	5	4	3	2	1	0
11. Manage working relationships with managers- establish/maintain good relations, explain recommendations.	5	4	3	2	1	0
12. Program design and development- design content, select methods, develop materials, evaluate, etc.	5	4	3	2	1	0
13. Manage training and development function- budget, plan, organize, staff, lead, and control.	5	4	3	2	1	0
14. Manage external resources- external instructors, materials, program logistics, consultants, etc.	5	4	3	2	1	0

Figure 8.1. Sample questionnaire (continued)

Increasing the structure increases the consistency from one interview to the next. When large numbers of people are being interviewed, for example, a highly structured format or schedule is necessary so that data can be compared later. One purpose of using an unstructured interview, on the other hand, is to explore all possibilities regarding the information sought. This type of interview helps identify and define important areas of information that might be studied through other techniques at another time.

Interviews are often useful in gathering data when the topic to be explored is "complex and emotionally loaded" (Sommer & Sommer, 1986). Interviews are also helpful when the chance for observation is limited; gathering opinions and facts from participants while observing their personal characteristics gives an added dimension to the observational data.

Choosing the documentation method is an important part of the planning. Data can be recorded in writing or electronically recorded on audio or video tape. When possible, electronically recorded interviews are preferable. Note taking may result in missed information and thereby reduce the validity of the interview results. On the other hand, some research participants are sensitive to electronic recording devices and may resist, not respond authentically, or even refuse to participate.

Direct interaction by research participants -- a characteristic of the interview technique -- is both an advantage and a disadvantage. Adaptability of the technique is the primary advantage of interviewing. "The well-trained interviewer can make full use of the responses of the subject to alter the interview situation. As contrasted with the questionnaire, which provides no immediate feedback, the interview permits the research worker to follow up leads that show up during the interview and thus obtain more data and greater clarity" (Borg, 1987, pp. 110-111). The interview technique also permits greater depth than other techniques. By using deliberate encouragement and establishing good rapport, a researcher can obtain information participants would reveal in no other way.

On the other hand, the interviewer must have skill and knowledge in order to gather valid and reliable data. An adequate amount of training is necessary; the specific amount is related to the complexity and sensitivity of the data to be gathered. More training is usually necessary for those who conduct unstructured interviews.

Interviewing is learned in a number of ways -- role playing, peer critiqueing, use of videotape, and observing experienced interviewers. However, skill comes only with practice and feedback on one's performance (Sommer & Sommer, 1986).

The interview should start with simple and interesting questions to engage the interviewee more readily and to obtain a good response. If the interview entails several subsections or topics, each section or topic should flow from the simple to the more complex. Questions should be introduced in a logical progression and asked completely and slowly. The full intent of the question should be made clear to the person being interviewed. Care should be taken not to interrupt the interviewee's train of thought. The interviewer must understand the response before moving on to the next question. Answers should never be assumed; let the interviewee articulate them. "The fundamental principle of qualitative interviewing," Patton (1980) emphasizes, "is to provide a framework within which respondents can express their own understanding in their own terms" (p. 205).

From the foregoing discussion of techniques, the reader probably recognizes that not all pertinent research data can be gathered by surveying. Other procedures and techniques may be needed to complement or replace the questionnaire or interview. The following section discusses another major way of gathering data -- observation.

Observation

Viewing events and behavior of people is not just an alternative method of getting the same type of information that research participants could give in response to an interview or questionnaire. Observational data is directly related to typical behavioral situations -- that is, people are seen in action. Because participants are frequently unaware of their behavior, having to recall or recount the past is not as productive as observing their behavior directly. "Anthropologists, for instance, in observing foreign cultures, often note facts that their best local informants would never have thought of reporting" (Selltiz, et al., 1959, p. 202).

Observation can serve several purposes. Since it can range from highly unstructured to highly structured, a great deal of flexibility is possible. In an exploratory study, for example, the technique of observation may be unstructured: the researcher observes while participating in a group activity related to the research. In contrast, when the research design calls for a comparison of events, a systematic rating scale is frequently used. The rating scale allows the researcher to concurrently observe the events and assess the degree to which an attribute, such as collaborative learning behavior, is exhibited by an individual or group. This makes comparison and analysis easier.

Observational techniques can be effective when participants in the research are unable or unwilling to respond in written or oral form. People who are physically handicapped, limited in their use of language, or highly sensitive to questioning or testing may have to be observed in order for the researcher to gather needed data.

Two problems associated with use of observation are the unpredictability of events the researcher wishes to sample and the "present" orientation of observation. Because forecasting all pertinent events the researcher needs to observe is difficult, the researcher may not be able to gather all needed data through observation. For example, following the activities of a group over several months in order to observe the point at which a gathering of individuals actually became a group may not be feasible. The technique of observation is also limited to sampling only the present; the story of a person's life, for instance, would be impossible to observe.

Planning the Observation—In planning the type of observation technique to fit the research problem, Selltiz et al., (1959, p. 205) suggest asking the following questions:

1. What should be observed?
2. How should observation be recorded?
3. What procedures should be used to try to ensure accuracy of observation?
4. What relationship should exist between the observer and the observed, and how can such a relationship be established?

Accuracy is the key to making the technique effective. Special training is needed to move from casual observer to systematic observer. Given the erratic nature of casual observation -- responding to any stimuli and to the impulse of motives unique to the observer -- this training is of utmost importance. Through training, the observer seeks to gain uniformity with other observers also attempting to describe accurately the same phenomenon.

In using structured observation techniques, the researcher typically is searching for the relationship of independent variables to a dependent variable. The independent variable may be a method of teaching used in the instruction of adults, or it may be the learner's behavior in pursuit of a learning project. In either example, the independent variable is defined in terms that make observation possible. If the teaching method is to be observed, a description of the method in behavioral terms is needed. Only after the events to be observed have been described precisely can the observation technique be a useful tool for gathering data. According to Kerlinger (1986), with structured observation "the fundamental task of the observer is to assign behaviors to categories" (p. 489).

A major concern of researchers planning structured observation is a balance between the "molecular approach" and the "molar approach" (Kerlinger, p. 490). This means choosing units of behavior that are small enough to ensure reliability in observation (molecular), while not reducing the size of units so much that they bear no resemblance to the context of human activity (molar). In the molecular approach to observation, verbal interaction, for example, is broken into words or phrases, whereas the molar observer first defines the variable broadly and then proceeds to identify several behaviors that fall into that one category. The molar observer "depends on his experience, knowledge, and interpretation of the meaning of the actions he is observing. The molecular observer . . . seeks to push his own experience and interpretations out of the observational picture. He records what he sees -- and no more" (Kerlinger, p. 490). A variety of rating scales can be used in observation -- checklists, forced-choice inventories, category rating scales, numerical rating scales, graphic rating scales -- and each is somewhat different in format. Checklists, for example, are used as a guide in the observation and simply include a list of behaviors of events that potentially could be viewed by the observer. The observer checks those things on the list that are actually seen.

The following is an example checklist that might be used to observe the interaction within an adult learning group:

___ collaborative
___ consensual
___ apathetic
___ goal-oriented
___ congenial
___ hostile

The observer checks all the descriptions that apply to the group during the observation period, if any.

Forced-choice scales, on the other hand, provide a limited number of alternatives (generally 4 to 6) from which the observer chooses just one. A forced-choice scale using the same items for the same purpose --to observe the interaction of a learning group -- might be ordered in the following way:

___ collaborative
___ goal-oriented
___ consensual
___ congenial
___ apathetic
___ hostile

In this case, the observer is to choose only one alternative -- the one that best represents the group. The descriptions on this scale are arranged in an order from bottom to top that represents increasing degrees of positive group interaction (collaborative being most positive and hostile being least positive).

Category, numerical, and graphic scales are arranged in a continuum or in an ordered series of categories with numerical values attached to each individual item as shown below.

hostile	apathetic	congenial	consensual	goal-oriented	collaborative
1	2	3	4	5	6

The observer rates the group by checking a point on the continuum that best represents what is being observed. The alternatives on a scale describe the degree an individual or group possesses certain traits. In the case of the adult learning group, the trait to be observed is group cohesiveness. Of the observation scales available, graphic scales are the most easily used and, therefore, are used frequently.

Problems of validity exist with use of rating scales. Raters tend to make "halo effect" errors; that is, they overlook specific characteristics due to the overall good impression made by the individual being rated. Other errors in rating judgment, according to Ary (1985) are *generosity* errors -- to give the benefit of the doubt; *severity* errors -- to rate very low in all categories; and *errors of central tendency* -- to avoid extremes in rating, thus placing all individuals in the middle of the scale (pp. 204-205). Once again, rater training is important in order to reduce errors and ultimately increase reliability. Another procedure that increases reliability is the use of multiple raters. As the number of raters increases, so does reliability.

The following discussion focuses on a particular type of structured observation -- content or document analysis.

Content Analysis—Content analysis is the systematic analysis of communications, whether it be in visual, aural, or printed form. It is defined by Holsti (1969) as "any technique for making inferences by objectively and systematically identifying specific characteristics of messages" (p. 14). Guba and Lincoln (1981) point out four major

characteristics of content analysis about which most research method-
ologists agree: (1) it is a rule-guided process -- certain steps are adhered
to in the analysis; (2) it is systematic -- the steps are completed rou-
tinely and consistently; (3) it is a process that aims for generality, or
application to other contents; and (4) it deals with manifest or apparent content -- what can be seen. Both quantitative and qualitative
approaches are used in content analysis. However, it is primarily a
quantitative technique, generally used to determine and quantify what
is emphasized in a document -- for example, the incidence of propo-
ganda, sexism, or racism. But the technique may also be used for a
qualitative purpose, such as to determine how the learning process
occurs by studying autobiographical material from a number of
accomplished learners. Content analysis can also be used for studying
the "mechanics" of the message in a document, such as reading difficulty, format, and style.

The researcher chooses units of content as the first step in the process of content analysis. Berelson (1968) gives five units of content:
words, themes, characters, items, and space-and-time measures. Typically, the smallest unit of content is the *word*, although a smaller unit,
such as a letter, is possible. By simply counting the number of times a
word is used, it is possible to infer the preferences or values of the one
who produced the material. Most often a theme -- a phrase or sentence
-- is the unit of content for analysis. For example, looking for the
number of sentences that contain reference to "training" rather than
"education" might suggest predisposition toward the type of learning
the producer of the material is, or wishes to be, engaged in. The third
type of content analysis is character analysis. This refers to studying
the personification of individuals portrayed in material, such as a
story, film, or play. The study of Eleanor Roosevelt as she is portrayed
in film is an example of character analysis. Item content analysis -- the
fourth unit of analysis -- is the study of an entire production, such as a
book, play, or autobiography. Effective use of item content analysis is
made in studying the learning activities of special persons in the past to
determine motivation and style of learning. A study of the autobiography of Malcolm X, for example, that analyzes his motivation for
education is content analysis. Space-and-time analysis -- the fifth type
of content unit -- refers to actual physical characteristics of content: the
number of words, paragraphs, column inches of written material or
number of minutes, frames, scenes, etc., in visual and aural media. The
ultimate goal in content analysis is to quantify the content for purposes
of comparison.

Broad application is one of the advantages of content analysis as a technique for research data gathering. It is also efficient, economical, and can be done with a great deal of objectivity and reliability.

Qualitative Observation—Observation is particularly suited to gathering qualitative data. Qualitative data is the "detailed description of situations, events, people, interactions and observed behaviors; direct quotations from people about their experiences, attitudes, beliefs and thoughts; and excerpts or entire passages from documents, correspondence, records and case histories" (Patton, 1980, p. 22). Where quantitative measurement uses objective and standardized instruments to limit data collection to prescribed categories of response, qualitative data "are open-ended in order to find out what people's lives, experiences, and interactions mean to them in their own terms and in their natural settings." (p. 22). Qualitative measures add depth and detail to data gathered from objective techniques, such as descriptive surveys or objective tests. Bogdan and Taylor (1975) describe qualitative methods by saying that "they allow us to know people personally and to see them as they are developing their own definitions of the world" (p. 4).

Participant observation is a frequently used and effective technique for gathering qualitative data (Merriam, 1988). This technique allows for data to be "systematically and unobtrusively collected" (Taylor and Bogdan, 1984, p. 15). Use of this technique requires the observer to take the role, at least partially, of a participant. The researcher participates but does not become totally absorbed in the activity because he or she must simultaneously stay sufficiently detached to observe and analyze. Furthermore, one has to be conscious of how the act of observation may change what is being observed. It is also assumed that the observer's views of what is being observed change as the research progresses.

Unobtrusive observation measures are those techniques of observation not inducing response or reaction from participants (Webb and others, 1966; 1981). Unobtrusive observation techniques assess behavior or behavior patterns "without the knowledge or awareness of those who are being observed" (Guba and Lincoln, 1981). The observation of traffic patterns in a museum and usage wear of books in a library are examples. Another example is the sampling of data from ongoing documents that record human events, such as minutes of meetings or birth and death records.

As with use of interview schedules, reliability of results rests to a great extent with the observer. Care in designing devices and scales does improve reliability. However, observers trained and practiced in coding and recording and aware of the potential biases they bring to research contribute significantly to reliability of results.

Testing

A third category of data-gathering techniques is the objective test. Basically, a test is a systematic procedure for obtaining from an individual a set of responses that may be converted to a numerical score. The test score represents the degree to which the individual possesses the characteristic(s) being measured. A major difference between a test and a scale is the idea of competition associated with the test -- achieving a certain mark as an indicator of progress or success. Essential to the concept of testing is objectivity, or the degree to which agreement can be reached between scorers of the test. Knowledge of the characteristics and methods of test construction is important to the researcher who wishes to use tests as means of gathering research data.

Test Validity—A major consideration for the researcher gathering quantitative data is the matter of content and construct validity. If a test or another scaled instrument for gathering data is used, the question arises: Does the instrument measure the attitude or characteristic it is intended to measure? The *content validity* of the research instrument represents the extent to which items on a test or scale match the behavior, skill, or effect the researcher intends them to measure. Judgment of content validity is done through a critical assessment of the test by the researcher to determine how representative sample items are.

Content validity has two forms -- concurrent validity and predictive validity. Both are of concern to the researcher if a comparison of the performance of participants is important in the analysis of data. Concurrent and predictive validity are sometimes referred to as criterion validity because they both are estimated through comparing performance with some criterion external to the test. Concurrent validity estimates the degree to which the performance scale or rating concurs with achievement. An example is the score on a preparatory examination for the GED test that concurs with the actual GED score an individual would achieve. Predictive validity estimates the extent to which performance on the test forecasts such things as achievement or job success. How well, for example, does passing the GED preparatory examination predict future success on the actual GED test?

Construct validity is established by both logical and empirical means. A construct is a theoretical explanation of an attribute or characteristic created by scholars for purposes of study. Constructs are abstract and, having not been observed directly, are not considered actual behaviors or events. Therefore, construct validity is first estimated logically by how well the various attributes, characteristics, and behaviors represent the particular construct. For example, the degree to which mental agility and physical dexterity actually represent intelligence is a question of construct validity. Then, an empirical analysis is done, comparing performance on the test that represents the construct -- intelligence -- with other tests measuring the same construct. Thus, construct validity is estimated both logically and empirically. For a detailed explanation of tests the reader is referred to authoritative sources of measurement and evaluation, such as Buros's *Mental Measurement Yearbooks* (1978).

Types of Objective Tests—Objective tests available to researchers are numerous, but all the various types of tests can be subsumed within five general categories: "intelligence and aptitude tests, achievement tests, personality measures, attitude and value scales, and miscellaneous objective measures" (Kerlinger, 1986, p. 451).

The tests in the first category -- intelligence and aptitude tests -- measure potential for achievement, whereas achievement tests -- the second category -- indicate present proficiency or knowledge within specific areas of content. Some tests are professionally developed and use scores based upon norms developed through field testing. Scores that are related to group norms make comparison for research purposes easier. These types of tests are typically called standardized tests.

Occasionally instructor-made or researcher-made tests are developed for measuring aptitude or achievement in specific content areas. This is very time consuming and should be done only when professionally developed instruments are unavailable. Since validity and reliability of the latter are the result of meticulous construction and field testing they should be used whenever possible. The researcher will be more assured of valid results with much less time expended. Some aptitude and intelligence tests used in adult education and human resource development research are the Graduate Record Examination (aptitude) and the Wechsler Adult Intelligence Scale.

The third type of objective test, personality measures, is one of the most complex areas of psychological testing. These tests measure personality traits -- the term trait being used to signify an organization of behaviors representing a personality pattern. The difficulty with measuring personality is being certain of how valid the measures really are.

Personality is so elusive -- based upon multiple traits, interactions, and influences of one trait upon another -- that it defies precise measurement. Personality is measured through attitude inventories, rating scales, and projective techniques.

In a personality inventory, the participant is supplied a host of statements describing various behavior patterns. By reponding "yes," "no," or "uncertain" to each statement on the list of behaviors, the participant indicates which are like him or her. A score is derived by summing the responses associated with a trait being measured. Personality inventories are simple and inexpensive to develop, but the problem with them, as with most personality measures, is lack of validity.

Another widely used technique to measure personality is the rating scale. The rater is instructed to place the person being rated on a continuum or in a category that is characteristic of the behavior that person exhibits. The graphic scale is one of the most commonly used scales for measuring personality.

In addition to intelligence, aptitude, achievement, and personality tests, a fourth category of objective tests includes attitude and value scales. This type of test attempts to elicit opinions from the participants that reflect their attitudes or values about a given topic or situation. When measuring attitude, the researcher is measuring "a predisposition to think, feel, perceive, and behave toward a referent or cognitive object" (Kerlinger, p. 453). An attitude is a set of beliefs that causes an individual to act selectively toward such things as ethnic groups, races, institutions, religious sects, political issues, and personal and Constitutional rights. Values, on the other hand, are the preferences one has for all those things as influenced by culture.

Several attitude and value scale techniques are available to the researcher; the most commonly used is the Likert technique. The examples in Figure 8.2 use the Likert technique to investigate attitudes of women returning to school. Individuals are asked to indicate one of five responses ranging from Strongly Agree (SA) to Strongly Disagree (SD). The scale is scored by adding the corresponding numerical weights below each response. Other types of scales are Thurstone scales -- based upon equal appearing intervals; Guttman scales, which use a cumulative technique in rating; and semantic differential scales, which are constructed around denotative and connotative meanings, measuring only one variable.

	SA	A	U	D	SD
Starting back to school as an adult was no different from starting as a child.	(-2)	(-1)	(0)	(1)	(2)
Returning to school was most difficult because of lack of support from my family.	(2)	(1)	(0)	(-1)	(-2)

Figure 8.2. Likert scale items

Scales used to measure attitude, such as the Kuder Preference Inventory and the Strong Inventory, are examples of standardized tests that use the Likert technique. (For a detailed description of scale construction, the reader is asked to refer to authoritative sources in test construction and evaluation procedures such as Kerlinger, 1986.)

Projective and Sociometric Techniques—A fifth major grouping of objective tests includes projective and sociometric tests. These methods are most commonly used in the fields of psychology, social psychology, psychiatry, and sociology to indirectly elicit feelings of clients. When projective techniques are used to study personality, an unstructured stimulus such as an ink blot (Rorschach Test) or a picture (Thematic Apperception Test) is introduced. The individual respondent is asked to supply a story that interprets the blot or picture. The purpose of the technique is to get a sample of behavior from which inferences can be drawn about personality, emotions, needs, internal conflicts, and self-images.

Projective techniques most applicable to research in adult education and training are (1) word association, (2) sentence completion, and (3) the open-ended question. Through these, the participants share feelings, attitudes, and thoughts that they might not share through direct means such as a questionnaire or an interview. Projective techniques are useful in determining the learning needs of adults.

Whereas projective techniques are used to study characteristics of individuals, sociometric techniques are used to study the organization of social groups. Sociometric techniques ask individuals to select first, second, and third choices of companions in some social situation, such as a team of workers or a learning group. Results of individual selections are then organized into a graphic figure called a sociogram. The sociogram visually represents the pattern of interpersonal relationships and can be quantified for use in research.

Summary

Data collection in the research process is the use of an intricate set of procedures and techniques aimed at getting the best information available (see Table 8.1). Procedures and techniques are selected on the basis of what is suggested by the chosen method of research, e.g., experimental, grounded theory, historical, or interactive. In turn, the choice of all three -- method, procedure, and technique -- results from the researcher's perception of the world and from the researcher's judgment of how best to address the research problem, given that perception.

A rational/empirical perception of reality, for example, usually leads to describing and proving things external to the researcher. Therefore, the trustworthiness of data is dependent upon the validity and reliability of the instruments used to gather the research data. A phenomenological perspective, on the other hand, suggests an intuitive method; thus, the researcher becomes more the instrument of data collection, and validity is an internal matter to the researcher.

No matter what perspective guides the process, a plan of procedures and techniques is essential in conducting quality research. Sometimes the plan cannot be completely formulated at the beginning of a project because of the intuitive and/or inductive nature of the research. However, systematic inquiry requires the documentation of *how* data were gathered as well as *what* was concluded from the data. A plan that is thoughtfully developed before the research project begins and that considers data sampling, types of intervention by the researcher, and ways the data are to be analyzed by the researcher in drawing conclusions is well worth the amount of time invested.

Table 8.1. Summary of research data gathering...

Types	Uses	Advantages	Limitations
Survey:			
Closed/Forced-Choice Questionnaire	Assessment of facts, attitudes, or opinions from research participants when the range and type of response generally can be anticipated by the researcher.	Easy to administer and decode data; a large group of participants may complete concurrently; may be administered through the mail and reach participants over a wide geographical area.	Provides little opportunity for divergent response or for in-depth material from participants; requires a great deal of preparation in instrument construction and validation prior to conducting the study.
Open-Form Questionnaire	Assessment of facts, attitudes, or opinions from research participants when the range and type of response cannot be anticipated, or the researcher does not wish to anticipate responses.	Allows participants to diverge, reflect, and respond in a more unique way than through structured formats (forced-choice questionnaires or interview schedules).	Focus is sometimes lost in relation to the purposes for the study; difficult to record, code, and analyze.
Structured Interview	Assessment of facts, attitudes, and opinions from research participants who cannot or will not respond to a written survey instrument (questionnaire).	Researcher interacts directly with the research participant, which permits assessment of nonverbal communications and encourages participation by the subjects; data easy to code and analyze.	Provides little opportunity for participants to diverge in response; more time consuming for the researcher and participant, as well as less convenient.
Unstructured	Assessment of facts, attitudes, or opinions from participants in research that requires data to be elicited through self-initiation or intuitive introspection.	Responses initiated by the research participants in most instances, which contributes to greater authenticity; allows the researcher to probe for the full meaning of response and typically results in more in-depth response and "richer" data.	Researcher has less control of the interview; data difficult to record, code, and analyze; more time consuming than the structured interview; requires training; can be threatening to participants.

Table 8.1. Summary of research data gathering techniques (cont.)

Types	Uses	Advantages	Limitations
Observation: (Structured)			
Checklists	Documentation and itemization of events, behaviors, or conditions.	Data easily coded and analyzed.	Requires training of the researcher; limits observation to predetermined list of descriptions or terms.
Rating Scales	Documentation and rating of degree that a particular characteristic, condition, or behavior is present in the observation.	Use of equal-interval scale adds power to researcher's ability to measure; indicates degrees of values being observed, thus more discriminating.	Requires intense and accurate observation; training is required in use of the scale.
Content Analysis	Documentation and quantitative analysis (primarily) of content in printed, aural, and visual media.	Few time constraints on the observation; the researcher can work at his or her own speed.	The researcher is limited to what is in print, recorded, or photographed; does not allow for interpretation beyond the material being analyzed.
(Unstructured) Unobtrusive Measures	Systematic observation of patterns of behavior or events in natural settings that does not induce response or reaction from subjects of the research.	Research subjects are not influenced by the research process; the researcher is not affected by extraneous factors that are presented while observing human interaction in progress.	The researcher does not interact with subjects of the research, and therefore may not detect the full depth of meaning in the data gathered.
Participant Observation	Comprehensive investigation of events or behavior in their natural setting.	Can combine the advantages of unstructured interview with observation to produce qualitative data; participants may be encouraged to respond more naturally in	Influence of the researcher's presence as a participant may result in limited or unauthentic response; time consuming; effective use requires training and experience.

Types	Uses	Advantages	
Tests: (Objective) Intelligence and Aptitude	Quantitative assessment of research participant's potential for achievement in areas such as education.	Relatively easy to administer and score; gives quantitative data that assists the researcher in making comparison of individual abilities.	Tests are limited by lack of knowledge of what actually constitutes human intelligence or aptitude; narrow in scope and tend to represent a limited aspect of potential for achievement.
Achievement	Appraisal of participant's proficiency or knowledge in given content areas (e.g., math or manual skills).	Easy to administer and score; gives an approximation of progress for comparison.	Limits measurement of achievement to what is performed on the test.
Personality	Assessment of traits possessed by an individual that reflect an organization of behavior.	Quantitatively separates various human behaviors for study.	Some tests lack validity.
Attitude and Value	Assessment of an individual's predisposition toward an object or situation.	Quantitatively separates affective dimension of human experience for comparison.	Some tests lack validity.
Projective and Sociometric	Sampling of behavior that results from an unstructured stimulus, from which inferences about needs, feelings, self-concept, etc., can be made.	Absence of structure may elicit more natural response and "richer" data.	Lacks validity; relies heavily on subjective judgment.
(Informal) Researcher Prepared	Instrument developed for assessment of knowledge, attitudes, or skills to provide data required in conducting the study, when a standardized test is unavailable.	Serves the need for special data that could be gathered in no other way.	Time consuming; may lack validity without substantial field testing; may be of limited value for comparison without norms.

REFERENCES

Ary, D., Jacobs, L. C., and Razavich, A. (1985). *Introduction to Research in Education.* (3rd ed.). New York: Holt, Rinehart and Winston.

Berelson, Bernard. (1954). "Content Analysis," in *Handbook of Social Psychology*, (ed.). G. Lindzed. Reading, Massachusetts: Additon-Wesley.

Bogdan, Robert and Steven J. Taylor. (1975). *Introduction to Qualitative Research Methods: A Phenomenological Approach.* New York: John Wiley and Sons.

Borg, Walter R. (1987). *Applying Educational Research.* New York: Longman.

Buros, Oscar. (1978). *The Eighth Mental Measurements Yearbook.* Highland, New Jersey: The Gryphon Press, Vols. 1 and 2.

Guba, Egon G., and Yvonna S. Lincoln. (1981). *Effective Evaluation: Improving the Usefulness of Evaluation Results Through Responsive and Naturalistic Approaches.* San Francisco: Jossey-Bass.

Hauser, Jean B. (1980). "A Study of Professional Development and Self Perceived Needs for Continuing Professional Education Among Selected Training Specialists," Unpublished Doctoral Dissertation, Northern Illinois University, pp. 143-144.

Holsti, Ole. (1968). "Content Analysis," in *Handbook of Social Psychology*, (eds.) G. Lindzey and E. Aronson. Reading, Massachusetts: Addison-Wesley, Ch. 16.

Kerlinger, F. N. (1986). *Foundations of Behavior Research.* New York: Holt, Rinehart and Winston (3rd ed.).

Manneheim, Henry L. (1977). *Sociological Research; Philosophy and Methods.* Homewood, Illinois: Dorsey Press.

Merriam, Sharan. (1988). *Case Study Research in Education: A Qualitative Approach.* San Francisco: Jossey-Bass Publishers.

Patton, Michael Q. (1980). *Qualitative Evaluation Methods.* Beverly Hills: Sage Publications.

Selltiz, Claire, et al. (1959). *Research Methods in Social Relations.* New York: Holt, Rinehart and Winston.

Selltiz, Claire, et al. (1976). *Research Methods in Social Relations.* New York: Holt, Rinehart and Winston.

Sommer, R. and Sommer, B. (1986). *A Practical Guide to Behavioral Research.* (2nd ed.). New York: Oxford University Press.

Stauss, A. L. (1987). *Qualitative Analysis for Social Scientists.* Cambridge University Press.

Taylor, Steven J. and Bogdan, Robert. (1984). *Introduction to Qualitative Research Methods: The Search for Meaning.* 2nd ed. New York: John Wiley and Sons.

Webb, Eugene T., et al. (1981). *Nonreactive Measures in the Social Sciences.* Boston: Houghton-Mifflin.

Webb, Eugene J. et al. (1966). *Unobtrusive Measures: Nonreactive Research in the Social Sciences.* Chicago: Rand McNally.

Wiersma, W. (1986). *Research Methods in Education.* Boston: UC (4th ed.).

CHAPTER 9

REPORTING AND
DISSEMINATING RESEARCH

Most people think of the research process as a matter of designing a study, collecting and analyzing data, and interpreting the results. But the process is incomplete without the very important final step of *reporting* the results. Unfortunately, much good research goes unnoticed because many investigators underestimate the time and discipline it takes to report their findings. Transforming the information and insights gleaned from any array of notebooks, audio tapes, or computer printouts into a written format that others can understand often becomes an insurmountable task. However, if the research is going to contribute to the knowledge base of a field or enhance practice in some way, this important step cannot be avoided. Report writing can be made easier. The researcher needs to become familiar with the traditional format for reporting social science research.

A research report describes what problem was studied, how it was studied, what the findings were, and what those findings mean. It does not attempt to persuade the reader to think in a certain way nor does it try to be entertaining. That is not to say that it is inherently dull or boring. Information can be imparted through an interesting and readable style.

Style and to some extent the structure of the report depend upon the intended audience. The same study might be written for the general public, for practitioners who are in a position to apply the results, for policy makers, for the funding source, or for professionals in the same field of study. Once the audience has been identified "two broad questions should be considered in planning the report: (1) *what* does this audience want or need to know about the study? and (2) *how* can this information best be presented?" (Selltiz et al., 1976, p. 501) Practitioners or the general public, for example, do not need to know why a particular statistical analysis was chosen, whereas for other researchers such a piece of information would be crucial to evaluating or replicating the work.

The purpose of a research report is to communicate information to the reader. This purpose, combined with constraints on length imposed by journals and other publication outlets, demands that the report be written simply, clearly, and impersonally. The report must also be factual and accurate. Agnew and Pyke (1978) point out that while

> the need for flowery descriptions is reduced; (sic) it is compensated for, to some extent, by the demands of caution. Rarely can researchers make a definitive statement in unequivocal terms about the implications of their findings. The world is filled with reasonable alternative explanations for the same set of data, and even with the admonition to be brief, some of those alternatives must be presented for the reader's consideration. (p. 171)

Unlike creative writing, which accommodates impressionistic or idiosyncratic style and structure, the research report is logical and systematic. The structure usually reflects the order of steps taken in the original investigation. There is, in fact, a standard format for research reporting in the social sciences, which can be adjusted to accommodate various audiences and different types of research. Familiarity with the format will better enable researchers to organize their data for dissemination.

Standard Format for a Research Report

A standard format for reporting research has evolved from the logical progression of steps in an actual investigation. The inherent logic of this format has resulted in its repeated use, which in turn has led to its being *required* by journals and other publication outlets. While no doubt some researchers feel constrained by the format and not all types of research can be made to fit, there are several advantages. First, the format offers the writer a ready-made outline for writing the research findings; no time is wasted devising an outline for each piece of research. Second, readers can easily extract desired information from any number of studies because the same type of information is found in approximately the same location in every report. Third, a uniform format allows for easier and faster distribution of work and supervision of those assisting in writing the results of a large-scale investigation. Overall, the standard format is flexible enough for writers to delete sections that are not needed and to add or change items that will contribute to the report's clarity.

The underlying structure of the standard research report can be divided into halves, and each half can be further divided into several sections (Fox, 1969). The first half represents "the thinking and action that occurred before the point at which the data were collected," and the second half reports "what happened after the data were collected" (p. 722). Fox (1969) more fully describes this basic dichotomy as follows:

> Before we report *any* of the data relevant to the hypotheses tested or questions studied, we must present all of the material on our thinking about the problem which structured the study, about the literature, about how we actually did the study, and any descriptive data about the people who comprised our sample. All of this must be out of the way so that the section reporting the data themselves can be free of this pre-data-collection information. (p. 722).

The first or "pre-results" half can be subdivided into the introduction of the research problem, the review of the literature, and data collection procedures. The second half of the report can be broken into three sections covering the results of the study, interpretation of the results, and conclusions and suggestions for further study. The structure of the report can be visualized in Figure 9. 1.

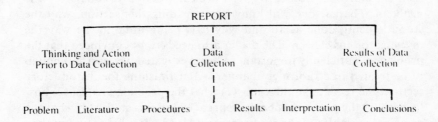

Figure 9.1. Structure of a research report

This subdividing, then, reveals the six sections that form the body of a research report; typically, a report also includes some standard introductory and closing material as well. A brief description of the various parts of a research report follows.

Introductory Materials—Depending upon the audience for whom the report is being written and the length of the report, preliminary materials might include a title page, preface and acknowledgments, table of contents, and a list of tables and/or figures. In most cases an abstract of the study is offered on a page prior to the report itself. Abstracts are brief summaries of the study presenting a statement of the problem, the procedures used to study the problem, and the results of the study. The purpose of an abstract is to help readers decide whether to read the report, to assist other researchers who scan great amounts of literature for information pertinent to their own work, or to provide a framework or advance organizer to someone intending to read the full report. Abstracts for journal articles rarely exceed 200 words; in longer, self-contained publications, such as a monograph or in-house report, abstracts may be one to two pages in length.

Presentation of the Research Problem—This section of the report tells the reader the purpose of the research, the nature and scope of the problem under study, and the need for the study. It is also important to discuss the theoretical framework from which the problem was derived or has emerged. This discussion helps to anchor the study in a larger context and usually reveals the significance of the particular aspect under study. It should also be clear from the introductory section what variables are being isolated for study and how these variables logically and reasonably relate to concepts and the problem area already identified. In short, the reader is given a clearly stated rationale for the problem. That is, one will know after reading this section, why the study is being done at all and why it is being done in the way the investigator has chosen. The reader also needs to be convinced that the problem is sufficiently important to be investigated, yet narrow enough to be treated in a thorough manner. After finishing the introductory section, the reader should know (1) what the problem area is; (2) how (generally) the problem is being approached in this study; (3) what the principal variables of the study are; and (4) why it is being undertaken at all.

The Literature Review—The several functions of the literature review have been discussed in detail in Chapter 3. Briefly, the literature review acquaints the reader with the history of the problem under consideration, establishes the fact that existing findings do not answer the questions related to the problem, and helps establish a conceptual framework for the immediate study. While the literature review usually comes after the introduction of the problem, in some highly theoretical or philosophical studies it may make more sense to reverse the two sections. In this way, the literature review leads to the conceptualization of the problem rather than to supporting a problem already formulated. In grounded theory studies, the literature can be integrated with the emerging theory rather than set off by itself (Glaser, 1978).

Research Procedures or Methodology—The purpose of this section is to tell the reader how the study was done. As has been discussed in Chapters 4 through 7, each methodology -- whether it is an experimental design or a historical inquiry or a trend analysis -- has systematic procedures for collecting and handling data. It is these procedures and how they have been used to solve the research problem that are detailed in this section. For example, a research problem dealing with predicting the number of trained personnel needed to work with the elderly in the year 2000 would require an explanation of trend analysis techniques. Likewise, a research question about how adult nonreaders cope in our society would require an explanation of a field-based methodology such as grounded theory or case study.

In general, this section of the research report presents a detailed explanation of the techniques and tools used to deal with the research problem such that another researcher could replicate the study. Regardless of the methodology, it is important to present the following information: the type of data used and reasons for its use; the way in which the data were selected; how the data were analyzed after being collected; and precautions the investigator has taken to ensure that the data and its analysis will justify inferences drawn from them.

Depending upon the type of study, methodology may include the following items:

1. Definition of Terms. While a conceptual discussion of terms is sometimes offered in the introduction section, a functional definition -- how the researcher is defining terms for this particular study -- usually evolves from the literature review and so is found in this section of the report.
2. Research Design. In general, the type of design used and a rationale for its selection are included here. Hypotheses or research questions used to guide the investigation follow the design discussion, if appropriate.
3. Sample Selection. A detailed description of the nature of the sample and how it was selected is included. This "sample" may be people, inanimate objects, events, etc.

4. Data Collection Procedures. A discussion of how the data were obtained may also include a discussion of a pilot study. All types of studies, including historical and philosophical, look at data. A discussion of how they were accumulated for analysis is thus an important section regardless of methodology.
5. Data Analysis. This part discusses how the data were processed in order to answer the questions raised by the study.
6. Assumptions and Limitations. The writer should make it clear what is being assumed and what the limits or weaknesses are of the particular methodology being used, with particular reference to how it is being applied to the problem under investigation.

Findings or Results—This section describes what the researcher has found as a result of the investigation. Findings may be presented in narrative form, in tables, graphs, charts, pictures, numbers, or formulas. In general, factual data are kept separate from inferences and interpretation, which usually, but not always, follow presentation of the actual findings. In historical, philosophical, case study, ethnographic, grounded theory, or interactive studies, interpretation may be interwoven with the factual results. If this is the case, it should be clear to the reader what is a finding and what is an interpretation of the finding. For example, to say that "17 percent of those interviewed were married" is a finding. To say that "only 17 percent of those interviewed were married" indicates surprise on the part of the investigator. Inherent in saying "only" is a value judgment that may be linked to interpretation as in "only 17 percent of those interviewed were married, which may explain why. . . ."

Discussion and Interpretation of Results—If not already integrated with the reported findings, the discussion and interpretation section allows the researchers to explain why the study produced the results that it did.

> The discussion is a much freer section than the results. Where the results are data-*bound*, the discussion is only data-*based*. This means that in the discussion the researcher is free to take off from the data and discuss what he believes they mean and how he believes they came about. Notice, however, that while the researcher has considerably more freedom in the discussion section, it is nevertheless based on the data. (Fox, 1969, p. 742)

In the discussion section, findings are tied back to the theory and rationale presented for the study in the first chapter. Insights gleaned from the literature review may also be referred to in interpreting the results of the study.

Summary, Conclusions, Recommendations—The entire study should be briefly summarized at the beginning of this section. Generalizations or conclusions safely supported by the study might also be presented here for the first time or succinctly summarized from the discussion section. Finally, the investigator may want to include recommendations for implementing the findings or suggestions for further research. Suggestions for further research can be particularly helpful to other researchers in that the investigator of the present study has learned much about the problem including what procedures or techniques were helpful or problematic, whether the question itself needs to be refocused, and what related questions might be worth pursuing.

References and Appendix—A list of the references used in the literature review and elsewhere in the report follows the body of the work. The style and arrangement of the reference section should reflect the audience for whom the report was written. A report for the general public will have few if any references, whereas a scholarly journal article will have a complete and accurate documentation of all references. The same is true for material in an appendix. Depending upon the audience, such material might include tests or survey forms, personal communications, charts or graphs in addition to those found in the results section, raw data such as transcribed interviews, or historical documents.

Reporting one's research findings is made easier by becoming familiar with the standard format. Other areas of importance to the research writer are: editorial style and documentations, writing and revising guidelines, tables and figures, and the use of statistics.

Editorial Style and Documentation

Editorial style refers to the mechanical details of putting together a research report. How one does footnotes, references, spacing of lines and paragraphs, headings, placement of tables and figures, and other mechanical aspects of a report depends upon the style used. There are many editorial styles, each providing "roughly the same information, which is sufficient to allow the reader to check the original sources of quotations, opinions, and facts used in the paper: the name of the author, the title of the publication, and facts about the publication --place of publication, publisher, date, pages" (Maimon et al., 1981, p. 110). Four of the more commonly used editorial styles are:

1. *Publication Manual* -- American Psychological Association-(APA). 3rd ed. Washington, D.C.: American Psychological Association, 1983. This style is used by over 200 journals in the social sciences and education.
2. *MLA Handbook for Writers of Research Papers, Theses, and Dissertations* -- Modern Language Association of America (MLA). Student ed. New York: Modern Language Association, 1980.
3. *A Manual for Writers of Term papers, Theses, and Dissertations* -- Kate L. Turabian. 4th ed. Chicago: University of Chicago Press, 1973.
4. *The Chicago Manual of Style* -- University of Chicago Press. 13th ed. Chicago: University of Chicago Press, 1982.

What and when to footnote is sometimes a problem for writers, especially with the recent confusion over copyright laws. The copyright law protects the author's rights to his or her own work, whether it is published or not. The copyright holder is the only one with authority or the right to sell, distribute, revise, or publish the work covered by copyright. The author of a published work, however, usually assigns the rights to the publisher who then becomes the author's agent for any further rights, sales, or permissions to reprint. When quoting a long passage from a copyrighted work, or a complete unit such as a graph or table, poem, or short story, permission must be obtained from the copyright holder. "Fair use" of copyrighted material means that others may use short, incomplete sections of a copyrighted work -- with acknowledgment -- in order to support a point in their writing. "Short" has come to be defined as a selection of 150 words or less.

In a recent book on writing in the arts and sciences, Maimon et al. (1981, pp. 107-109) outline four types of material that must be documented:

1. Direct quotations -- used when the way someone else said something cannot be improved upon, or when the authority of the person is important and a quotation from that person will add weight to your argument;
2. "Other people's judgments, ideas, opinions, and inferences, even if you rephrase their material" (p. 107) -- if other people's ideas have had an impact upon your own thinking, or if you link your ideas or support your ideas with someone else's but don't use their exact words, you still need to acknowledge the source;

3. "Facts that other people have discovered and that are not generally known by the reading public" (p. 107) -- facts about a topic that are common knowledge (they reappear in most of your sources) do not have to be documented; however, if you uncover what appears to be a new piece of information, the author of the information should be referenced. For example, it has become common knowledge that most adults continue learning into very old age. The fact that 90 percent of adults conduct at least one independent learning project a year, though, discovered by Allen Tough (1976), is not common knowledge and should be documented appropriately.

4. "Experiments performed by other people" (p. 109) -- previous research studies referred to in your own research report should be documented so that others might refer to them if they desire.

Writing and Revising—Some Guidelines

For most people, writing a report is a tedious undertaking. There is nothing worse than facing a blank page and not being able to fill it with coherent sentences and paragraphs. Those who do quite a bit of writing have found ways of facilitating the process. Most shortcuts arise out of an individual's own special working pattern. To develop shortcuts, you need to first establish a pattern of writing that feels comfortable. Getting started may be the most difficult part, but there is no rule that says you have to start at the beginning of a report. In fact, an introduction is one of the hardest things to write. It might be easier to begin with the procedures section of the study. What you did and how you did it is concrete enough to help you get started. Once started, proceed to the next easiest part of the report. Mullins (1980) calls this approach the "block" method. It is something of a compromise between the "beginning to end" and the "bits and pieces" method.

In the "beginning to end" method, an outline is generally followed. In a research report, you would begin with the introduction of the problem and proceed to the literature review. The "bits and pieces" approach, on the other hand, is for those who "dislike any kind of formally organized procedure" (Mullins, 1980, p. 142). You begin with what you feel like writing at the moment and proceed by bits and pieces. This method is more time consuming than the others, but it is better than being "stuck" in an outline or not writing at all.

Other suggestions that might be useful to establishing your own writing pattern include the following:

- Determine in what type of environment you are most productive.
- Determine the time of day when you write best; is it early morning, late at night, midday?
- Expect that there will be times when conditions are perfect but you still cannot write; do something else and try again later.
- "Talk" your way through. Describe to yourself or to others what you intend to write; this almost always helps to clarify what you will write next and may cause you to realize that more reading or thinking needs to be done.
- Before stopping for a day, list what you intend to do during the next writing session; this should reduce the time needed to get started again.
- Set aside what you have written to be reread after some time has lapsed.
- Don't let yourself get bogged down in the technical aspects of writing such as spelling and grammar; these can be corrected later.

Once a draft of the report has been completed, you are ready to revise. "To revise means literally 'to see again.' The key task during the revision process is to see your paper as others will see it" (Maimon et al., 1981, p. 14). Most writers consciously or unconsciously assume too much on the part of the reader. Readers are usually not that familiar with the topic, and they have not read the vast amount of material that the author has. Thus, readers are not capable of moving from point to point and of seeing how points connect in the way that the writer can. Readers "need to be reminded frequently of what you are talking about. If you want them to connect two ideas, you have to do the work of forming the connection" (Maimon et al., 1981, p. 15). Neither can the writer become bogged down in unnecessary details -- readers "want to know your point in writing, and they want to know this point as efficiently as possible. They do not want to wade through a chronological account of your research process" (Maimon et al., 1981, p. 15).

The best way to determine if your report is clear and readable is to have several other people read it. This

will help you see quite clearly the differences between writer-based and reader-based prose. You will find that there is frequently a subtle battle going on between a writer and a reader, with each one trying to expend the lesser amount of energy. When you have a stake in getting your information or ideas across, you are entering a buyer's market, and you should learn all that you can about accommodating the needs of your buyers, your readers. (Maimon et al., 1981, p. 14)

Readers who have to expend energy trying to understand what you have written will have no energy left to make use of your findings or may just give up reading your report altogether. The task in revising is to see that all obstacles that hinder the transmission of information from writer to reader are removed. Steps in the revision process might include: (1) checking the overall organization of your report by making an outline from your draft; (2) "interviewing" each paragraph by asking " 'What is the point of this paragraph?' " (Maimon et al., 1981, p. 15); (3) cutting out repetitive sections and unnecessary words; (4) smoothing out clumsy sentence structures; and (5) checking for spelling, grammar, and typographical errors.

Occasionally it is necessary to shorten the report to satisfy certain journal requirements or to have an abbreviated form of the report available for newsletters or in-house publications. It is easier to pull together a shortened version of a longer draft than to create a shortened version from nothing. Once you have drafted a report, it can be cut in several places. The literature review may be eliminated and the crucial points summarized with reference to the supporting literature. The bare skeleton of the theoretical framework needs to be preserved, but a detailed discussion can be eliminated. Sample questions from data collection instruments can be given instead of inserting the entire instrument. Finally, findings can be stated without supporting tables or charts, or certain findings can be highlighted and separated articles written for other findings (Selltiz et al., 1976).

Thus, while there is no magic formula for writing and revising a research report, the task can be made easier by establishing a pattern for your writing, by continually striving for clarity and precision, and by writing for the reader, not yourself. In a humorous book on how to start and finish your thesis, book, or article, Becker (1986, p. 43) underscores these points by noting that people make the job of writing "harder than it need be when they think that there is only One Right Way to do it, that each paper they write has a preordained structure they must find. They simplify their work, on the other hand, when they recognize that there are many effective ways to say something and that their job is only to choose one and execute it so that readers will know what they are doing."

Tables and Figures

Visual presentations can be dramatic and revealing in explaining important information to the reader. But care in the construction of tables and figures is necessary if they are to enhance and not confound the report of research findings.

Tables are used to display quantitative data in some logical pattern. The pattern of organization -- chronological, alphabetical, numerical, or qualitative -- must be readily apparent to the reader. The table should be understandable by itself without accompanying text. This is not to say that tables can supplant text; rather, tables offer detail that would be tedious to put into the text. Tables are never totally independent of text. Fox (1969) discusses the responsibility of the reader and the writer with regard to tables:

> This perception of the table as supplementary and yet independent means that in preparing the research report the researcher can place some responsibility for the full understanding of the data upon the reader. But he cannot place all of it there. That is, he cannot go to the extreme of presenting a table with no comment other than an introductory sentence. . . .If we have nothing to say about the table, the chances are excellent that there is no reason to include the table in the report. . . .Obviously then the researcher's problem is to hit the appropriate middle way in which he reports, in the text, the highlights of the data in the table. (p. 739)

Some general guidelines might prove helpful to those interested in constructing tables. To begin with, the "well-constructed table, like a well-written paragraph, consists of several related facts that are integrated to present *one main idea*" (Van Dalen, 1966, p. 428). A very complex table showing numerous relationships or interactions needing many pages of explanation is self-defeating. The major focus of the table should be easily grasped by the reader. To test whether one's table is clear, ask someone unfamiliar with the study to take any item or number in the table and explain what it means (Fox, 1969). This will also check whether the horizontal and vertical axes have been clearly labeled.

Labeling is important. The title itself should contain four bits of information: "(1) the variable or variables for which data are being presented; (2) the groups on whom the data were collected; (3) the subgroups within the table; and (4) the nature of the statistic included within the table" (Fox, 1969, p. 720). For example, in a hypothetical table titled "Percent of Adult Men and Women Enrolled in Six Different Degree Programs at County Community College," enrollment is the variable for which data are being presented, adults is the group on whom the data were collected, men and women are subgroups, and percent is the statistic. In addition to a precise title, column headings and row labels should be accurate and as brief as possible.

Mechanically, there are several conventions for including tables in a research report. Some of the more common practices include the following:

- The table is placed immediately after it is first referred to in the text, or on the next page.
- Tables should be no larger than the page size of the text. Larger tables can be reduced or placed in the appendix.
- Capitalization and punctuation should follow a consistent format.
- Rulings or lines should be used sparingly and only toenhance readability.

As an alternative to presenting data in tables, many types of figures can be used. Figures include charts and graphs, diagrams, blueprints, maps, and photographs. Each of these categories can be subdivided; for example, there are pie charts, flow charts, organizational charts, line graphs, histograms, and bar graphs. Selecting the best type of figure to present data depends upon the type of data. In ethnographic research, for example, photographs are often used to convey culturally based results; in case studies, organizational charts are commonly used.

Figures are visual presentations and typically contain a minimum of numbers and words. A figure "is used only if it snaps important ideas or significant relationships into sharp focus for the reader more quickly than other means of presentation" (Van Dalen, 1966, p. 431). Figure 9.2 is an example of a bar graph that dramatically displays the rise in life expectancy since 1900.

The point being made by the graph -- that life expectancy has been substantially increasing since 1900 -- is more easily grasped by this visual presentation than by offering the same explanation in words. It is also clearer than the table of vital statistics from which the data were derived.

Appropriate use of figures can do much to add interest to a research report. Several cautions about using figures are worth mentioning.

- Keep the figure simple, including only that information that is necessary to understanding the presentation. Too much information will clutter the figure; a complex figure can be divided into two simple ones.
- Fewer figures representing important ideas will draw attention to those ideas; keep the number of figures to a minimum.
- Integrate the figure with references to it in the text, keeping the figure as close to its discussion as possible.

Average Life Expectancy

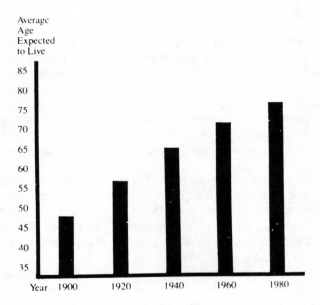

Figure 9.2. A sample bar graph

In summary, by constructing tables and figures that are easy to read and interpret, you may enable the readers to understand the study results more easily and forcefully than they would by reading only the text itself. Tables and figures accompanied by brief explanations give the reader a double opportunity to understand what information the writer is trying to convey.

Reporting Statistics

Statistics are typically used in tables and figures to summarize and explain data economically. A statistic is a piece of data (fact, event, characteristic) converted to a numerical unit that permits uniform comparison of data. There are two types of statistics -- descriptive and inferential. *Descriptive statistics* allow the researcher to summarize information or make simple comparisons of data. A descriptive statistic can summarize the distribution of a group of data, indicate the degree to which a particular score deviates from the average, or describe the degree to which one event or characteristic is related to other events or characteristics. *Inferential statistics* are used to test hypotheses as well as to estimate the parameters of the population used in the study. An inferential statistic is a more powerful statistic than a descriptive statistic. The researcher can say more about the individual data from which the statistic is derived, as well as speak to characteristics of the total population that the statistic represents. Inferential studies "have the purpose of drawing implications from data to some setting, subjects, or material other than those that were directly involved in the completed study" (Drew, 1980, p. 266).

In using either descriptive or inferential statistics to report findings, researchers should take care that their statistical presentation enlightens rather than confuses the reader. Nearly everyone at one time or another has had the frustrating experience of being unable to interpret a table or graph or statistical procedure in a research report. And nearly everyone can remember the satisfaction and feeling of power when the meaning of those numbers was finally revealed. These contrasting feelings represent, at least in part, the weaknesses and strengths of using statistics to transform raw data into meaningful concepts that are embedded in research findings. On one hand, we can be confused, misled, and possibly turned off by the foreign language of numbers. On the other hand, being able to comprehend relationships between several variables by glancing at a single page in a report is compelling. It gives us the feeling of being in command -- a "master" of the data.

Using statistics to enlighten rather than confuse a reader means avoiding some common problems in the reporting of statistics. The following are four errors to be avoided:

1. *Use of descriptive statistics to infer beyond the present study.* Misuse of descriptive statistics is the result of not understanding

the assumptions of inferential and descriptive procedures. It is a temptation, for example, to assume that two groups are significantly different if the means of the two groups appear to be very different. Without the test of an inferential statistic to see if the difference is significant, what *appears* to be a real difference could have happened by chance. Statistical significance cannot be assumed simply on the basis of descriptive analysis.

2. *Lack of consistency of selection in displaying statistical data.* It is helpful to the reader of research reports to have statistical tables or figures presented in a consistent pattern. Also, it should not be assumed that all statistical data generated in conducting a study must go into the final report. Only selected, essential data should be included if statistics are to make reporting more clear and concise as intended. Much may be deduced from a few carefully chosen and consistently displayed sets of statistics.

3. *Improper placement of statistics.* In a discussion of findings, statistical procedures should be subordinate to the findings themselves, even to the point of putting certain statistics in parentheses at the end. For example, it is much clearer to say "the responses of the trained managers were correct significantly more often than the responses of those who had no training (p = .05)," than to write "the chi-square tests of differences between samples were calculated determining at the .05 level of significance that the trained managers' responses differed from those that had received no training." Highlight the findings by subordinating the statistics.

4. *Overuse of statistics.* Just because statistics are produced by and are available to the researcher does not mean that they have to be reported. An important contribution of statistics is helping the researcher better grasp meaning from raw data. Meaning is not the statement of a statistic, but what is inferred from the statistic. Therefore, a discussion may be more effective in conveying meaning than simply supplying numbers. Readers of research need assistance in understanding the essence of what has been discovered. This is particularly true in exploratory studies. For example, if a study is intended to develop theory about the concept of competency, well-documented lists of competencies from practitioners may be useful data to gather and include. But a discussion of findings, rather than a quantitative summary, is likely to be more helpful to the reader who is trying to understand the concept.

In summary, statistics, well chosen and properly handled, can bring clarity and understanding to the findings of a research study. They should not take the place of a verbal discussion of a study's results; rather, they should be used in support of the findings.

Disseminating Research

The decisions an investigator makes when writing the research report depend upon (1) the audience for whom the report is intended, and (2) the purpose of disseminating research results. While many researchers are content to add to the stock of knowledge in a field, others are also concerned with the implementation of their findings into practice. Since this text is intended for those in the applied fields of adult education and training, the issue becomes one of how best to disseminate findings to maximize their chance of being applied to practice. Answering this question involves taking into account the issue -- whether real or imagined -- of the gap between research and practice in an applied field of study.

Practitioners stereotype researchers as ivory-tower residents who investigate questions no one needs to answer. Researchers, on the other hand, characterize practitioners as naive about research and too tied to everyday concerns to see the larger questions. Such attitudes thwart advancements that could be effected through the close cooperation of researchers and practitioners in applied areas. Fortunately, efforts are being made in many fields to bring researchers and practitioners together on common problems. One method is to involve the subjects of research in all aspects of the investigation from the conceptualization of the problem, to collecting and analyzing data, to disseminating the findings. This particular approach is discussed in detail in Chapter 7 under "interactive research." Interactive research includes what has commonly been called action research and participatory research.

A second avenue for bringing practitioners and researchers closer together has been through graduate programs in which both groups become more sophisticated in doing and appreciating research. Practitioners working in master's degree programs usually complete a research component as part of their studies. And those who intend to be researchers and scholars receive advanced training in investigating the complex problems in the world of practice.

A third mechanism by which researchers and practitioners have become more aware of one another has been through structured activities, such as conferences, where researchers stress the practical implications of their work. Some large organizations have also created liaison positions or offices where research is collected and interpreted to appropriate audiences. Such a person or office is likely to be found in the research and development section of large corporations, government agencies, private foundations, and universities.

Undoubtedly there are other ways social science researchers and practitioners are working together to address the problems encountered in a society as complex as ours. The apparent lag in the adoption of new practices may also have less to do with the so-called "gap" between research and practice, and more to do with the cautious assessment of new discoveries or human nature's natural resistence to change:

> There are built-in aversive properties of any new findings. Any new idea or new practice, almost by definition, implies that the old idea was wrong and that the practitioner's current methods are ineffective or at least inadequate. . . .In addition to being told one is wrong, anyone who accepts new findings and their implications for practice faces the arduous task of unlearning old ways of responding and of acquiring a newly organized repertory of behaviors. (Helmstadter, 1970, p. 402)

Thus the "why" of disseminating research in applied fields of study is to improve practice. This is not to suggest contributing to knowledge alone in one's field is not a worthwhile goal. But it is only through dissemination that knowledge is accumulated and practice has a chance of being improved.

How to Disseminate Findings

There are many ways to transmit research results to relevant audiences. Three of the more common ways are journal articles and books, sponsored publications, and conferences.

Most researchers strive to publish their research in refereed journals. Depending upon the journal, this can be the most prestigious and the most difficult method. *Refereed* means that the report is sent to editorial consultants who critique the article and determine whether it is appropriate for publication. The review is usually done blindly; that is, neither author nor reviewer knows the identity of the other. Many people assume, erroneously, that only recognized authorities in a field are allowed to publish in major journals. While an important person might be invited to write an article on occasion, most journals consider all submissions regardless of who the author is. Other criteria -- such as the appropriateness of the content, the significance of the problem, and the clarity of presentation -- determine the acceptability of the manuscript.

Prior to submitting an article for publication, the researcher should determine which journal most closely matches the article's content area. A copy of the journal should then be studied for style, format, and procedures for submission (usually found on the inside cover). Most journals follow the standard format for reporting research. If one is not sure which journal would be appropriate, there are guidebooks available that detail such information. *The Directory of Publishing Opportunities in Journals and Periodicals* (1981), for example, has catalogued 3,900 journals in the humanities and social sciences. Each entry contains the following information: name of editor and address, when it was first published, how often it comes out and the annual subscription rate, circulation, an editorial description listing the subject matter and audience for whom the journal is intended, and complete information for the submission of manuscripts. In addition to comprehensive directories, each discipline has its own directory of periodicals. The *Guide to Periodicals in Education and Its Academic Disciplines* (1975) lists 602 education-related periodicals in the United States with the same information as above.

Typically, research results are not disseminated in book form unless the research was a large-scale undertaking with significant results appealing to a wide audience. Often these books are produced by presses associated with the university or organization where the study was done. Occasionally a commercial press will publish research results that have wide appeal (Sheehy's book *Passages: The Predictable Crises of Adult Life*, 1976, for example). The individual researcher might consider publishing results in a monograph form if the study is too big for a journal article and too small for a book. Monographs are similar to books, but smaller and more focused. Some academic presses, private agencies, and foundations publish monographs. As with journal articles, there are directories of publishers that give the necessary information on how to submit a manuscript.

A second major means of disseminating research is through publications sponsored by organizations that have some interest in the research problem. Such groups might include professional associations, foundations, social service agencies, and community organizations. Perhaps such a body has contributed to the funding of the project or collaborated by providing other forms of support such as personnel or computer time. The organization may want to disseminate the study's results through a newsletter, monograph, an in-house journal, audio-visual tape, or oral presentation. Such research is likely to be action oriented with highly practical applications for the sponsoring agency or institution. Professional journals (already discussed) and conferences offer avenues for the researcher who desires to disseminate findings beyond the collaborating and related agencies.

Conferences are sponsored by professional organizations, institutions, and agencies. They can be designed for anyone interested in the topic, for certain professional groups such as nurses or trainers, for employees of certain agencies and so on. Any conference is potentially a forum for disseminating research results. There are, however, conferences that have as their sole purpose the presenting of research. Information about conferences and procedures for submitting research proposals can be found by consulting recent journals and newsletters in the field appropriate to your topic. If a proposal is accepted for presentation, it is common practice to prepare a paper to be distributed at the conference. Such papers usually follow the traditional format for reporting research. The oral presentation itself is less formal than a journal article and may be a report of research in progress rather than completed work. Conference presentations often result in the formation of networks of people interested in the same problem area. Such networks facilitate the accumulation of knowledge in a field and result in greater dissemination of recent research findings.

Conferences, sponsored publications, and refereed journal articles are three common means of disseminating one's research findings. The method chosen depends upon the audience one is trying to reach and to some extent the type of research that has been conducted. In any case, reporting and disseminating is a crucial part of the research process and demands a commitment on the part of the researcher from the very outset of the project. Not to make this effort deprives the field of a potential contribution and brings into question the importance of the undertaking in the first place.

REFERENCES

Agnew, Neil and Sandra Pyke. 1978. *The Science Game*. Englewood Cliffs, New Jersey: Prentice-Hall, Inc.

Becker, Howard S. 1986. *Writing for Social Scientists*. Chicago: The University of Chicago Press.

Camp, William and Bryan L. Schwark. 1975. *Guide to Periodicals in Education and Its Academic Disciplines*. Metuchen, New Jersey: The Scarecrow Press, Inc.

Drew, Clifford J. 1980. *Introduction to Designing and Conducting Research*. St. Louis: The C. V. Mosby Company.

Fox, David J. 1969. *The Research Process in Education*. New York: Holt, Rinehart and Winston, Inc.

Glaser, Barney G. 1978. *Theoretical Sensitivity*. Mill Valley, California: The Sociology Press.

Helmstadter, G. C. 1970. *Research Concepts in Human Behavior*. New York: Appleton-Century-Crofts, Inc.

Maimon, Elaine P. et al. 1981. *Writing in the Arts and Sciences*. Cambridge, Massachusetts: Winthrop Publishers, Inc.

Marquis Academic Media. 1981. *Directory of Publishing Opportunities in Journals and Periodicals*. (5th ed.) Chicago: Marquis Academic Media.

Mullins, Caroloy J. 1980. *The Complete Writing Guide*. Englewood Cliffs, New Jersey: Prentice-Hall, Inc.

Selltiz, Claire, et al. (1976). *Research Methods in Social Relations*. 3rd Ed. New York: Holt, Rinehart and Winston.

Sheehy, Gail. 1976. *Passages: The Predictable Crises of Adult Life*. New York: E. P. Dutton and Company.

Tough, Allen. 1971. *The Adult's Learning Projects*. Toronto: Ontario Institute for Studies in Education.

Van Dalen, Deobold B. 1966. *Understanding Educational Research*. New York: McGraw-Hill Book Company.

CHAPTER 10

GRADUATE RESEARCH

Professionals in applied fields are typically more concerned with the daily tasks of administration, planning, teaching, or counseling than with doing research. While a few practitioners and some professors engage in research, much more is conducted by students pursuing graduate degrees. And even though graduate research is primarily a learning experience for those involved, it is one way in which significant contributions to the theory and practice of a field can be made. Students, after all, especially those supported by assistantships or grants, have time to devote to their research. Also, students who are practicing professionals or those on temporary leave from their jobs are in positions both to detect important problems that need investigating, and to access sources of data to deal with those problems. Finally, graduate students do not work in a vacuum: they are guided by experienced researchers whose job it is to ensure that a study is well conceptualized and well planned. Rarely do professionals who want to do research have such support once their formal academic preparation is complete.

In an undergraduate program a student is introduced to and acquires the basic knowledge of a field; at the graduate level more is learned about a particular field, and a student is introduced to the methods by which knowledge is tested. Graduate programs in such fields as engineering, education, business, and nursing have the additional goal of preparing people to make an impact upon the practice of their specific vocation. The standard requirements of graduate programs have been adjusted by most institutions to fit this applied emphasis. Course work often includes internships (work experience in the field); computer or statistics courses may take the place of the more traditional foreign language requirement; and research projects tend to evolve from practice.

All doctoral programs and some master's programs require students to conduct research as part of their graduate preparation. The difference between research at the master's level and research at the doctoral level is one of degree. Theoretically, doctoral research involves a problem of greater magnitude, the significance and ramifications of which will have a potentially greater impact on the field:

> Because the problem is more complex, the candidate must draw upon a greater breadth of understanding in his field in solving it; and because he must demonstrate that he can perform independent research, he must exercise his own initiative and demonstrate professionalism to a greater extent than is expected in a MS project. (Davis, 1980, vi)

In practice, however, some master's research is as rigorous as that conducted at the doctoral level. Differentiating between the two is further obscured by the fact that the term "thesis," while usually applied to master's research, is sometimes used to refer to doctoral research. "Dissertation" is the more appropriate term for the latter. This chapter will focus upon doctoral-level graduate research with the realization that most of the information presented is equally applicable to master's level research. Specifically, this chapter will deal with the practical aspects of selecting a topic, forming a committee, writing a proposal, carrying out the research, and defending the research.

Selecting a Topic

Selecting a topic is the first step in the dissertation process. Many students find this a difficult task because so much is involved. To begin with, you have to be relatively certain that no one is investigating precisely the same problem. You must also be prepared to make a mental, emotional, and perhaps financial investment in the topic -- an investment that will take at least a year's time. Finally, all the members of your committee must agree that the topic is worth investigating.

Often students engage in practices that appear to speed up the selection of a topic, but actually hinder the process. Some students have an area of interest in mind and expect that a topic will present itself or be handed to them by someone else; however, no one should expect to focus on a topic without first reading widely in the problem area and reviewing all the previous research. Other students are hindered in topic selection because they first decide to use a particular instrument, methodology, population, or data set, and then try to find the problem. The problem should come first, followed by a selection of the best means of approaching it. Another block occurs when a student settles on a topic but fails to anchor it in a conceptual/theoretical framework and, as a result, finds it difficult to articulate the significance of doing the study.

There are ways a student can facilitate the selection of a topic. First, no later than halfway through course work, you should begin thinking about a problem area in terms of its potential for producing a suitable dissertation topic. Papers and presentations in courses can then be used to explore the topic, to learn what has and has not been done, and perhaps to test an idea on a small scale. Second, you should be attuned to the multitude of sources from which ideas can be generated, such as current journals, class work, dissertations, newspapers, conversations, media events, or research agendas. Keeping an ongoing list of tentative topics from various sources provides a starting point when the time comes to decide upon one topic.

Basically, a research problem is something you wonder about, something that puzzles or confuses. Determining more exactly what you are puzzled by, curious about, or confused about will help focus the study further. For example, wondering if something *works* leads to an experimental or evaluation study; needing to *understand* a process involves exploratory research such as case study; and asking about the *variance* of a phenomenon necessitates a descriptive approach.

Martin (1980, pp. 39-40) suggests that problems arise out of four circumstances:

1. Little or no research exists on a particular topic. How entry level people in applied fields become "professionalized" is an example where there is little data-based research.
2. "There is some research, but it has not been applied to enough samples or in enough situations to be considered a reliable phenomenon. . . the limits of the extent to which the phenomenon can be generalized are unknown" (p. 39). Much of the research on adult development has been done with male, middle-class samples. How the findings apply to other groups, such as women or lower-class males, is not known.
3. There might be a great amount of research, but the results of some studies are inconsistent with those from other studies. This is characteristic of the research on group versus self-directed learning.
4. There are two theories that explain the same phenomenon but that recommend or predict different outcomes of a common action. At one time, for example, the disengagement theory predicted the withdrawal of older people from social interaction after retirement; another theory predicted a changing pattern of interaction, but not withdrawal.

Whatever the source of the research topic, at least three criteria need to be applied to the final selection: the interest of the student in the problem, the feasibility of actually carrying out the study, and the significance of the problem itself. A person who is about to invest a year or more in a research endeavor should be vitally interested in the topic. In the long run, genuine interest is more motivating than the desire to finish and get the degree. Also, this interest may carry over into professional life after formal study is completed and perhaps lead to further work in the area. Feasibility is a consideration -- that is, is the population accessible? is there money for mailing? does the project demand extensive travel? how much must other people be depended upon? does the library have the necessary documents? and so on. It is not enough to be personally interested in a topic -- the study must also be manageable.

The third criterion, that of significance, is more complex than the other two, for there is some debate about what constitutes a significant research topic. Significance is related to the original purpose of research -- to contribute to knowledge. This raises the question of what constitutes a contribution to knowledge. According to Allen (1973),

> A contribution represents some advancement in the state of the art; a breakthrough in some theory; formulation of a new theory; refutation of an existing theory; addition to an existing theory; new insights into human, physical, or natural sciences; establishing of new relationships; or a creative accomplishment. (p. 2)

Many years before Allen, Almack (1930) dealt with this same question. For him, research was significant if it contributed to the fund of knowledge (by adding a new principle, law, or historical information), if it contributed to technique (by developing a new use of an old procedure, by developing a new instrument, or by refining an old one), if it contributed to both knowledge and technique, or if it made available to many what only a few had before (translating a book, for example) (p. 281).

In applied fields significance typically answers the question "How is getting an answer to this problem going to make some difference in the world?" The results of a significant study should have some implication for practice. To get thinking along these lines, the student might try to answer these questions: Who will benefit from the findings? In what way(s) will they benefit? Of what value is it to them to know the answer to this problem?

A helpful aid to students in the process of selecting a thesis or dissertation topic is the "Thesis/Dissertation Generator" shown in

Figure 10.1. Students can use it as a worksheet to bring their topic into focus.

The Thesis/Dissertation Generator

1. State in two sentences or fifty words a question, issue, activity, or situation that makes you curious, angry, or enthusiastic. (For example: "What is the process people go through who make career changes?" or "Why do so many adults drop out of Adult Basic Education programs?")

2. You have just written a problem statement. Now complete the following: "The purpose of the proposed study is to. . . ."

3. You have just written a purpose statement. Now explain in fifty words or less why you think the problem is worth solving.

4. Without being overly technical, state how you might go about solving the problem.

5. You have just developed a strategy for approaching the problem. What research methodology most nearly reflects your approach?

Figure 10.1. The thesis/dissertation generator

In summary, the selection of a dissertation topic need not be an overly anxious or time-consuming undertaking. The emphasis should be on delineating a topic that is both interesting and feasible and that contributes to either knowledge or practice in a field. Avoiding what appear to be shortcuts (selecting a methodology and then looking for a problem, for example) will also facilitate the selection of an appropriate topic.

Forming a Committee

A faculty person with some expertise and interest in the problem area you are pursuing will most likely become the director of your dissertation and chair of your committee. In addition to advising on specific matters concerning the preparation of your dissertation, this person may have previously helped you to focus in on your topic and will later guide you in developing and presenting a proposal to your committee.

Procedures and criteria for the composition of dissertation committees vary among universities. Usually the student works closely with the major advisor in selecting members of the committee. There are several criteria you can use in deciding whom to invite to serve on the committee. First, you should look for highly *qualified* persons:

> Successful and qualified people rarely have 'insecure egos' that need to be fed by putting others down. The 'tougher' your committee (meaning the more qualified) the 'easier' it will be. First, they are capable of recognizing an 'outstanding' proposal. On the other hand, they will have little patience with a poorly thought out proposal. If you have a good committee, they can make suggestions based on their own experience in doing research that can be very helpful to you. (Gardner and Beatty, 1980, p. 81)

Successful people are usually very busy people however, and so it is important to consider the *availability* of prospective committee members. A nationally recognized researcher may not be around enough to be of any real assistance.

In addition to being qualified and available, a prospective committee person should be *interested* in your topic. This is probably a more important consideration than the time availability criterion. "If a faculty member is truly interested in a particular topic, she/he will usually find the time to help a student investigate that topic" (Martin, 1980, p. 32).

Finally, there is the *personality* factor to consider in the selection of a committee. You should feel that you can work with each member of the committee *and* that the committee members can work with one another. In theory, committee members are professionals who can separate personal concerns from their academic pursuits. In practice some people cannot work with certain other people. Personality traits, biases, private agenda, and so on may interfere with getting the task accomplished. With most committees there is a strong tendency

> toward negotiation and compromise. This process breaks down when one committee member is clearly more expert in the topic area of the student's research than the chairperson and when the chairperson does not acknowledge this in making decisions. The

process can also break down in cases where two 'experts' with different approaches to a problem, e.g., persons having different theoretical orientations, are on the same committee. To avoid this problem, the student should choose as the committee chairperson the faculty member with the most interest and expertise in the area of the proposed research and ask for suggestions from this chairperson when selecting other members. (Martin, 1980, p. 33)

The extent of contact a student has with the advisor and committee during the dissertation process is determined by the working styles and wishes of those involved. In some cases, after the committee has accepted a proposal, students will work almost exclusively with their advisor until a draft of the dissertation is ready to present to the entire committee. Other committees may want to see each chapter as it is written, or certain members may want to review particular chapters during the process. The procedure is usually established at the time the committee approves the proposal.

How to work best with an advisor is an individual matter, but it is helpful if each person's expectations are communicated to the other. At the very least, students should remember that advisors are also teaching, doing research, and advising other students. Students can maximize advisement time by seeking their advisor's help only for the problems of their study ("nuts and bolts" type questions can be answered by a graduate school manual or by more experienced graduate students), and by summarizing the work they have accomplished to date at the beginning of each conference. Students, however, have the right to expect reasonable access to their advisor and a reasonable turnaround time on the work they submit for their advisor's review.

Presenting a Proposal

The dissertation proposal presents an overview of the research you are "proposing" to do. It should tell the reader what your specific problem is, how you intend to do the research, why it is significant, and how it is different from other research on the same topic. There are two major reasons why a proposal is a valuable component of the dissertation process. First, it forces you to structure the entire project. The proposal serves "as a 'road map' for your research, always letting you know where you have been and where you are going" (Allen, 1973,

p. 34). Second, it protects both the student and the committee. It is a type of contractual agreement in which the committee endorses the study as proposed, and the student agrees to carry out the investigation in the manner stipulated in the proposal.

The format of a proposal differs from one institution to another. You can learn the form expected at a particular school by referring to that school's doctoral handbook, by reviewing proposals that have been accepted there, or by consulting your advisor. In most cases, the proposal addresses, in abbreviated fashion, the same areas that will be treated in depth in the dissertation. Proposals can be divided into three sections that reflect the content of the first three chapters of the dissertation. Most proposals are at least twelve pages in length and most (in the experience of the authors of this text) average twenty pages. Figure 10.2 outlines the parts of a typical proposal. Of course not all the parts shown here are appropriate for all investigations.

The proposal may also include a time line that projects when different phases of the research will be conducted, a bibliography of literature to be reviewed in the Review of the Literature section, sample letters of introduction and/or permission, sample interview questions, data collection, and any supporting material that will be involved in the study.

Just as the format for a proposal is likely to differ among universities, so too is the system for getting a proposal approved. Committee members may approve a proposal on an individual basis with the chair signing a form or the proposal itself. Some universities require that the proposal be defended before the committee as a whole. In this case a formal committee meeting is held, at which time the student presents a brief synopsis of the proposed research and defends it in response to questions asked. Gardner and Beatty (1980) list six areas most often questioned in a proposal hearing:

1. Why the subject should be studied
2. Reliability and validity of instrumentation
3. Length and type of treatment (or survey procedures)
4. Population
5. Research design
6. Data analysis procedures (pp. 85-86)

In summary, the research proposal sketches out the entire project. It offers an overview of the problem, justifies the need for doing the

→ add
divorce rates

Proposal

A. Introduction and Problem (Chapter 1 of dissertation)
Introduction to the study
Background of the problem —
Statement of the problem (What is the problem, the area of concern?)
Purpose of the study (specific purposes and/or objectives)
Rational or theoretical basis for the study
Hypotheses or questions to be answered   *end*
Importance or significance of the study
Definition of terms (operational definitions)   *?*
Assumptions and limitations of the study
Organization of the remainder of the study

B. Review of the literature (Chapter 2)
Introduction and organizational structure of the chapter
An abbreviated review of pertinent literature, grouped around major topics or themes

C. Methodology (Chapter 3)
Introduction reviewing purpose of the study
Description of methodology to be used (e.g., experimental, case study, historical)
Design of the study (operationalize variables)
Sample and population or source of data *n/a*
Instrumentation
Data collection and other procedures
Data analysis (how you expect to analyze the data once it is collected)

Figure 10.2. A typical proposal outline

research, relates the study to other literature, delineates just how the study is to be carried out, and proposes how the data are to be analyzed. Spending the time to be thorough in developing the proposal will save the student time in completing the dissertation because the structure of the proposal mirrors that of the dissertation. So if the proposal is approved, the student not only has committee support for the study itself, but also has an outline of the first three chapters of the dissertation.

Completing the Research

The thesis or dissertation has come to connote a formal paper detailing the process and results of a research investigation. More precisely, it is "a substantial paper that is submitted to the faculty of a university by a candidate for an advanced degree that is typically based on independent research and that if acceptable usually gives evidence of the candidate's mastery both of his own subject and of scholarly method" (Webster's Third New International Dictionary of the English Language, Unabridged, 1981). The format for the organization of the dissertation has also become fairly standardized. In addition to the three chapters already discussed, the typical dissertation has two concluding chapters. The fourth chapter presents the findings of the study. It is a nonevaluative reporting of data, including tables, figures, and charts. If hypotheses or research questions guided the study, data are reported relative to each question or hypothesis. Depending upon the topic and type of data used, conclusions may also be interwoven with the results in this chapter.

The purpose of the fifth chapter is to present an analysis and interpretation of what was found in the study and to recommend ideas for additional research. This final chapter can be divided into three major sections:

1. Summary. The summary should contain an overview of the entire study: a brief description of the problem, the research methodology, the findings, and the conclusions. It should be thorough enough to allow someone to get the gist of the research without reading the entire dissertation in detail.

2. Conclusions and/or Discussion. If conclusions were not integrated with the findings in the fourth chapter, they may be presented here. The discussion of the findings typically goes beyond the data in an attempt to place the findings in a broader

perspective. Such a discussion should also tie in some of the pertinent literature reviewed in the second chapter. Creativity is allowed in interpreting the data as long as the implications are suggested by the data.

3. Recommendations. This section should specify areas of additional needed research and may suggest a different procedure that would bring about more substantive results.

The closing material in a dissertation includes a complete bibliography and appendices. Appendices contain all information not immediately germane to the body of the paper, but of interest to the reader such as data-gathering instruments, survey forms, supplemental data analysis, etc.

The dissertation, with its stylized format, has not always been so prescribed or research-focused. "To dissertate" originally meant to discuss a topic in a learned and formal manner. The meaning underwent gradual change over the centuries, until today a dissertation has come to signify "an original research project that contributes to knowledge" -- quite an imposing image and intimidating to many students. The Carnegie Foundation for the Advancement of Teaching expressed their concern with this emphasis:

> Some graduate departments have magnified the thesis beyond reason, both in size and in emphasis upon it as an original contribution. There is no demonstrable relationship between the size of the dissertation and its quality. Some believe that the emphasis on an original contribution to knowledge is the most important factor in forcing students into more and more abstruse and narrow topics.
>
> The important thing to keep in mind is that it is not so much what the individual can 'prove' or 'contribute' that counts in a dissertation; it is what the individual shows of how his mind works, of his literacy, of his quality of thought. . . .Published contributions are only one desirable consequence of research training. Other consequences are scholarly judgment, critical acuity, knowledge in depth, and the capacity to teach in an inspired fashion. (quoted in Koefod, 1964, p. 94)

Nearly half the students who begin doctoral study fail to finish. For some, adult responsibilities to family and work have to take precedence over school. Sometimes those who have entered programs to change, upgrade, or prepare for a job find that the right job comes along before completing the degree and the new position leaves little time for a major research project.

These practical barriers are accompanied by motivational problems. There are few, if any, rewards or reinforcements once students have passed comprehensive exams until the degree is awarded, and so they must set their own schedules of reinforcement. Once students finish courses and turn their attention to a dissertation, they enter a different world. No other people are structuring their work, setting their deadlines, or providing them various forms of support. They rarely have contact with fellow students or faculty other than their advisor. Many students cannot cope with the lack of structure and the loneliness of the task.

There are several ways to deal with these motivational barriers. The problem of being overwhelmed by the complexity of the task can be alleviated by dividing the task into many smaller, manageable units. Set deadlines for the completion of each unit and reward yourself when the deadline is met. It might also help to remind yourself that you would not have been admitted to the program or not have gotten this far if you were not capable of completing the dissertation. A dissertation requires perseverance, not brilliance. In a discussion of self-control techniques and the dissertation, Martin (1980, pp. 73-78) offers five ideas to help students complete their dissertation:

1. The student must schedule regular and frequent work periods. Try being possessive of your time and setting aside certain periods each week. The longer the time lapses between sessions, the harder it is to begin again.
2. Work periods should take place in the same spot each time and the place should be conducive to work. "Behavior analysis has documented the fact that if a behavior is carried out repeatedly in one setting, the setting will come to be associated with that behavior and will tend to foster the continual occurrence of that behavior" (p. 75).
3. "A goal should be set for the amount of work to be produced each day or each week and a record should be kept of the amount of work accomplished in order to determine if the goal has been met" (p. 76). This technique will both motivate and reinforce your efforts.
4. Set up reinforcements or punishments if needed. Martin recounts the example of a person who gave a friend money to send in five

dollar amounts to a proselytizing church "that the subject disliked" if she did not complete five or more pages in a week (p. 78).

5. "Anticipate lower rates of production after a large segment of work has been completed" (p. 79). Stronger reinforcements can be established for anticipated periods of low production.

Defending the Research

The final step in the dissertation process is the oral defense. The oral defense is a vestige of the European tradition of graduate education. In medieval Europe, students desiring to become masters, doctors, or professors (the terms were synonymous) demonstrated mastery of a subject through a public examination or series of lectures (Davinson, 1977, p. 19). Except for Scandinavian countries where the rigorous public examination of doctoral students still exists (Davinson, 1977), contemporary dissertation defenses are private affairs. Present are the student and the committee, perhaps a few additional faculty members who may examine the candidate, and possibly other doctoral students who are merely observing the process.

Most oral defenses begin with the chair introducing the session and laying out suggested procedures for questioning the candidate. At this point the student is usually asked to review briefly how interest in the topic developed, what the purpose of the study was, how it was carried out, and the major findings. Since everyone present has read the entire study, it is important that this overview be kept brief and to the point. The chair then invites questions from committee members, sometimes suggesting where the questioning might begin.

Students, perhaps because they are more expert in content than methodology, anticipate and prepare for difficult methodological questions. Unless there are blatant methodological problems, committee members are more likely to ask questions related to significance and generalizability. Allen (1973) lists several questions that a student might expect, none of which deals directly with methodology:

(1) A dissertation is supposed to be a contribution to the literature. What is your contribution? (2) Who, in your area of study, would agree with your findings? Why? Who would disagree? Why? (4) What questions were you unable to answer with your research? (5) What areas for further research did you

uncover? (6) How did you reduce your biases and prejudices? (7) What additional work do you intend to undertake as a result of your study? (8) Where could you publish your findings to reach the audience that could profit most from your work? (9) What did this exercise in research teach you? (10) How do you intend to use your findings? (p. 86)

Once the questioning has been completed, the committee must decide whether or not the student has passed the oral exam. Typically, the student and other visitors are asked to leave while the committee deliberates. Depending upon the university, the committee may exercise one of several options: the student can pass, fail, pass on condition that certain revisions are made, or if major revisions are needed, a committee may have the option of postponing a decision and rescheduling a hearing. The student is informed immediately of the decision. A student who passes is considered a holder of the doctoral degree even though formal graduation ceremonies are still to come. It is a rare dissertation that survives the defense without some revisions being needed. These revisions are often handled by the advisor and the candidate, but on occasion other members of the committee may want to approve them.

A student can prepare for the defense in several ways. Anxiety can be reduced by realizing that the committee cannot challenge you on the basic structure of the study because they approved it at the proposal stage. Secondly, no one else knows as much about the study as you do at this time -- you *should* be able to defend it. Finally, most advisors will not take a candidate to the oral defense unless the advisor is satisfied with the product. More often than not, an advisor who has approved your work will be supportive of you during the hearing. Other suggestions for preparing are:

1. Carefully read through the dissertation the night before.
2. Check the room where the defense is to be held and make sure any necessary aids are there.
3. Practice your introductory remarks with a friend.
4. Check -- or have your advisor check -- with the other committee members ahead of time for serious or major concerns.
5. Attend a few oral defenses prior to yours in order to familiarize yourself with the process.

The oral defense culminates a person's career as a doctoral student. It can be a stimulating experience in which you feel a great sense of achievement. It offers an opportunity to discuss your research with interested faculty. Finally, the defense signals a rite of passage from student status to professional colleague.

Summary

The process of graduate research is not unlike doing research in other contexts. In community settings, in business and industry, in education, the person who engages in research must first focus the problem and then select a strategy for investigating the problem. In many instances a proposal is presented to a funding source, and a committee may be formed to guide the research. Finally, the research needs to be carried out followed by a "defense" in the form of a journal article, conference presentation, or final report to the funding source. Most of these aspects have been covered in other chapters of this text. This chapter has concentrated on the *practical* aspects of graduate research. For students interested in more detailed discussions of the research process, Table 10.1 lists the parts of the graduate research process (left-hand column) and corresponding chapter discussions.

Table 10.1. The Process of graduate research

Discussion Found in Text

	Chapter 1 The nature of Systematic Inquiry	Chapter 2 Focusing the Research	Chapter 3 The Literature Review	Chapter 4 Experimental and Descriptive Research	Chapter 5 Historical and Philosophical Inquiry	Chapter 6 Ethnography, Case Study, Grounded Theory	Chapter 7 Interactive, Ecological and Futures Research	Chapter 8 Data Collecting Procedures and Techniques	Chapter 9 Reporting and Disseminating Research	Chapter 10 Graduate Research
A. Selecting a Topic		■								■
B. Forming a Committee										■
C. Presenting a Proposal										■
*1. The Problem		■								■
*2. Review of Literature			■							
*3. Methodology				■			■			
D. Completing the Research							■	■	■	■
*4. Findings								■	■	
*5. Conclusions and Implications									■	■
E. Defending the Research										■

•Note: Sections 1 through 5 reflect the chapter divisions of a typical dissertation and the sections of the standard research report

REFERENCES

Almack, John C. 1930. *Research and Thesis Writing*. Boston: Houghton Mifflin Company.

Allen, George R. 1973. *The Graduate Students' Guide to Theses and Dissertations*. San Francisco: Jossey-Bass.

Davinson, Donald. 1977. *Theses and Dissertations*. Hamden, Connecticut: Linnet Books.

Davis, Richard M. 1980. *Thesis Projects in Science and Engineering*. New York: St. Martin's Press.

Gardner, David C. and Grace J. Beatty. 1980. *Dissertation Proposal Guidebook*. Springfield, Illinois: Charles Thomas.

Koefod, Paul E. 1964. *The Writing Requirements for Graduate Degrees*. Englewood Cliffs, New Jersey: Prentice-Hall, Inc.

Martin, Roy. 1980. *Writing and Defending A Thesis or Dissertation in Psychology and Education*. Springfield, Illinois: Charles Thomas.

Prior, Moody E. 1965. "The Doctor of Philosophy Degree," *Graduate Education Today*, (ed.) Ewert Walters. Washington, D.C.: American Council on Education.

Webster's Third New International Dictionary. 1981. Springfield, Massachusetts: G & C Merriam Company.

GLOSSARY

ABSTRACT. A brief summary of a research study presenting the problem statement, the procedures used, and the results of the study.

ACTION RESEARCH. A type of interactive research that aims to solve a specific and current problem.

APPLIED RESEARCH. A type of research that is directed toward solving immediate and practical problems.

A PRIORI THEORY. A mode of inquiry in which a theory is proposed and hypotheses are made in advance of gathering data about a specific phenomenon (also called hypothetical-deductive theory).

BASIC RESEARCH. A type of research that is motivated by intellectual interest alone and is concerned with knowledge for its own sake.

CASE HISTORY. An analysis that traces the past of a person, group, or institution.

CASE METHOD. An instructional technique whereby the major ingredients of a case study are presented to students for illustrative or problem-solving purposes.

CASE STUDY. An intensive description and analysis of a particular social unit that seeks to uncover the interplay of significant factors that is characteristic of that unit.

CASE WORK. The remedial or developmental procedures that are undertaken after the causes of a maladjustment have been diagnosed.

CAUSAL/COMPARATIVE RESEARCH. A form of descriptive research in which the investigator looks for relationships that may explain phenomena that have already taken place (also called *ex post facto* research).

COLLECTIVE BIOGRAPHY. An application of quantitative analysis in which the historical researcher looks at biographical characteristics of a particular group of people.

CONCEPTS. Abstract ideas that develop from observation and are used to explain and describe the phenomena being studied.

CONCEPTUAL LITERATURE. *See* THEORETICAL LITERATURE.

CONSTRUCT VALIDITY. The extent to which a test measures the abstract, theoretical ideas (constructs) that it is designed to measure.

CONTENT ANALYSIS. An application of quantitative analysis in which the researcher establishes the frequency with which certain words, ideas, or attitudes are expressed in a particular body of material.

CONTENT VALIDITY. The extent to which items on a test or scale match the behavior, skill, or affect the researcher intends them to measure.

CRITICAL RESEARCH. A methodology that emphasizes the examination of epistemological, cognitive, cultural and political bases of policy and practice through dialectic intercourse, leading to knowledge of practical interest and "new world" perspectives by those engaged in the process.

CROSS-SECTIONAL RESEARCH. A design in which data are gathered from different groups (usually age groups) at a single point in time.

DESCRIPTIVE RESEARCH. A method used to describe systematically the facts and characteristics of a given population or area of interest.

DESCRIPTIVE STATISTICS. A set of procedures that can be used to summarize data or to make simple comparisons of data.

DIALECTIC METHOD. A type of philosophical inquiry in which disputes and contradictions are disclosed, examined, and reconciled.

DISSERTATION. Commonly used at the doctoral level to mean a formal paper that details the process and results of a research investigation.

ETHNOGRAPHY. A research methodology that includes both a set of techniques used to uncover the social order and meaning that a setting has for the people participating in it and the written record that is the product of using those techniques.

EX POST FACTO RESEARCH. *See* CAUSAL/COMPARATIVE RESEARCH.

EXTERNAL VALIDITY. The degree to which the results of a study are generalizable to other situations under similar conditions.

FACTORIAL DESIGN. A method used to study the effects of more than one independent variable on more than one dependent variable.

FUTURES RESEARCH. A methodology that frequently uses the past as a means of illuminating the study of possible futures.

GROUNDED THEORY. A research methodology that is characterized by inductive fieldwork and the goal of having theory emerge from the data.

HISTORICAL DEMOGRAPHY. An application of quantitative analysis in which the researcher studies the composition of a population by examining public records.

HYPOTHETICAL-DEDUCTIVE THEORY. *See* A PRIORI THEORY.

INFERENTIAL STATISTICS. A set of procedures that can be used to test hypotheses or to estimate the parameters of the population used in the study.

INTERACTIVE RESEARCH. A methodology in which the design is formulated while the research is in progress, the researcher serves as a facilitator for problem-solving, and the results are intended for immediate application by those who participated in the research.

INTERNAL VALIDITY. The degree to which the research procedure measures what it purports to measure.

INTERVIEW SCHEDULE. A highly structured format of questions that will be asked of a research participant.

LITERATURE REVIEW. A narrative essay that integrates, synthesizes, and critiques the important thinking and research on a particular topic.

LOGISTIC METHOD. A type of philosophical inquiry in which knowledge is examined by understanding the elements of which it is composed.

LONGITUDINAL RESEARCH. A design in which data are gathered from the same sample on several occasions.

MOLAR APPROACH. A procedure used with structured observation in which the observer groups several behaviors into broadly defined categories.

MOLECULAR APPROACH. A procedure used with structured observation in which the focus is on units of behavior that are small enough to ensure reliability in observation.

PARTICIPATORY RESEARCH. A type of interactive research that aims at the political empowerment of people through group participation in the search for knowledge.

PRIMARY SOURCES. Oral or written accounts by someone who was an eyewitness to the event.

PROBLEMATIC METHOD. A type of philosophical inquiry in which problems are solved one at a time and without reference to an all-inclusive whole or a simplest part.

PROCEDURE. The steps or activities that describe the general way data are gathered.

PROJECTIVE TECHNIQUES. A group of methods used for getting participants to share their feelings, attitudes, and thoughts.

PSYCHOSOCIAL HISTORY. An approach that uses modern psychological and sociological theories and concepts to interpret personalities, events, groups, or movements of the past.

QUALITATIVE DATA. Data that are not transferable to numbers and not comparable by statistical procedures.

QUANTITATIVE DATA. Data that are coded and represented by statistical scores (also call statistical data).

QUANTITATIVE HISTORY. An approach that analyzes a historical period or event by focusing upon phenomena that can be counted or measured.

RATING SCALE. A measuring instrument on which the researcher assigns observed behaviors to numbered categories.

RESEARCH AND DEVELOPMENT (R&D). A term used in business and industry to refer to applied research that is directed toward product development.

RESEARCH STUDIES. Writings that are based on the collection and analysis of data gathered from sources extraneous to the author.

SECONDARY SOURCES. Oral or written accounts by someone who did not witness an event.

SOCIOMETRIC TECHNIQUES. A group of methods used for studying the organization of social groups.

STATISTICAL DATA. See QUANTITATIVE DATA.

SUBSTANTIVE THEORY. An explanation that emerges from a grounded-theory study and deals with phenomena that are limited to particular real-world situations.

SURVEY. A broad category of techniques that use questioning as a strategy to elicit information.

TECHNIQUE. The specific device or means of recording the data.

THEORETICAL LITERATURE. Writings that are based on an author's experience or opinions (also called conceptual literature).

THESIS. Commonly used at the master's level to mean a formal paper describing a culminating research project.

INDEX

Social change through interactive research, 107-115
Social Science Index, 34
Sociological Abstracts, 35
Sociometric techniques, 145-146
Sommer, Robert and Barbara B. Sommer, 135
Sources of knowledge. *See* Knowledge
Spiegelberg, Herbert A., 85-86
Stanage, Sherman, 83, 84
Statistical data. *See* Quantitative data
Statistics
advantages, disadvantages in research, 64
reporting of, 165-167
Strauss, A. L., 20, 97, 103
Stubblefield, Harold, 70
Style. *See* Editorial style
Substantive theory, 16, 99-100. *See also* Grounded theory, 99-103
Survey, 62, 97, 129-136
Survivor bias, 60
Systematic inquiry, 1-10
definitions and sources of, 2-6
process of, 7-10
purposes and types, 6-7

T

Tables, use and placement in research reports, 161-165
Taylor, Steven J. and Robert Bogdan, 141
Testing, 142-146
objectivity in, 143
types of, 143-146
attitude and value scales, 144-145
personality measures, 143-144
projective and sociometric, 145-146
researcher-made, 143
standardized, 143
validity, 142-143

Testing effects and instuments used in adult development studies, 61-62
Thematic investigation, 112
Theoretical framework, relationship to research process
functions of, 16-21
importance, 8-10
Theoretical literature, functions relating to research, 8, 29-31. *See also* Literature review.
Theoretical sampling, 101
Theory
as a source of hypotheses, 22-24
as a source of research problems, 8-10
characteristics of, 23-24
functions of, 16-21
See also Literature review, functions of, 29-31, 152
inductive, 3, 18
hypothetical-deductive, 3, 17-19
scientific, 4-5, 16-19
Theory building, 20, 90-91, 99-103
Thesis, 173-174, 177
Thesis/Dissertation Generator, Figure 10.1, 177
Thomas, Lewis 4
Training and Development Handbook: A Guide to Human Resource Development, 33
Trend analysis, 155
Trend extrapolation, 121
Turabian, K. L. *See Manual for Writers of Term Papers, Theses, and Dissertations.*

U

UNESCO simulation games developed by, 124

V

Validity
in interactive research, 107

of questionnaires, 132
of tests, 142-143
  concurrent, 143
  construct, 143
  predictive, 143
  external, 55-56
  internal, 55-56
Van Dalen, Deobold B., 162
Variables
  dependent, 50-52, 54-55
  extraneous, 54
  independent, 50-52, 54-55

W

Wagner, P., 101
Walker, Susan, 24-26
Webb, Eugene and others, 14, 141

Wiersma, William, 59, 132
Williams, G. B., 53
Wilson, Ian H., 122
Witkin, Herman A. and Donald Good-
  enough, 25
Wolcott, H. F., 95
Wright, Lewis E., 115

Y

Yearbooks, 32-33
*Yearbook of Adult and Continuing
  Education*, 33
Young, J. D., 53

Z

Zeph, Catherine, 99